Developing Web Services with Apache Axis2

By

Kent Ka Iok Tong

TipTec Development

Publisher: TipTec Development

Author's email: freemant2000@yahoo.com

Book website: http://www.agileskills2.org

ISBN: 978-99937-929-1-8

Edition: Second edition March 2008

Foreword

Learn web services and Apache Axis2 easily

If you'd like to learn how to create web services (in particular, using Apache Axis2) and make some sense of various standards like SOAP, WSDL, MTOM, WS-Addressing, WS-Security, WS-Policy, XML Encryption and XML Signature, then this book is for you. Why?

- It has a tutorial style that walks you through in a step-by-step manner.
- It is concise. There is no lengthy, abstract description.
- Many diagrams are used to show the flow of processing and high level concepts so that you get a whole picture of what's happening.
- The first 46 pages are freely available on http://www.agileskills2.org. You can judge it yourself.

Unique contents in this book

This book covers the following topics not found in other books on Axis:

- How to work with Axis2 1.3.
- How to use Eclipse Europa (WTP 2.0) with Axis2.
- How to invoke asynchronous operations using WS-Addressing.
- How to encrypt and sign SOAP messages using Rampart.
- How to send user authentication information using Rampart.
- How to send and receive binary files using MTOM.
- How to integrate Axis2 with Spring.

Target audience and prerequisites

This book is suitable for those who would like to learn how to develop web services in Java.

In order to understand what's in the book, you need to know Java and to have edited XML files. However, you do NOT need to know the more advanced XML concepts (e.g., XML schema, XML namespace), servlet, Tomcat or PKI.

Acknowledgments

I'd like to thank:

- The Axis developers for creating Axis.
- The WSS4J developers for creating WSS4J.
- Anne Thomas Manes, an expert in web services, for reviewing the book (first edition).
- Helena Lei for proofreading this book.
- Eugenia Chan Peng U for doing book cover and layout design.

Table of Contents

Chapter 1

Designing the interface for a simple web service

What's in this chapter?

In this chapter you'll learn how to design the interface for a simple web service.

Providing cross platform operations across the Internet

Suppose that you'd like to provide a service to the public or to some business partners: They can send you two strings and you will concatenate them and return the string. Of course, in the real world you provide a more useful service.

There are several major requirements: First, the users may be using different languages (Java, C# and etc.) and using different platforms (Windows, Linux and etc.). Your service must be accessible by different languages and platforms. Second, they will call your service across the Internet and there may be firewalls in between. Your service must be able to go through firewalls.

Given these requirements, the best solution is to provide a so-called "web service". For example, you may make a web service accessible on the host www.ttdev.com and accessible as /SimpleService (see the diagram below), so the full URL is http://www.ttdev.com/SimpleService. This is called the "endpoint" of the web service. Your web service may support one or more operations. One operation may be named "concat":

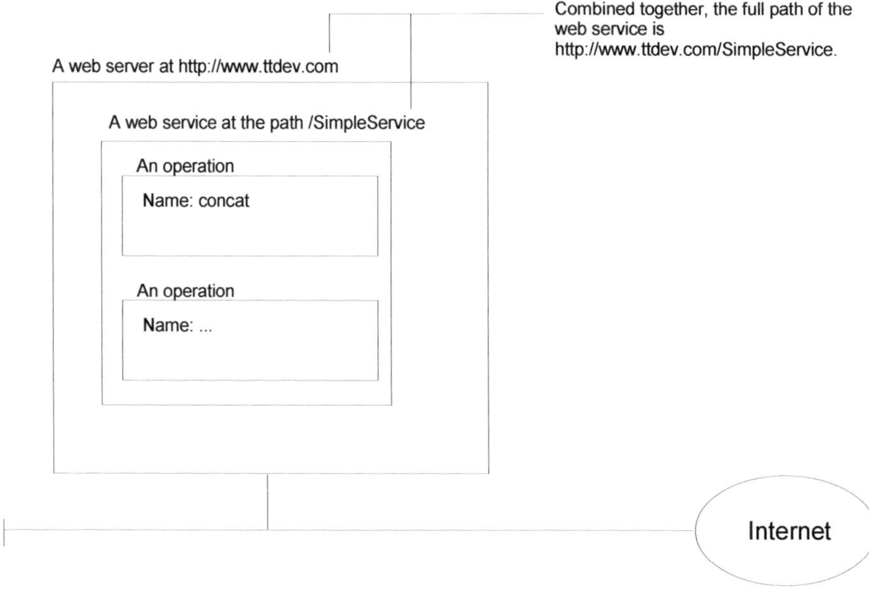

However, you hope to provide a globally unique name to each operation so that you can have your "concat" operation while another person may have his "concat" operation. So, in addition to the name, you may declare that the "concat" name above is in the "namespace" of http://ttdev.com/ss (see the diagram below). A namespace is just like a Java package, but it is not in a dot format like com.ttdev.foo; it is in the format of a URL. So, the full name of the operation will be "concat" in namespace http://ttdev.com/ss. The name "concat" is called the "local name". The full name is called a "QName (qualified name)":

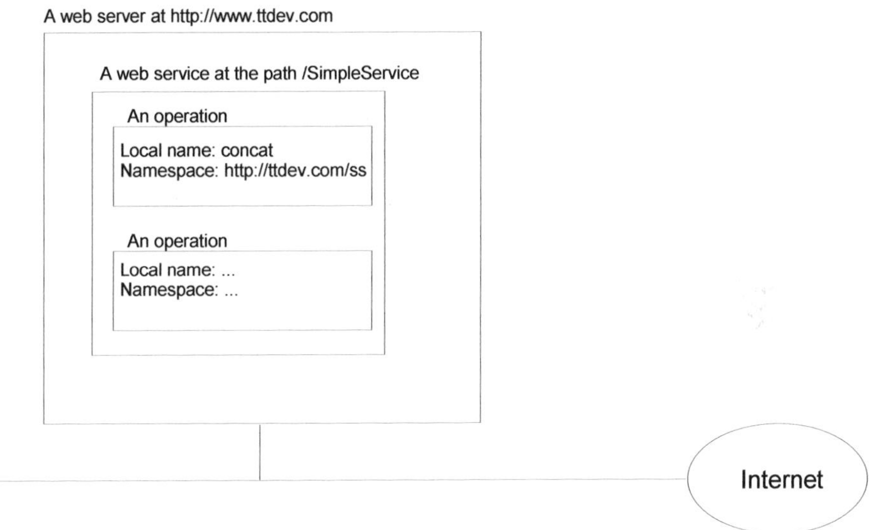

You may wonder what this http://ttdev.com/ss namespace means. The answer is that it has no particular meaning. Even though it is a URL, it does NOT mean that you can use a browser to access this URL to get a web page (if you do, you may get a file not found error). The only important thing is that it must be globally unique. As I have registered the domain name ttdev.com, it must be globally unique.

Note that the namespace is a completely different concept from the endpoint. The endpoint really is the location, while the namespace is just a unique id. I could easily move the web service to another web server and thus it will have a different endpoint, but the namespaces of its operations will remain unchanged.

RPC style web service

Your concat operation may take two parameters. One is named "s1" and is a string. The other is named "s2" and is also a string. The return value is also a string:

An operation

```
Local name: concat
Namespace: http://ttdev.com/ss
Parameters:
  s1: string
  s2: string
Return:
  string
```

However, what does the above "string" type mean? Is it the Java string type? No, you can't say that because it must be language neutral. Fortunately, the XML schema specification defines some basic data types including a string type. Each of these data types has a QName as its id. For example:

Data type	***Local name***	***namespace***
string	string	http://www.w3.org/2001/XMLSchema
integer	int	http://www.w3.org/2001/XMLSchema
...	...	...

So, the interface of your operation should be written as:

An operation

```
Local name: concat
Namespace: http://ttdev.com/ss
Parameters:
  s1: string in http://www.w3.org/2001/XMLSchema
  s2: string in http://www.w3.org/2001/XMLSchema
Return:
  string in http://www.w3.org/2001/XMLSchema
```

Actually, in web services, a method call is called an "input message" and a parameter is called a "part". The return value is called an "output message" and may contain multiple parts. So, it is more correct to say:

An operation

```
Local name: concat
Namespace: http://ttdev.com/ss
Input message:
  Part 1:
    Name: s1
    Type: string in http://www.w3.org/2001/XMLSchema
  Part 2:
    Name: s2
    Type: string in http://www.w3.org/2001/XMLSchema
Output message:
  Part 1:
    Name: return
    Type: string in http://www.w3.org/2001/XMLSchema
```

When someone calls this operation, he can send you an XML element as the input message like:

```
Local name: concat
Namespace: http://ttdev.com/ss
Input message:
  Part 1:
    Name: s1
    Type: string in http://www.w3.org/2001/XMLSchema
  Part 2:
    Name: s2
    Type: string in http://www.w3.org/2001/XMLSchema
Output message:
  Part 1:
    Name: return
    Type: string in http://www.w3.org/2001/XMLSchema
```

The QName of this XML element is exactly that of the operation he is trying to call

There is a child element for each part. Each child element has the same name as that part ("s1" in this case).

foo is a "namespace prefix" representing the http://ttdev.com/ss in the rest of this element including its children.

```
<foo:concat xmlns:foo="http://ttdev.com/ss">
  <s1>abc</s1>
  <s2>123</s2>
</foo:concat>
```

When you return, the output message may be like:

```
Local name: concat
Namespace: http://ttdev.com/ss
Input message:
  Part 1:
    Name: s1
    Type: string in http://www.w3.org/2001/XMLSchema
  Part 2:
    Name: s2
    Type: string in http://www.w3.org/2001/XMLSchema
Output message:
  Part 1:
    Name: return
    Type: string in http://www.w3.org/2001/XMLSchema
```

The QName of this XML element is exactly that of the operation being called

Each child element has the same name as a part in the output message ("return" in this case).

```
<foo:concat xmlns:foo="http://ttdev.com/ss">
  <return>abc123</return>
</foo:concat>
```

This kind of web service is called "RPC style" web service (RPC stands for

"Remote Procedure Call"). That is, the operation QName and the names of the parts are used to create the input and output messages.

Document style web service

The above way is not the only way you design the interface of your web service. For example, you may say that its input message only contains a single part (see the diagram below) which is an element defined in a schema. In that schema, it is defined as an element named "concatRequest" that contains two child elements <s1> and <s2>:

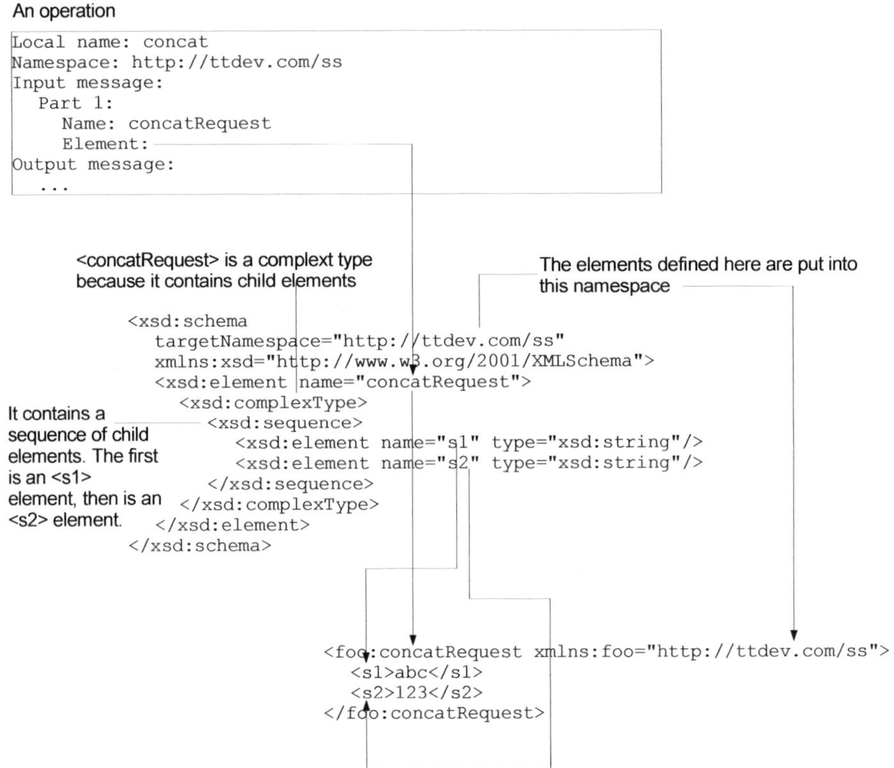

An operation
Local name: concat
Namespace: http://ttdev.com/ss
Input message:
Part 1:
Name: concatRequest
Element:
Output message:
...
<concatRequest> is a complext type because it contains child elements
The elements defined here are put into this namespace
<xsd:schema
targetNamespace="http://ttdev.com/ss"
xmlns:xsd="http://www.w3.org/2001/XMLSchema">
<xsd:element name="concatRequest">
<xsd:complexType>
<xsd:sequence>
<xsd:element name="s1" type="xsd:string"/>
<xsd:element name="s2" type="xsd:string"/>
</xsd:sequence>
</xsd:complexType>
</xsd:element>
</xsd:schema>
It contains a sequence of child elements. The first is an <s1> element, then is an <s2> element.
<foo:concatRequest xmlns:foo="http://ttdev.com/ss">
<s1>abc</s1>
<s2>123</s2>
</foo:concatRequest>

Note that the schema is included in the interface of your web service:

A web service

A schema

```
<xsd:schema
  targetNamespace="http://ttdev.com/ss"
  xmlns:xsd="http://www.w3.org/2001/XMLSchema">
  <xsd:element name="concatRequest">
    <xsd:complexType>
      <xsd:sequence>
        <xsd:element name="s1" type="xsd:string"/>
        <xsd:element name="s2" type="xsd:string"/>
      </xsd:sequence>
    </xsd:complexType>
  </xsd:element>
</xsd:schema>
```

An operation

```
Local name: concat
Namespace: http://ttdev.com/ss
Input message:
  Part 1:
    Name: concatRequest
    Element: concatRequest in http://ttdev.com/ss
Output message:
  ...
```

As you can see above, a part may be declared as a particular element (<concatRequest> defined in your schema) or as any element having a particular type (string defined in XML schema specification). In either case it is identified using a QName.

When someone calls this operation, he will send you a <concatRequest> element as the input message like:

```
<foo:concatRequest xmlns:foo="http://ttdev.com/ss">
  <s1>abc</s1>
  <s2>123</s2>
</foo:concatRequest>
```

Similarly, for the output message, you may specify that it contains only one part and that part is a <concatResponse> element:

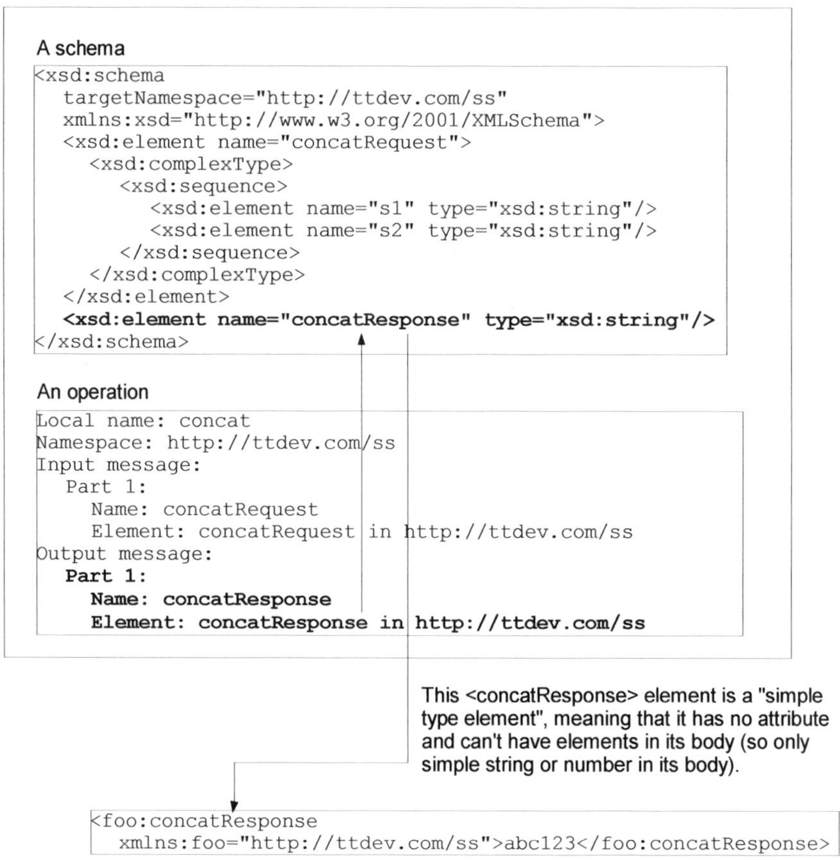
A web service
A schema
<xsd:schema
targetNamespace="http://ttdev.com/ss"
xmlns:xsd="http://www.w3.org/2001/XMLSchema">
<xsd:element name="concatRequest">
<xsd:complexType>
<xsd:sequence>
<xsd:element name="s1" type="xsd:string"/>
<xsd:element name="s2" type="xsd:string"/>
</xsd:sequence>
</xsd:complexType>
</xsd:element>
<xsd:element name="concatResponse" type="xsd:string"/>
</xsd:schema>
An operation
Local name: concat
Namespace: http://ttdev.com/ss
Input message:
Part 1:
Name: concatRequest
Element: concatRequest in http://ttdev.com/ss
Output message:
Part 1:
Name: concatResponse
Element: concatResponse in http://ttdev.com/ss
This <concatResponse> element is a "simple type element", meaning that it has no attribute and can't have elements in its body (so only simple string or number in its body).
<foo:concatResponse
xmlns:foo="http://ttdev.com/ss">abc123</foo:concatResponse>

This kind of web service is called "document style" web service. That is, the input message will contain a single part only which is well defined in a schema. The same is true of the output message.

If you go back to check the input message for the RPC style service, it should be revised as:

```
<foo:concat>
  xmlns:foo="http://ttdev.com/ss"
  xmlns:xsd="http://www.w3.org/2001/XMLSchema"
  xmlns:xsi="http://www.w3.org/2001/XMLSchema-Instance">
  <s1 xsi:type="xsd:string">abc</s1>
  <s2 xsi:type="xsd:string">123</s2>
</foo:concat>
```

This attribute is used to explicitly state the XML data type of the body of an element ("abc" here). This is useful when the element (<s1>) itself is not defined in a schema. This "type" attribute is defined in the http://www.w3.org/2001/XMLSchema-Instance namespace, so you need to introduce a prefix for it:

This is because <foo:concat>, <s1> and <s2> are not defined in any schema and therefore you must explicitly state the XML element types of the content of <s1> and <s2>.

Now, let's compare the input messages of the RPC style web service and the document style web service:

RPC style	`<foo:concat>`
	`  xmlns:foo="http://ttdev.com/ss"`
	`  xmlns:xsd="http://www.w3.org/2001/XMLSchema"`
	`  xmlns:xsi="http://www.w3.org/2001/XMLSchema-Instance">`
	`  <s1 xsi:type="xsd:string">abc</s1>`
	`  <s2 xsi:type="xsd:string">123</s2>`
	`</foo:concat>`

Document style	`<foo:concatRequest xmlns:foo="http://ttdev.com/ss">`
	`  <s1>abc</s1>`
	`  <s2>123</s2>`
	`</foo:concatRequest>`

Not much difference, right? The significant difference is that the former can't be validated with a schema while the latter can. Therefore, document style web service is becoming the dominant style. According to an organization called "WS-I (web services interoperability organization)", you should use document style web services only.

Determining the operation for a document style web service

To call an operation in a document style web service, one will send the single part of the input message only. Note that it does NOT send the operation name in any way. Then if there are more than one operations in the web service (see the diagram below), how can it determine which one is being called? In that case, it will see if the input message is a <concatRequest> or a <someElement> to determine. What if both take a <someElement>? Then it is an error and it won't work:

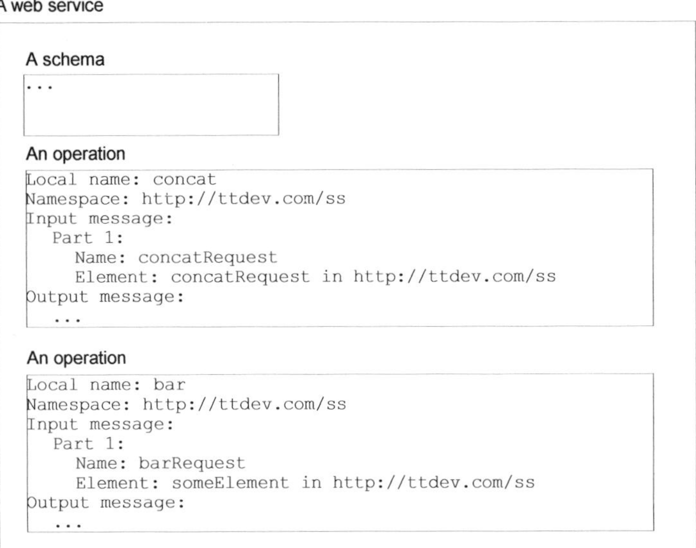

A web service
A schema
...
An operation
Local name: concat
Namespace: http://ttdev.com/ss
Input message:
Part 1:
Name: concatRequest
Element: concatRequest in http://ttdev.com/ss
Output message:
...
An operation
Local name: bar
Namespace: http://ttdev.com/ss
Input message:
Part 1:
Name: barRequest
Element: someElement in http://ttdev.com/ss
Output message:
...

Port type

Actually, a web service doesn't directly contain a list of operations. Instead (see the diagram below), operations are grouped into one or more "port types". A port type is like a Java class and each operation in it is like a static method. For example, in the web service above, you could have a port type named "stringUtil" containing operations for strings, while having another port type named "dateUtil" containing operations for dates. The name of a port type must also be a QName:

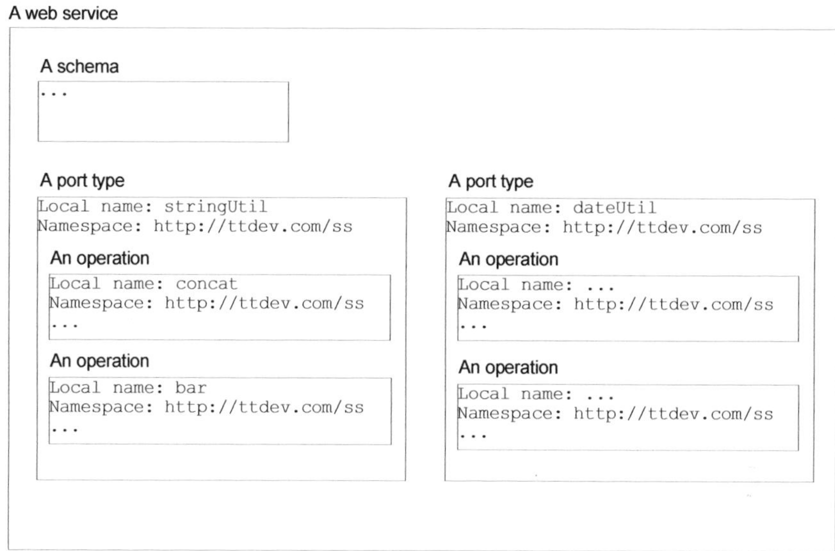

Binding

Actually, a port type may allow you to access it using different message formats. The message format that you have seen is called the "Simple Object Access Protocol (SOAP)" format. It is possible that, say, the stringUtil port type may also support a plain text format:

```
concat(s1='abc', s2='123')
```

In addition to the message format, a port type may allow the message to be carried (transported) in an HTTP POST request or in an email. Each supported combination is called a "binding":

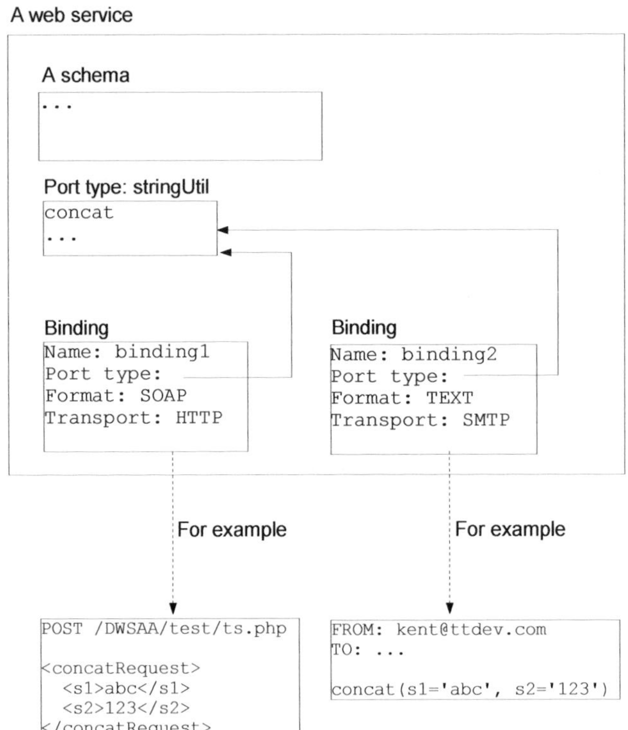

What bindings should your port type support? SOAP+HTTP is the most common combination. So, you should probably use this binding in practice.

Port

Suppose that there are just too many people using your web service, you decide to make it available on more than one computers. For example (see the diagram below), you may deploy the above binding 1 on computers c1, c2 and c3 and deploy binding 2 on c3. In that case it is said that you have four ports. Three ports are using binding 1 and one using binding 2:

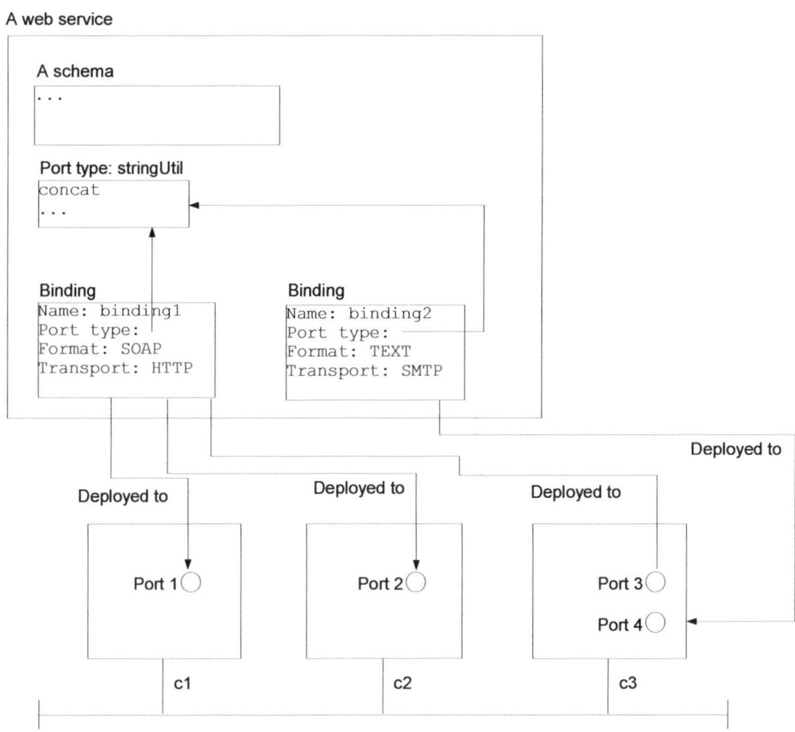

Note that it does NOT mean that the requests received by these three computers will be forwarded to a computer hiding behind for processing. Instead, it means that there is some software implementing the port type installed on these three computers. There is no requirement that the same piece of software is installed onto the different computers. For example, on c1, port 1 may be written in Java, while on c2, port 2 may be written in C#. The important point is that they both support the operations specified in port type stringUtil and the message format and transport specified in the binding 1. Port 4 must also implement the same operations too (same port type) but the message format and transport are different.

To tell others about this arrangement, you include these ports in the interface of the web service:

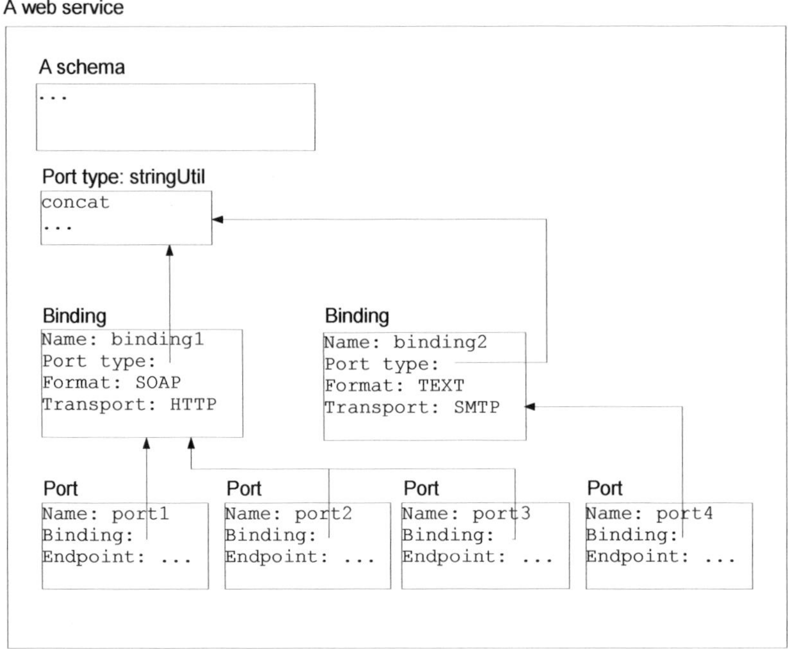

Target namespace

You have been using the same namespace for the operation names, port type names and etc. in this web service. Do they have to be in the same namespace? By default, this is the case: There is a single namespace for a web service to put the names into. This is called the "target namespace" for the web service:

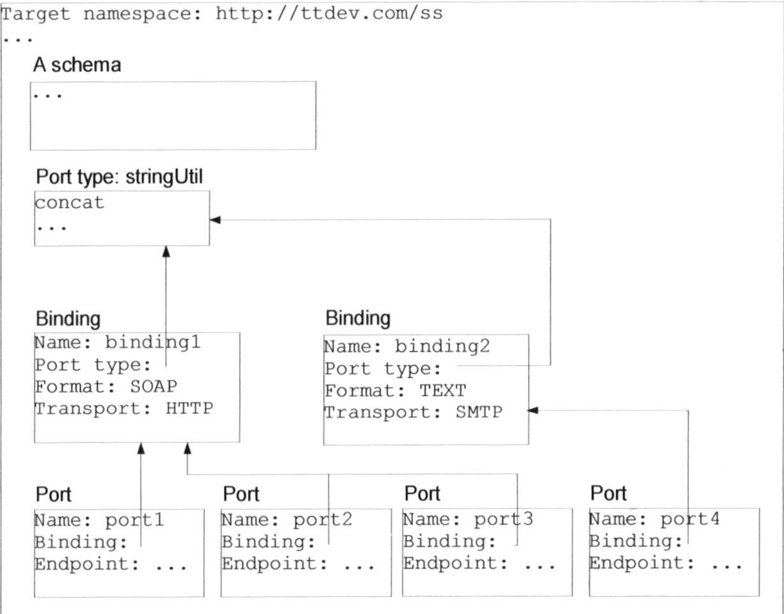

You've been using http://ttdev.com/ss as the target namespace. Is it a good choice? Basically a namespace is good as long as it is globally unique. So this one should be good. However, people may try to download a web page from this URL. When it doesn't work, they may suspect that your web service is out of order. To avoid this confusion, you may use something called URN (Uniform Resource Name) as the namespace.

A namespace must be a URI. URI stands for Uniform Resource Identifier. There are two kinds of URI. One is URL such as http://www.foo.com/bar. The other is URN. A URN takes the format of urn:<some-object-type>:<some-object-id>. For example, International ISBN Agency has made a request to the IANA (International Assigned Numbers Association) that it would like to manage the object type named "isbn". After the request has been approved, the International ISBN Agency can declare that a URN urn:isbn:1-23-456789-0 will identify a book whose ISBN is 1-23-456789-0. It can determine the meaning of the object id without consulting IANA at all.

Similarly, you may submit a request to IANA to register your Internet domain name such as foo.com as the object type. Then on approval you can use URNs like urn:foo.com:xyz to identify an object xyz in your company. What xyz means or its format is completely up to you to decide. For example, you may use urn:foo.com:product:123 (so xyz is product:123) to mean the product #123 produced by your company, or urn:foo.com:patent/123 (so xyz is patent/123) to mean a patent coded 123 in your company.

However, this will create a lot of workload on you and on IANA (one registration per company!). As you have already registered the domain name foo.com, it is unlikely that someone will use it in their URN's. So, you may want to go ahead and use foo.com, or, as many people do, foo-com as the object type without registration with IANA and hope that there won't be any collision.

An XML namespace must be a URI. You can use a URL or a URN. Functionally there is no difference at all. For example, you may use say urn:ttdev.com:ss as the target namespace for your web service instead of http://ttdev.com/ss without changing any functionality.

By the way, if you are going to lookup references on URN, do NOT try to find terms like "object type" or "object id". The official terms are:

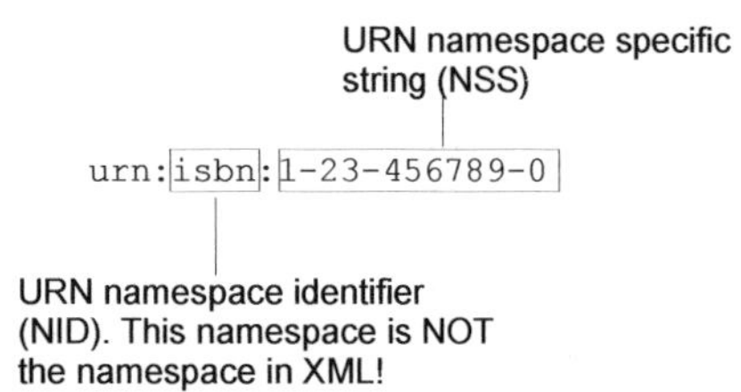

WSDL

By now you have finished designing the interface for your web service:

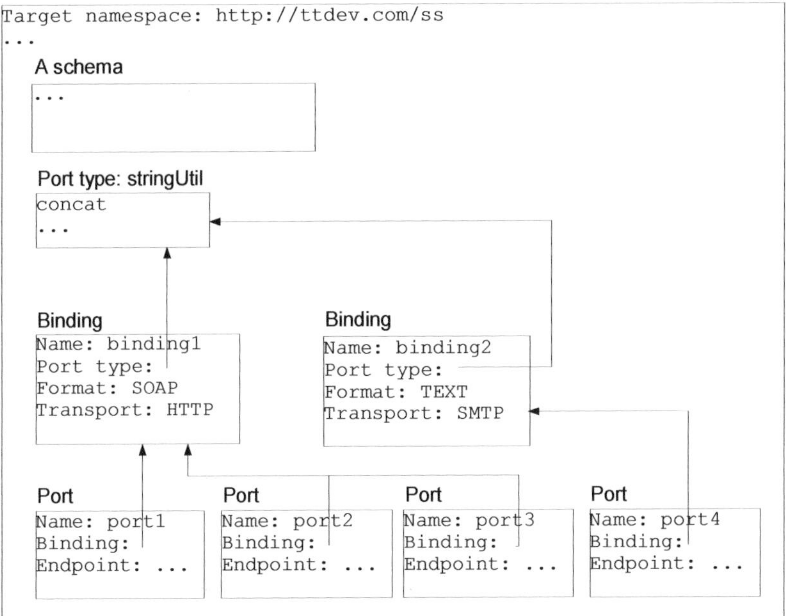

It fully describes your web service. This description language (terms and concepts) is called "WSDL (Web Services Description Language)".

Summary

A web service is platform neutral, language neutral and can be accessed across the Internet.

A web service has one or more ports. Each port is a binding deployed at a certain network address (endpoint). A binding is a port type using a particular message format and a particular transport protocol. A port type contains one or more operations. An operation has an input message and an output message. Each message has one or more parts. Each part is either a certain element defined in the schema of the web service, or any element belonging to a certain element type in that schema. All this information is fully described in WSDL.

To call a RPC style web service, one will create an XML element with the name of the operation and a child element for each of its input message part. To call a document style web service, one will just send the one and only part of its input message. Because the XML element used to call a RPC style web service is not defined in any schema, for better interoperability, one should create document style web services.

The web service, and each of its ports, bindings, port types and operations, has a QName uniquely identifying it. A QName has a local part and an XML namespace. An XML namespace is a URI that is globally unique. By default the names of all these components are put into the target namespace of the web service.

There are two kinds of URI: URL and URN. URN takes the form of urn:<NID>:<NSS>. You can use either as an XML namespace. The only difference is that a URL is suggesting that it is the location of an object, while a URN is purely an id of the object.

Chapter 2

Implementing a web service

What's in this chapter?

In this chapter you'll learn how to implement the web service interface designed in the previous chapter.

Installing Eclipse

You need to make sure you have Eclipse v3.3 (or later) installed and it is the bundle for Java EE (the bundle for Java SE is NOT enough). If not, go to http://www.eclipse.org to download the Eclipse IDE for Java EE Developers (e.g., eclipse-jee-europa-fall-win32.zip). Unzip it into c:\eclipse. Then, create a shortcut to run "c:\eclipse\eclipse -data c:\workspace". This way, it will store your projects under the c:\workspace folder. To see if it's working, run it and make sure you can switch to the Java EE perspective:

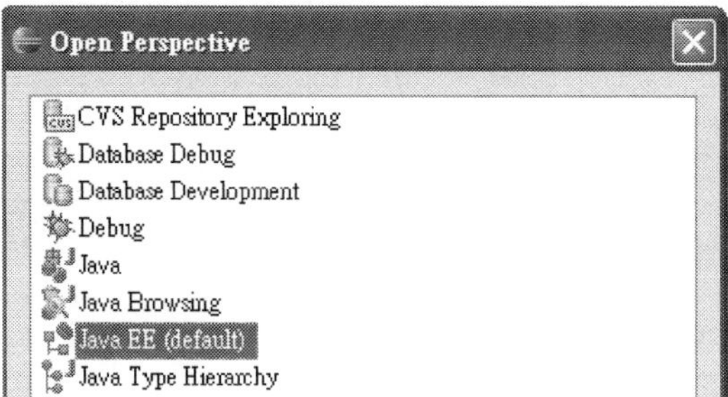

BUG ALERT: If you're using Eclipse 3.3.1, there is a serious bug in it: When visually editing WSDL files Eclipse will frequently crash with an OutOfMemoryError. To fix it, modify c:\eclipse\eclipse.ini:

Installing Axis2

Next, go to http://ws.apache.org/axis2 to download the "Standard Binary Distribution" (e.g. axis2-1.3-bin.zip). Unzip it into c:\axis. To run the Axis server, change into c:\axis\bin and run axis2server.bat. You should see:

```
$ axis2server.bat
Using JAVA_HOME    C:\Program Files\Java\jdk1.5.0_02
Using AXIS2_HOME   c:\axis2-1.3\bin\..
[INFO] [SimpleAxisServer] Starting
[INFO] [SimpleAxisServer] Using the Axis2 Repositoryc:\axis2-1.3\bin\..\reposito
ry
[SimpleAxisServer] Using the Axis2 Repositoryc:\axis2-1.3\bin\..\repository
[SimpleAxisServer] Using the Axis2 Configuration Filec:\axis2-1.3\bin\..\conf\ax
is2.xml
[INFO] Deploying module: addressing-1.3
[INFO] Deploying module: metadataExchange-1.3
[INFO] Deploying module: ping-1.3
[INFO] Deploying module: script-1.3
[INFO] Deploying module: soapmonitor-1.3
[INFO] script module activated
[INFO] Deploying Web service: version.aar
[INFO] [SimpleAxisServer] Started
[SimpleAxisServer] Started
[INFO] Listening on port 8080
```

Then open a browser and access http://localhost:8080. You should see:

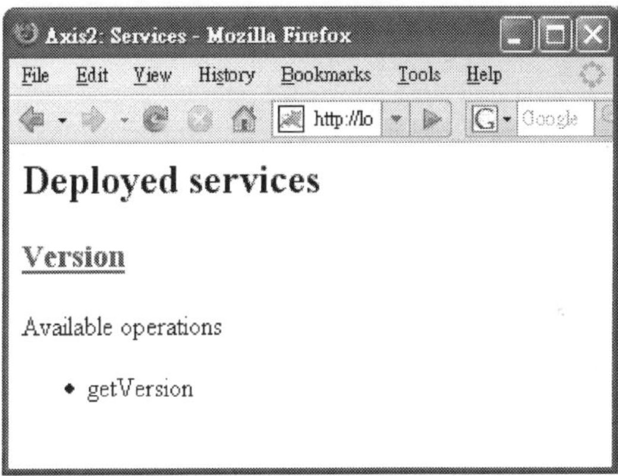

It means that there is an existing web service called "Version" available. Click on that "Version" link and you should see its WSDL file:

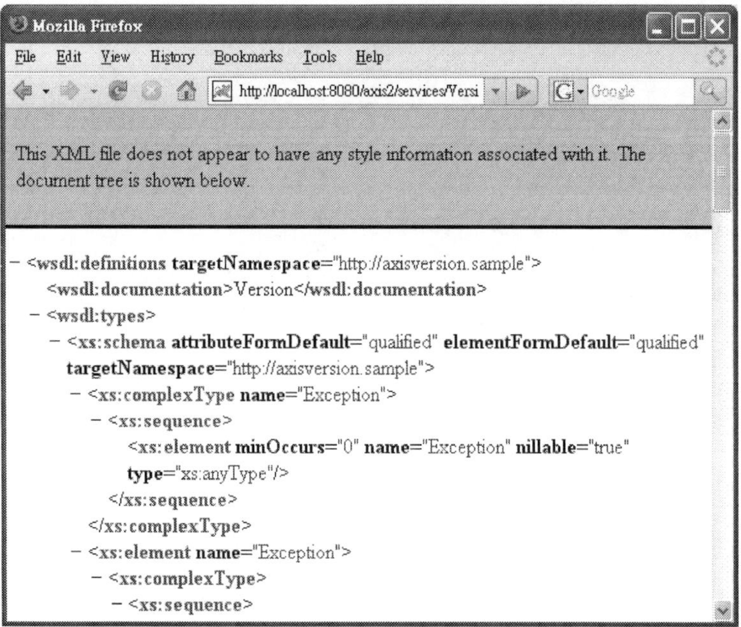

Installing the Axis2 plugin for Eclipse

Go to http://ws.apache.org/axis2/tools/index.html and download the Code Generator Wizard - Eclipse Plug-in. BUG ALERT: v1.4 of the plugin contains a critical bug. Use v1.3 instead! Suppose that it is axis2-eclipse-codegen-wizard.zip. Unzip it into the c:\eclipse\plugins folder. Restart Eclipse if required. To check if it's working, choose "File | New | Other" and you should see the "Axis2 Code Generator":

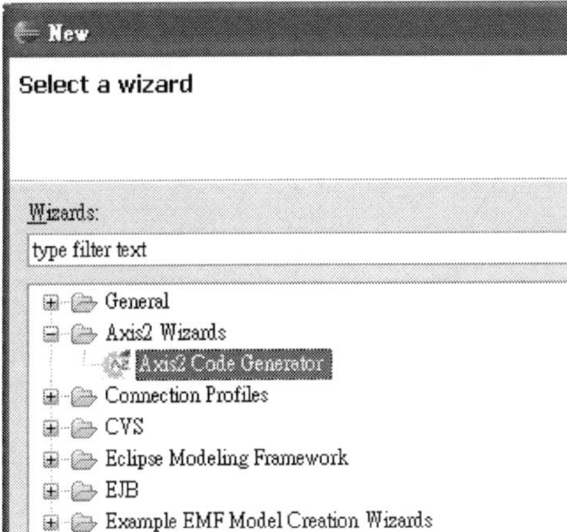

WSDL file for the web service

Suppose that you'd like to create a web service described in the previous chapter:

```
Target namespace: http://ttdev.com/ss

 Schema
 <xsd:schema
   targetNamespace="http://ttdev.com/ss
   xmlns:tns="http://ttdev.com/ss"
   xmlns:xsd="http://www.w3.org/2001/XMLSchema">
   <xsd:element name="concatRequest">
     <xsd:complexType>
       <xsd:sequence>
         <xsd:element name="s1" type="xsd:string"/>
         <xsd:element name="s2" type="xsd:string"/>
       </xsd:sequence>
     </xsd:complexType>
   </xsd:element>
   <xsd:element name="concatResponse" type="xsd:string"/>
 </xsd:schema>

 Port type
 Name: ...
 Operations:
   Name: concat
   Input msg:
     Part 1:
       Name: concatRequest
       Element: concatRequest element as defined in the schema
   Output msg:
     Part 1:
       Name: concatRequest
       Element: concatResponse element as defined in the schema

 Binding
 Name: ...
 Port type:
 Format: SOAP
 Transport: HTTP

 Port
 Name: ...
 Binding:
 Endpoint: ...
```

To write it using the real WSDL language, it should be:

The names of the port types, operations, bindings and ports will be put into this namespace

All the elements and element types defined in the schema will be put into this namespace

```
<?xml version="1.0" encoding="UTF-8"?>
<wsdl:definitions xmlns:soap="http://schemas.xmlsoap.org/wsdl/soap/"
  xmlns:tns="http://ttdev.com/ss"
  xmlns:wsdl="http://schemas.xmlsoap.org/wsdl/"
  xmlns:xsd="http://www.w3.org/2001/XMLSchema" name="SimpleService"
  targetNamespace="http://ttdev.com/ss">
  <wsdl:types>
    <xsd:schema
      targetNamespace="http://ttdev.com/ss"
      xmlns:tns="http://ttdev.com/ss">
      <xsd:element name="concatRequest">
        <xsd:complexType>
          <xsd:sequence>
          <xsd:element name="s1" type="xsd:string"/>
          <xsd:element name="s2" type="xsd:string"/>
          </xsd:sequence>
        </xsd:complexType>
      </xsd:element>
      <xsd:element name="concatResponse" type="xsd:string"/>
    </xsd:schema>
  </wsdl:types>
  <wsdl:message name="concatRequest">
    <wsdl:part name="concatRequest" element="tns:concatRequest" />
  </wsdl:message>
  <wsdl:message name="concatResponse">
    <wsdl:part name="concatResponse" element="tns:concatResponse" />
  </wsdl:message>
  <wsdl:portType name="SimpleService">
    <wsdl:operation name="concat">
      <wsdl:input message="tns:concatRequest" />
      <wsdl:output message="tns:concatResponse" />
    </wsdl:operation>
  </wsdl:portType>
  ...
</wsdl:definitions>
```

Put the schema into the <types> section

The input message contains a single part. The name of the part is unimportant.

The output message contains a single part. The name of the part is unimportant.

concat operation

This defines the schema and the port type. To define the binding and the port:

```
<?xml version="1.0" encoding="UTF-8"?>
<wsdl:definitions xmlns:soap="http://schemas.xmlsoap.org/wsdl/soap/"
  xmlns:tns="http://ttdev.com/ss"
  xmlns:wsdl="http://schemas.xmlsoap.org/wsdl/"
  xmlns:xsd="http://www.w3.org/2001/XMLSchema" name="SimpleService"
  targetNamespace="http://ttdev.com/ss">
  <wsdl:types>
    ...
  </wsdl:types>
  <wsdl:message name="concatRequest">
    <wsdl:part name="concatRequest" element="tns:concatRequest" />
  </wsdl:message>
  <wsdl:message name="concatResponse">
    <wsdl:part name="concatResponse" element="tns:concatResponse" />
  </wsdl:message>
  <wsdl:portType name="SimpleService">
    <wsdl:operation name="concat">
      <wsdl:input message="tns:concatRequest" />
      <wsdl:output message="tns:concatResponse" />
    </wsdl:operation>
  </wsdl:portType>
  <wsdl:binding name="SimpleServiceSOAP" type="tns:SimpleService">
    <soap:binding style="document"
      transport="http://schemas.xmlsoap.org/soap/http" />
  </wsdl:binding>
  <wsdl:service name="SimpleService">
    <wsdl:port binding="tns:SimpleServiceSOAP"
      name="SimpleServiceSOAP">
      <soap:address
        location="http://localhost:8080/axis2/services/SimpleServiceSOAP"/>
    </wsdl:port>
  </wsdl:service>
</wsdl:definitions>
```

The binding uses the SOAP format and HTTP transport. SOAP supports RPC and document styles. Here you use the document style.
This binding implements this port type
The port supports this binding
The port
URL to the Axis server
Must be the word "services"
Name of the port
The endpoint of the port

In fact, in a SOAP binding, you need to specify some more details:

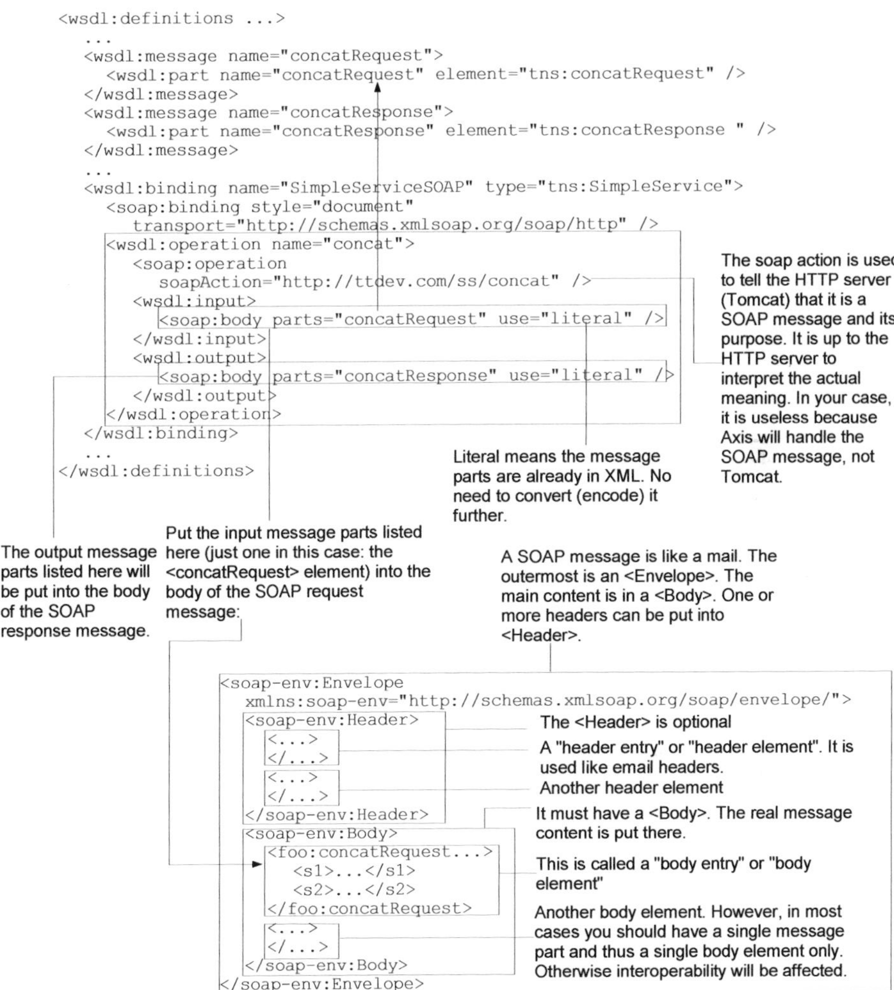

RPC version of the web service

If the web service was a RPC style service, then the WSDL file would be like:

```
<wsdl:definitions ...>
  <wsdl:types>
    <xsd:schema ...>
      <xsd:element name="concatRequest">
        <xsd:complexType>
          <xsd:sequence>
            <xsd:element name="s1" type="xsd:string"/>
            <xsd:element name="s2" type="xsd:string"/>
          </xsd:sequence>
        </xsd:complexType>
      </xsd:element>
      <xsd:element name="concatResponse" type="xsd:string"/>
    </xsd:schema>
  <wsdl:types/>
  <wsdl:message name="concatRequest">
    <wsdl:part name="s1" type="xsd:string" />
    <wsdl:part name="s2" type="xsd:string" />
  </wsdl:message>
  <wsdl:message name="concatResponse">
    <wsdl:part name="return" type="xsd:string" />
  </wsdl:message>
  <wsdl:portType name="SimpleService">
    <wsdl:operation name="concat">
      <wsdl:input message="tns:concatRequest" />
      <wsdl:output message="tns:concatResponse" />
    </wsdl:operation>
  </wsdl:portType>
  <wsdl:binding name="SimpleServiceSOAP" type="tns:SimpleService">
    <soap:binding style="rpc"
      transport="http://schemas.xmlsoap.org/soap/http" />
    <wsdl:operation name="concat">
      <soap:operation
        soapAction="http://ttdev.com/ss/concat" />
      <wsdl:input>
        <soap:body parts="s1 s2" use="literal" />
      </wsdl:input>
      <wsdl:output>
        <soap:body parts="return" use="literal" />
      </wsdl:output>
    </wsdl:operation>
  </wsdl:binding>
  ...
</wsdl:definitions>
```

Don't need these any more

The input message has two parts. Each part is of element type xsd:string (not elements).

The output message has one part. It is of element type xsd:string (not elements).

RPC style

Two message parts are listed. So, they will be included into the <Body> (but not directly). As it is a RPC style service, the caller must create an element with the QName of the operation and then add each message part listed here as a child element. So it should still have a single element in the <Body>:

```
<soap-env:Envelope
  xmlns:soap-env="http://schemas.xmlsoap.org/soap/envelope/">
  <soap-env:Header>
    ...
  </soap-env:Header>
  <soap-env:Body>
    <foo:concat ...>
      <s1>...</s1>
      <s2>...</s2>
    </foo:concat>
  </soap-env:Body>
</soap-env:Envelope>
```

No schema to validate it

As RPC style is not good for interoperability, you'll continue to use the document style version.

Creating the WSDL file visually

It may be error prone to manually create such a WSDL file. Instead, you may use the Eclipse to do it. First, create a new Java project named SimpleService in Eclipse:

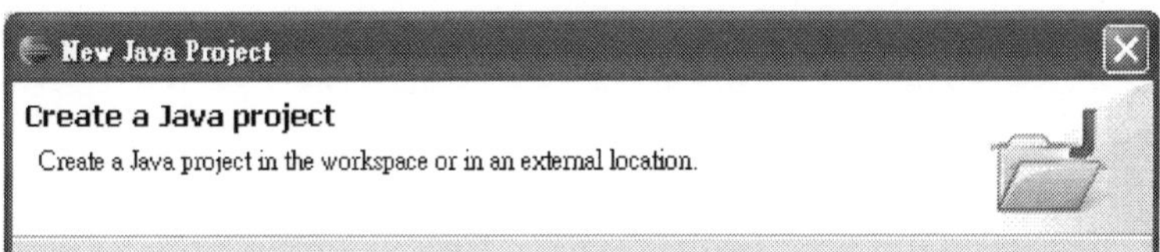

Make sure you use separate folders for sources and class files. Then go ahead and complete the creation of the project. Next, right click the project and choose "New | Other" and then "Web Services | WSDL":

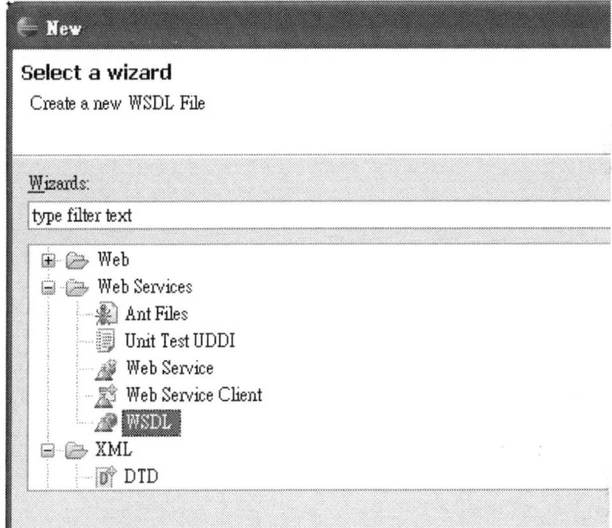

If you don't see this option, it means that you haven't installed the Java EE version of Eclipse. If it is working, click "Next" and enter SimpleService.wsdl as the filename:

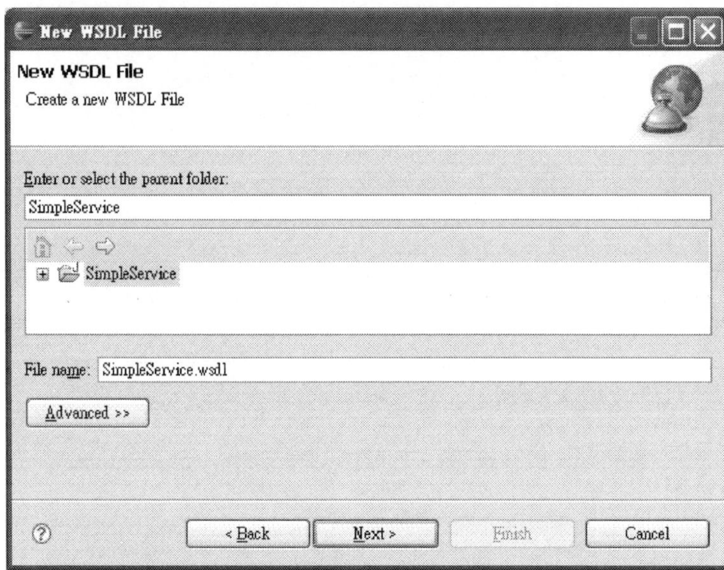

Click "Next". Then input as shown below:

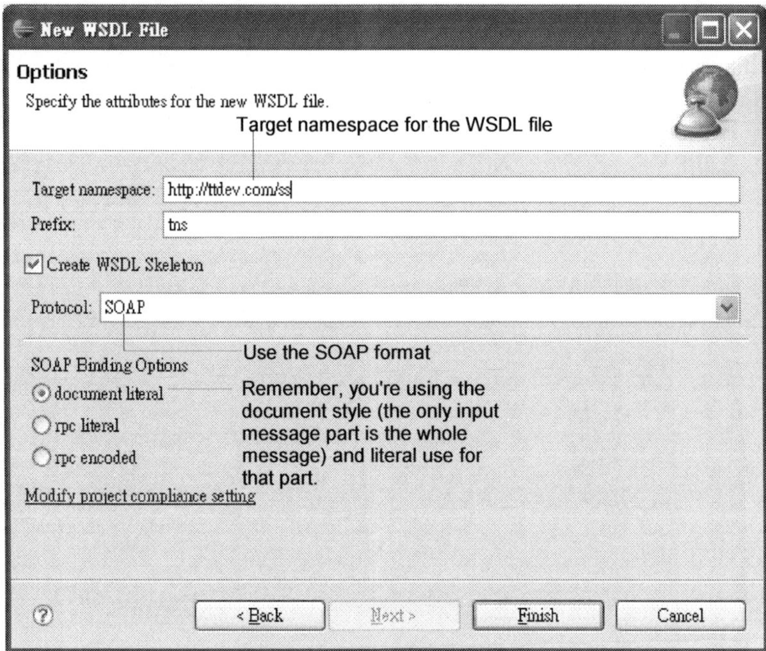

Click "Finish". Then you will see something like:

SimpleService.wsdl

```
<?xml version="1.0" encoding="UTF-8"?>
<wsdl:definitions xmlns:wsdl="http://schemas.xmlsoap.org/wsdl/" xmlns:s
  <wsdl:types>
    <xsd:schema targetNamespace="http://ttdev.com/ss" xmlns:xsd="http:/.
      <xsd:element name="NewOperation">
        <xsd:complexType>
          <xsd:sequence>
            <xsd:element name="in" type="xsd:string"/>
          </xsd:sequence>
        </xsd:complexType>
      </xsd:element>
      <xsd:element name="NewOperationResponse">
        <xsd:complexType>
          <xsd:sequence>
            <xsd:element name="out" type="xsd:string"/>
          </xsd:sequence>
        </xsd:complexType>
      </xsd:element>
    </xsd:schema>
  </wsdl:types>
  <wsdl:message name="NewOperationRequest">
    <wsdl:part element="tns:NewOperation" name="parameters"/>
  </wsdl:message>
  <wsdl:message name="NewOperationResponse">
    <wsdl:part element="tns:NewOperationResponse" name="parameters"/>
  </wsdl:message>
  <wsdl:portType name="SimpleService">
    <wsdl:operation name="NewOperation">
      <wsdl:input message="tns:NewOperationRequest"/>
      <wsdl:output message="tns:NewOperationResponse"/>
    </wsdl:operation>
  </wsdl:portType>
```

Design Source

This is the WSDL code. To edit it visually, click the "Design" tab at the bottom of the editor window. Then you'll see:

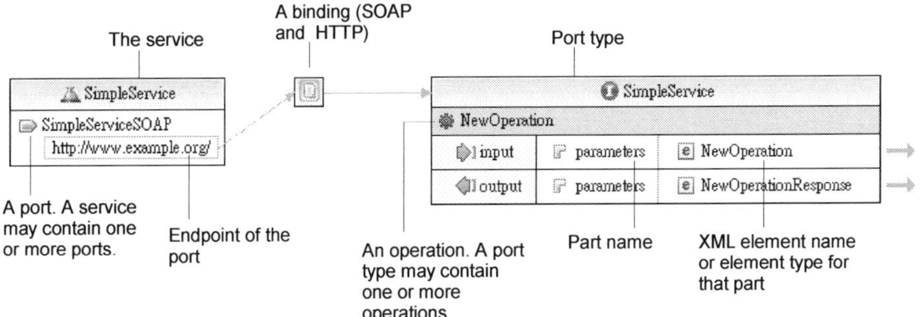

Double click on the endpoint to change it to http://localhost:8080/axis2/services/

SimpleService:

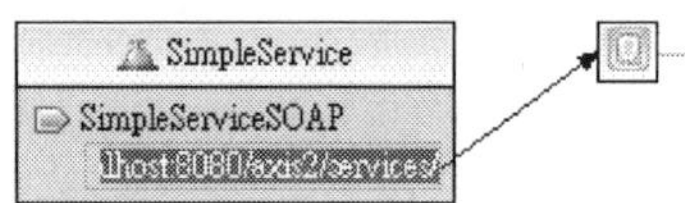

Double click on the name of operation and change it to "concat":

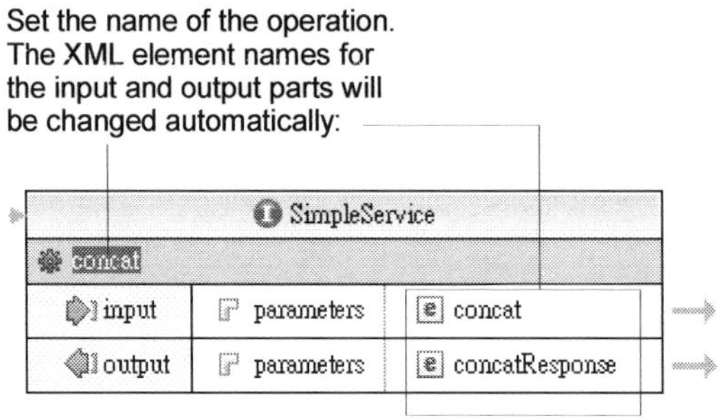

For the moment, the input part is an <concat> element. You'd like to change it to <concatRequest>. But for now, put the cursor on the arrow to its right first. The arrow will turn into blue color. Wait a couple of seconds then a preview window will appear showing the definition of the <concat> element:

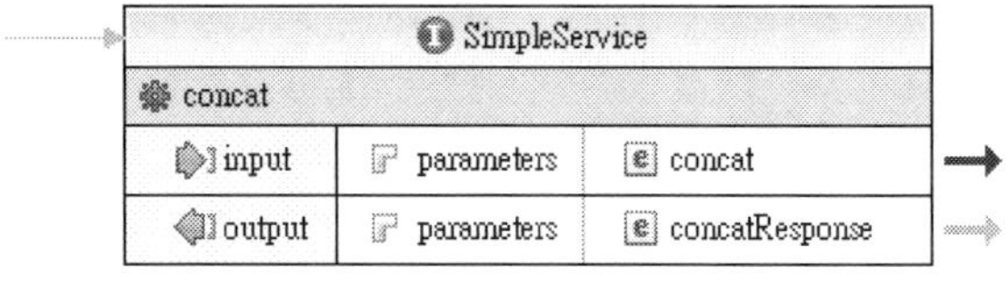

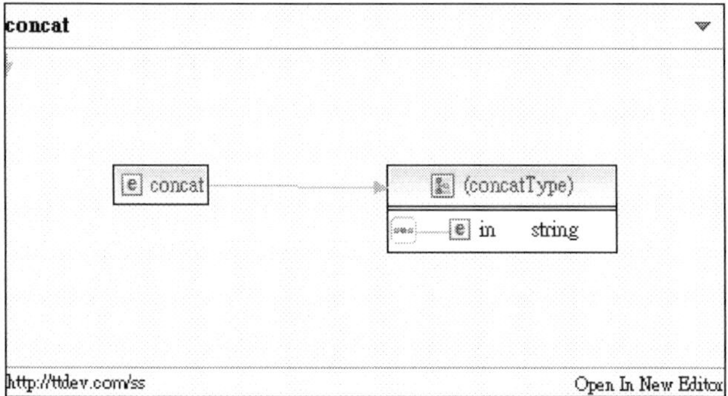

Clicking anywhere else will make that preview window disappear. To edit the schema definition, click on the blue arrow. A new editor window will appear:

*SimpleService.wsdl | *Inline Schema of SimpleService.wsdl

```
<xsd:element name="concat">
  <xsd:complexType>
    <xsd:sequence>
      <xsd:element name="in" type="xsd:string"/>
    </xsd:sequence>
  </xsd:complexType>
</xsd:element>
<xsd:element name="concatResponse">
  <xsd:complexType>
    <xsd:sequence>
      <xsd:element name="out" type="xsd:string"/>
    </xsd:sequence>
```

To edit it visually, click the "Design" tab at the bottom, you'll see:

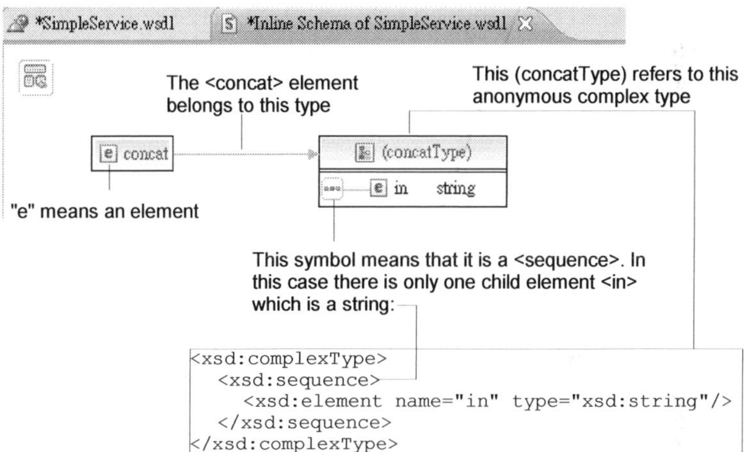

Double click on "in" and change it to "s1":

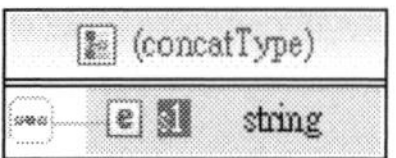

Right click it and choose "Add Element" and set the name to "s2":

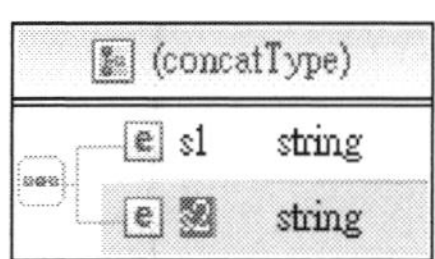

By default the type is already set to string. If you wanted it to be say an int instead, you would double click on the type and it would become a combo box and then you could choose "int":

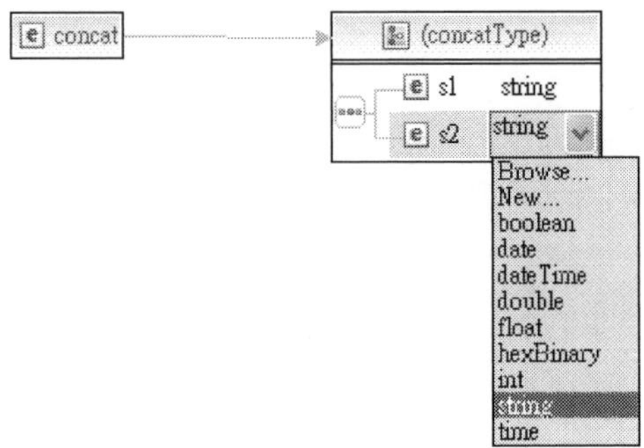

If you wanted s2 to appear before s1 in the sequence, you could drag it and drop it before s1:

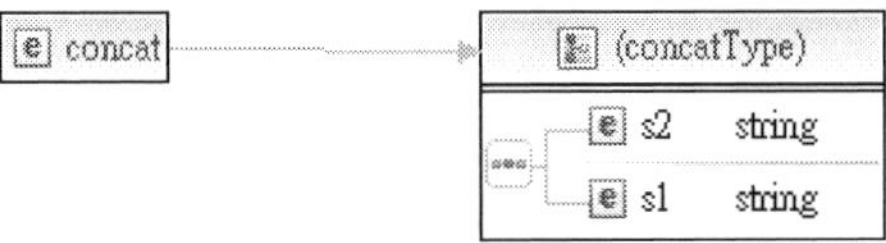

But for now, make sure it is s1 first and then s2. Next, right click on the <concat> element and choose "Refactor | Rename", then change its name to concatRequest:

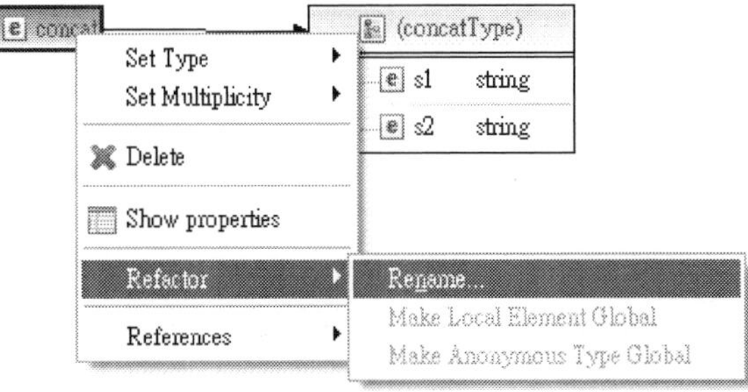

You're done with the <concatRequest> element. Now return to the WSDL editor to work on the response message. For the moment, the <concatResponse> is like:

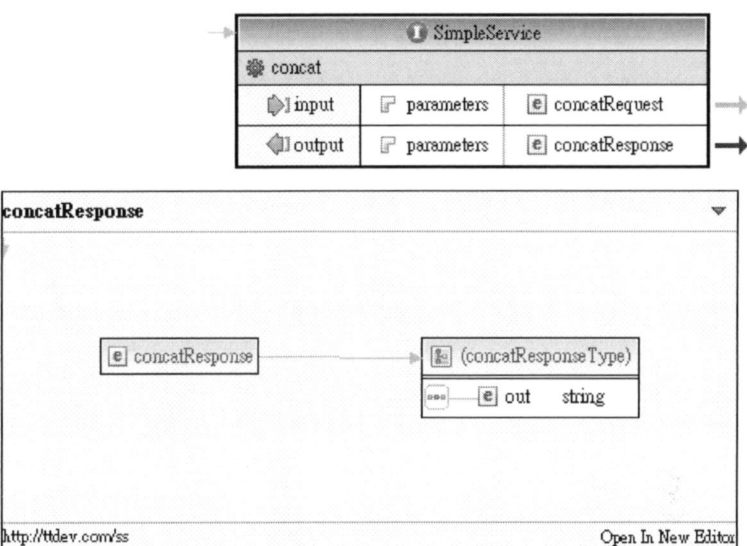

That is, it is an element that contains a sequence of <out> element:

```
<foo:concatResponse>
  <foo:out>abc</foo:out>
</foo:concatResponse>
```

However, in your design, the response is simple type element, not a complex type element:

Its body contains a string instead of other elements

```
<foo:concatResponse
  xmlns:foo="http://ttdev.com/ss">abc123</foo:concatResponse>
```

To do that, go into the schema editor to edit the <concatResponse> element:

Right click it and choose "Set Type | Browse":

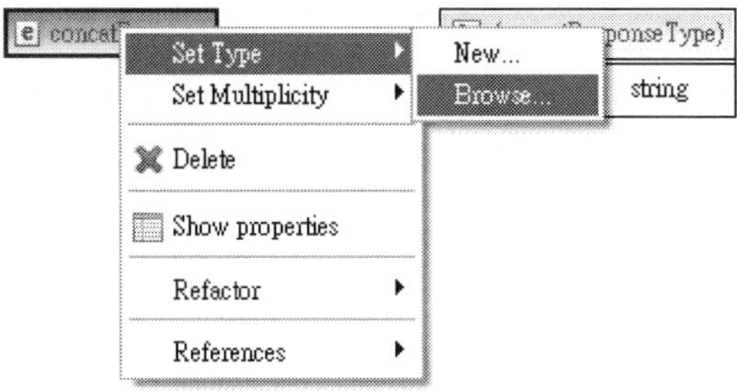

Choose "string":

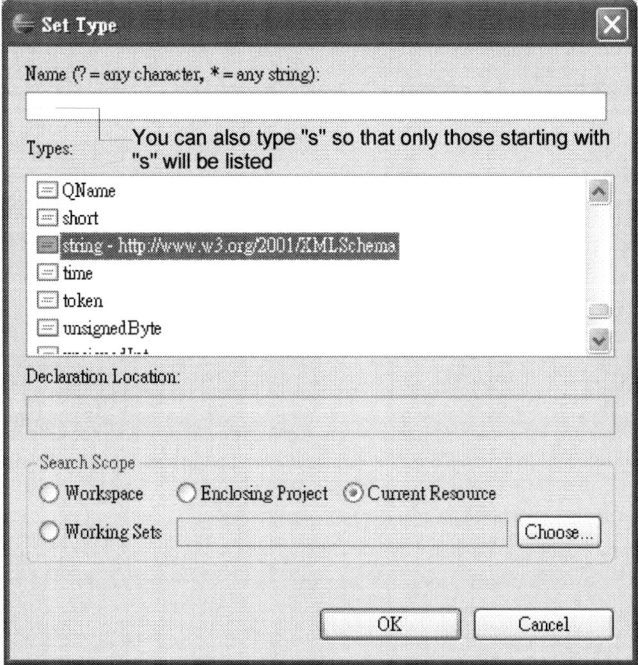

Then it will be like:

That's it. To review the whole schema, click on the icon at the upper left corner:

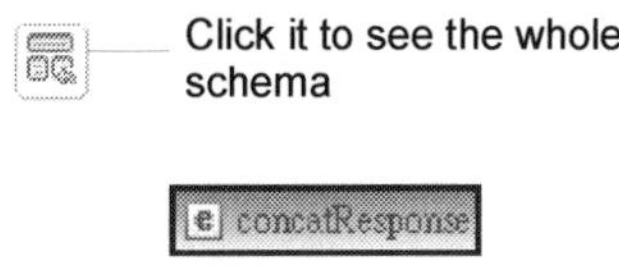

Then you'll see:

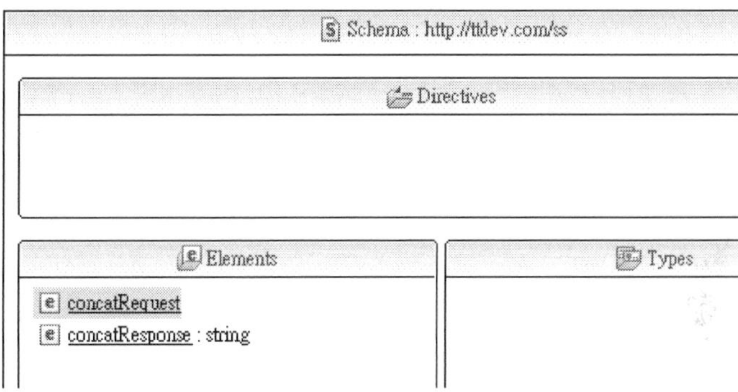

This looks fine. Now, save the file.

Validating the WSDL file

The next step is to validate the WSDL file to make sure it conforms to the various web services standards. To do that, right click the SimpleService.wsdl file in Eclipse and choose "Validate". If there were anything wrong, they would be reported in the Problems window. For example, here I had introduced an error into the file:

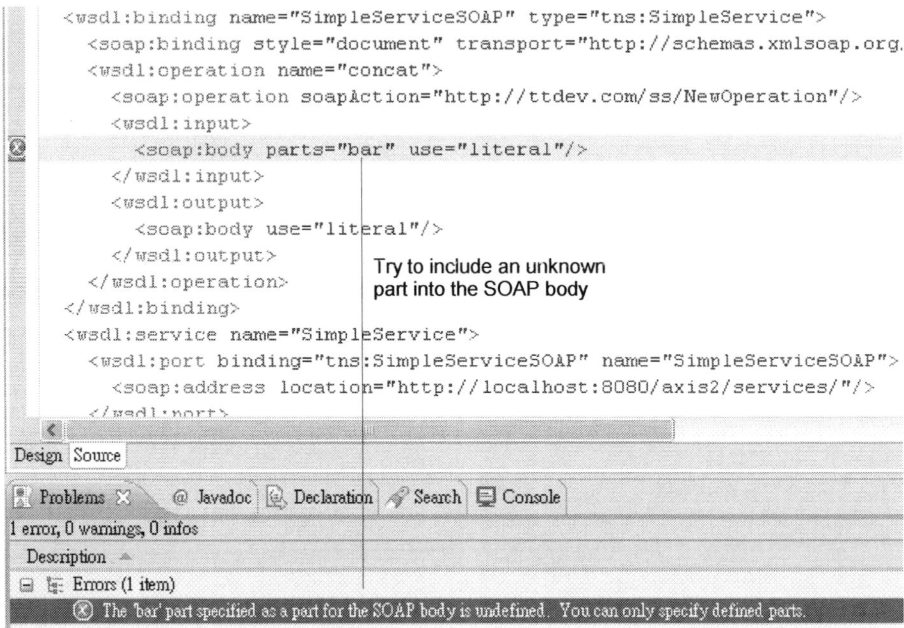
<wsdl:binding name="SimpleServiceSOAP" type="tns:SimpleService">
<soap:binding style="document" transport="http://schemas.xmlsoap.org.
<wsdl:operation name="concat">
<soap:operation soapAction="http://ttdev.com/ss/NewOperation"/>
<wsdl:input>
<soap:body parts="bar" use="literal"/>
</wsdl:input>
<wsdl:output>
<soap:body use="literal"/>
</wsdl:output>
</wsdl:operation>
</wsdl:binding>
<wsdl:service name="SimpleService">
<wsdl:port binding="tns:SimpleServiceSOAP" name="SimpleServiceSOAP">
<soap:address location="http://localhost:8080/axis2/services/"/>
Try to include an unknown part into the SOAP body
Design
Source
Problems
Javadoc
Declaration
Search
Console
1 error, 0 warnings, 0 infos
Description
Errors (1 item)
The 'bar' part specified as a part for the SOAP body is undefined. You can only specify defined parts.

Generating a service stub

Next, in order to implement the web service, you will generate a "service stub" (see the diagram below). When a request message comes in, the service stub will convert the <concatRequest> XML element into a ConcatRequest Java object. Then it will pass it to the concat() method in a service skeleton to be supplied by you. Your concat() method will create and return a ConcatResponse Java object. The service stub will convert it into a <concatResponse> XML element and return it to the client:

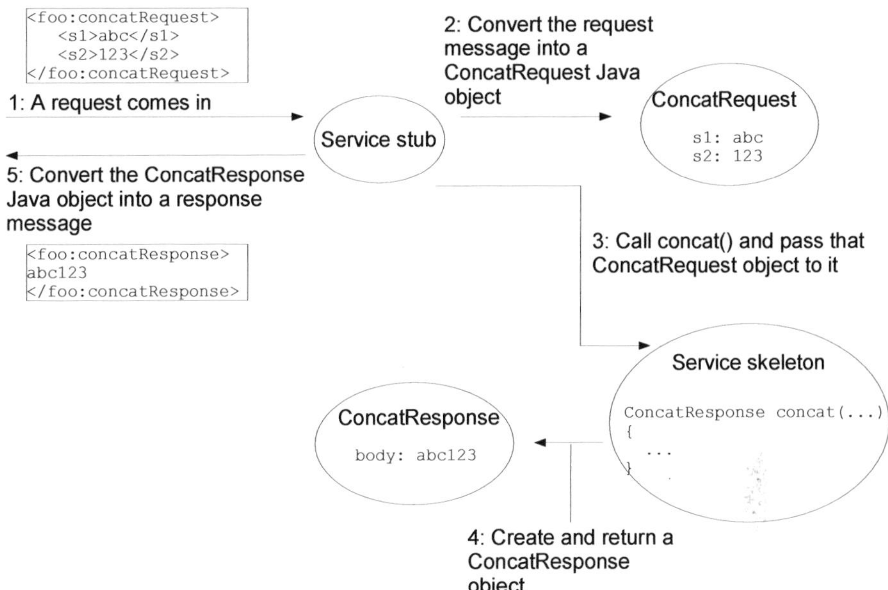
<foo:concatRequest>
<s1>abc</s1>
<s2>123</s2>
</foo:concatRequest>
1: A request comes in
Service stub
2: Convert the request message into a ConcatRequest Java object
ConcatRequest
s1: abc
s2: 123
5: Convert the ConcatResponse Java object into a response message
<foo:concatResponse>
abc123
</foo:concatResponse>
3: Call concat() and pass that ConcatRequest object to it
Service skeleton
ConcatResponse concat(...)
{
...
}
ConcatResponse
body: abc123
4: Create and return a ConcatResponse object

To implement this idea, in Eclipse choose "File | New | Other" and choose "Axis2 Code Generator" (see below). The default is to generate Java code from WSDL. This is what you want:

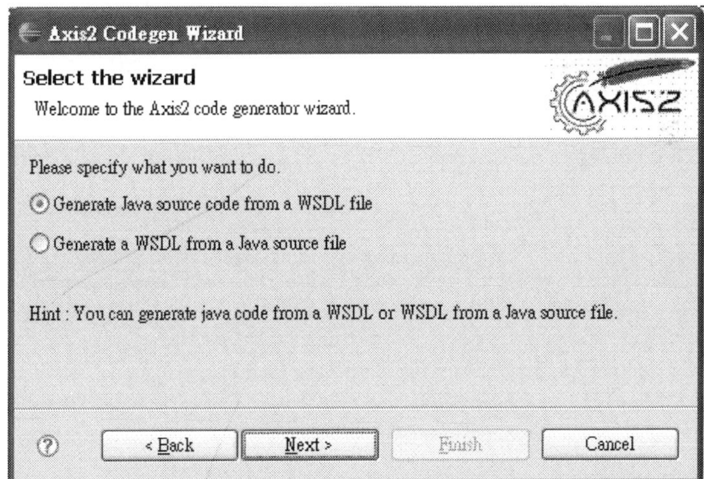
Axis2 Codegen Wizard
Select the wizard
Welcome to the Axis2 code generator wizard.
AXIS2
Please specify what you want to do.
Generate Java source code from a WSDL file
Generate a WSDL from a Java source file
Hint : You can generate java code from a WSDL or WSDL from a Java source file.
< Back
Next >
Finish
Cancel

Click "Next" (see below). Click "Browse" to locate your SimpleService.wsdl file:

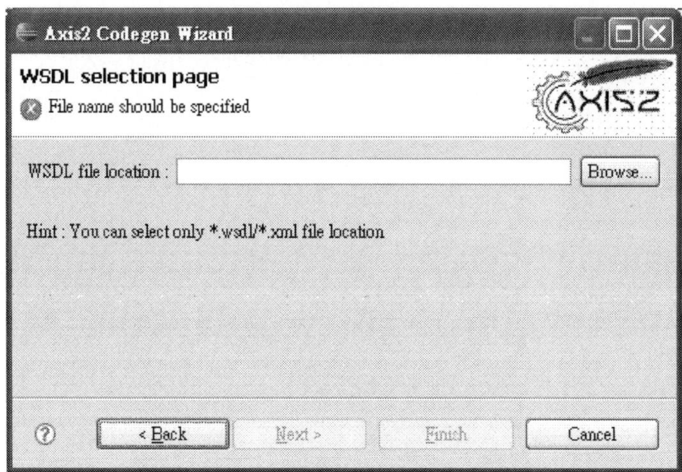

Click "Next" (see below). Set the options as shown below:

Axis2 Codegen Wizard

Options

Set the options for the code generator. If you wish to edit the codegen options, Select custom option from Codegen Option drop down list.

Codegen option	custom
Output language	java
Service Name	SimpleService
Port Name	SimpleServiceSOAP
Databinding Name	adb
Custom package name	com.ttdev.ss

Set to "custom" in order to enable the options below.

☐ Generate test case

☐ Generate client side code

○ Generate both sync and async ○ Generate sync style only ○ Generate async style only

Generate server side code (the code implementing the service)

☑ Generate server side code

☑ Generate a default services.xml ☑ Generate an Interface for Skeleton

☐ Generate Both with all classes for every elements on Shemas

Namespace to package mappings

Namespace	Custom package name
http://ttdev.com/ss	com.ttdev.ss
http://www.w3.org/2001/XMLSchema	org.w3.www._2001.xmlschema
http://schemas.xmlsoap.org/wsdl/soap/	org.xmlsoap.schemas.wsdl.soap
http://schemas.xmlsoap.org/wsdl/	org.xmlsoap.schemas.wsdl

< Back Next > Finish Cancel

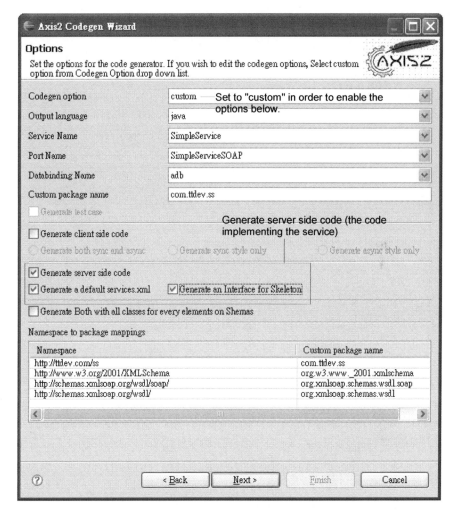

Note that by default how the namespaces will be mapped to Java packages. For example, your SimpleService port type in http://ttdev.com/ss namespace will be mapped to a SimpleService Java interface in the com.ttdev.ss Java package:

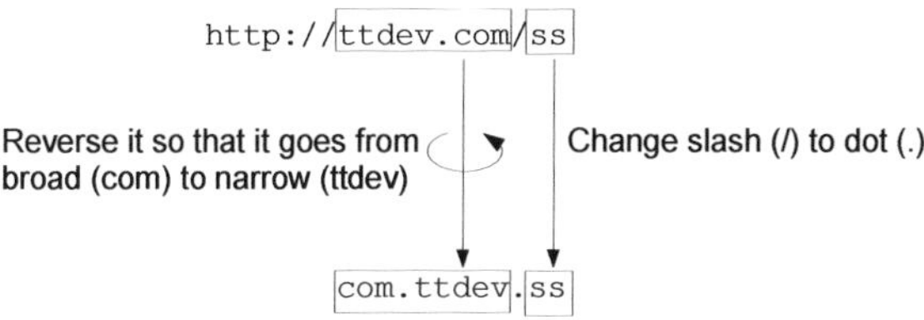

Of course this is just the default. You can change the Java package names in

the dialog box above. But for our purpose the default mapping is just fine. So, click "Next" (see below) and enter the information as shown below:

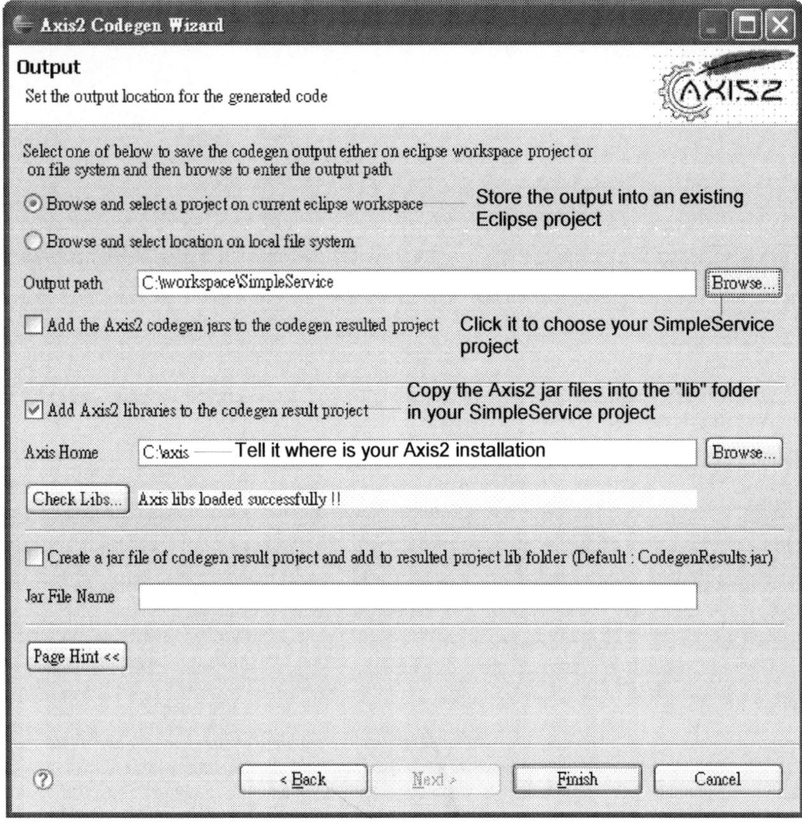

Click "Finish". Right click your project and choose "Refresh". Then you'll see some files have been generated:

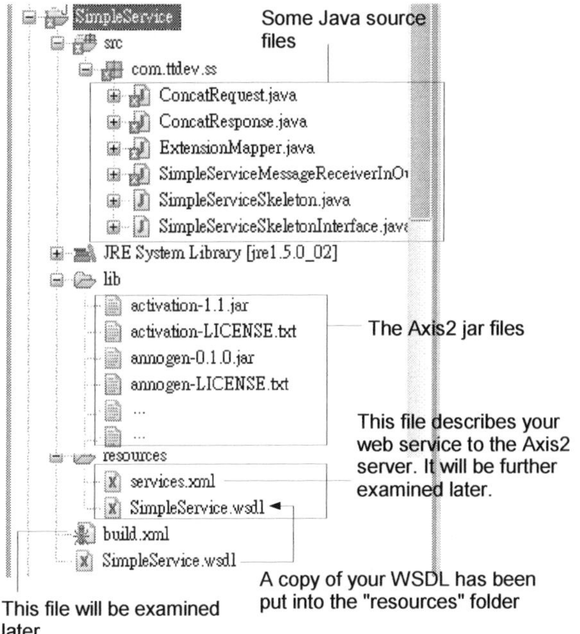

The Java source files are in errors because they are referring to the Axis2 jar files but they are not on the build path. So, go to the build path dialog and click "Add JARs":

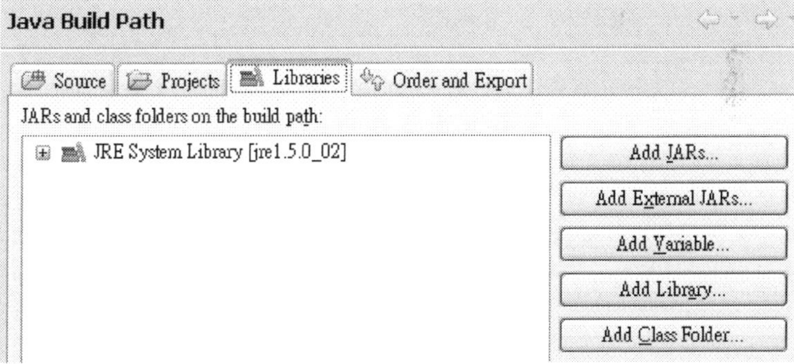

Choose all the jar files in the "lib" folder in your project:

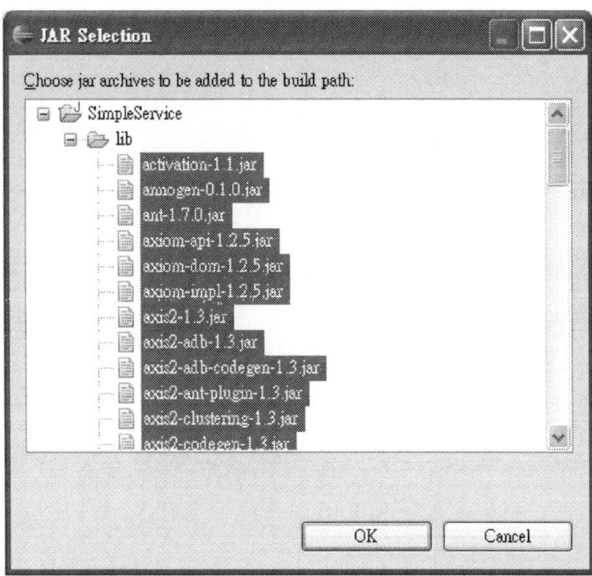

Then the errors will disappear.

Implementing the web service

To implement the web service, modify the SimpleServiceSkeleton.java which is the service skeleton:

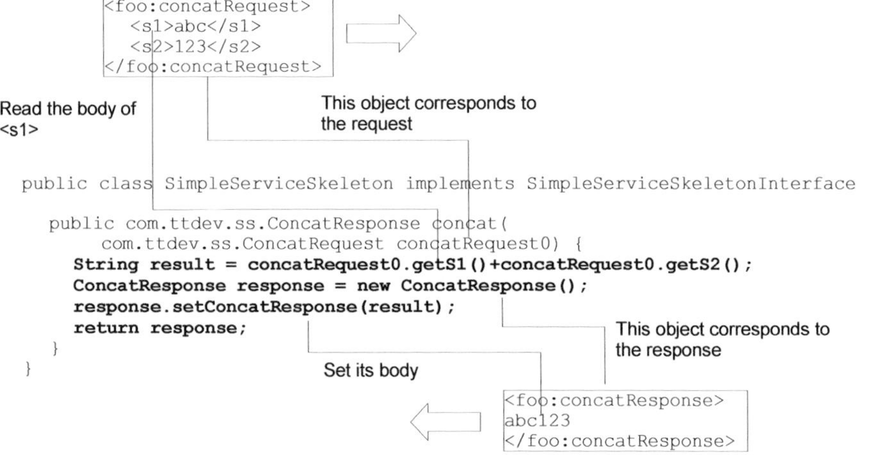

Where do the ConcatRequest class and ConcatResponse class come from? They were generated by the Axis2 Code Generator Wizard:

Deploying a web service

To deploy the web service with the Axis2 server, copy the files as shown below:

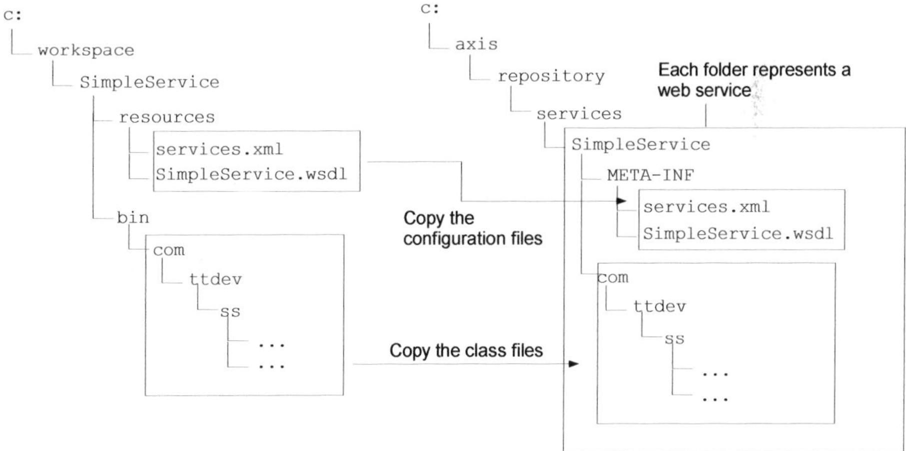

Now, start the Axis2 server by running c:\axis\bin\axis2server.bat. You should see that it is picking up your SimpleService:

```
c:\axis2-1.3\bin>axis2server.bat
Using JAVA_HOME    C:\Program Files\Java\jdk1.5.0_02
Using AXIS2_HOME   c:\axis2-1.3\bin\..
[INFO] [SimpleAxisServer] Starting
[INFO] [SimpleAxisServer] Using the Axis2 Repositoryc:\axis2-1.3\bin\..\reposito
ry
[SimpleAxisServer] Using the Axis2 Repositoryc:\axis2-1.3\bin\..\repository
[SimpleAxisServer] Using the Axis2 Configuration Filec:\axis2-1.3\bin\..\conf\ax
is2.xml
[INFO] Deploying module: addressing-1.3
[INFO] Deploying module: metadataExchange-1.3
[INFO] Deploying module: ping-1.3
[INFO] Deploying module: script-1.3
[INFO] Deploying module: soapmonitor-1.3
[INFO] script module activated
[INFO] Deploying Web service: SimpleService
[INFO] Deploying Web service: version.aar
[INFO] [SimpleAxisServer] Started
[SimpleAxisServer] Started
[INFO] Listening on port 8080
```

Go to http://localhost:8080 and you should see your SimpleService listed:

To see its WSDL file, just click the "SimpleService" link:

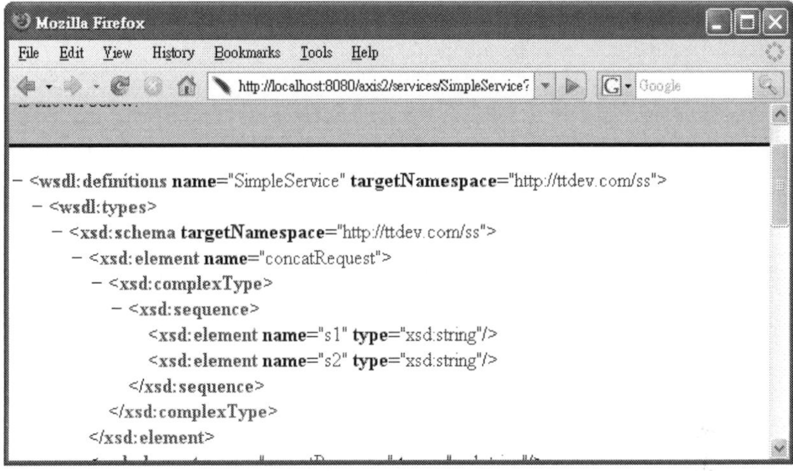

Creating a client using a client stub

To call this web service, you can use the Axis2 Code Generator Wizard to generate a "client stub". When you call a method on it (see the diagram below), it will convert your Java data/objects into the right format (XML), create a request message in the right format (SOAP), send it over the Internet to the right endpoint using the right transport protocol (HTTP) to invoke that operation, wait for the response message, convert the XML back into Java data/object and then return it to you:

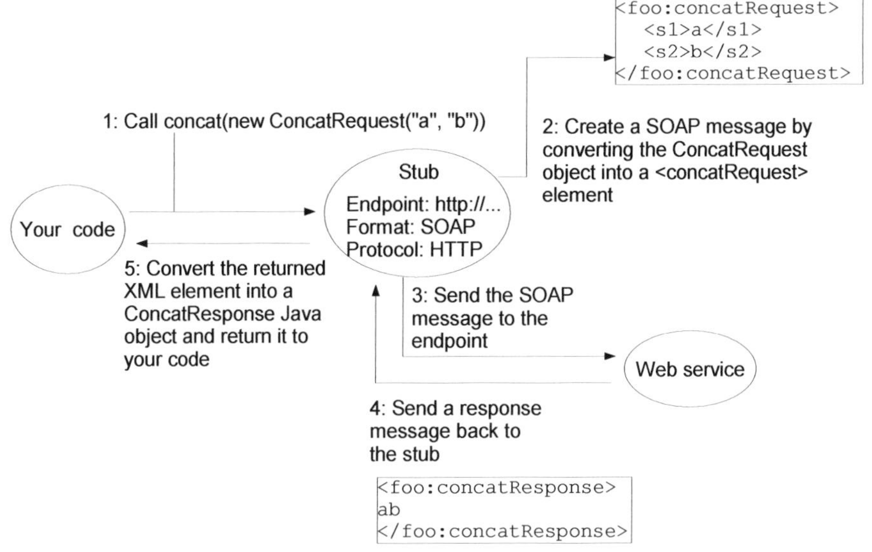

To implement this idea, run the Axis2 Code Generator Wizard as before until you see the follow screen. Then tell it to generate client side code instead of server side code:

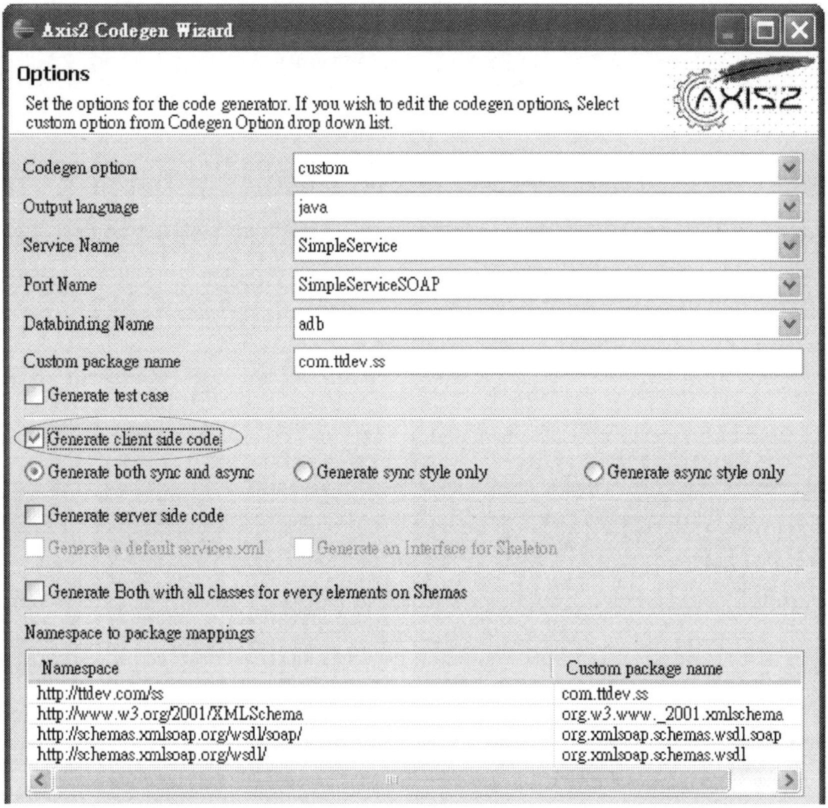

Axis2 Codegen Wizard

Options

Set the options for the code generator. If you wish to edit the codegen options, Select custom option from Codegen Option drop down list.

AXIS2

Codegen option: custom

Output language: java

Service Name: SimpleService

Port Name: SimpleServiceSOAP

Databinding Name: adb

Custom package name: com.ttdev.ss

☐ Generate test case

☑ Generate client side code

◉ Generate both sync and async ○ Generate sync style only ○ Generate async style only

☐ Generate server side code

☐ Generate a default services.xml ☐ Generate an Interface for Skeleton

☐ Generate Both with all classes for every elements on Shemas

Namespace to package mappings

Namespace	Custom package name
http://ttdev.com/ss	com.ttdev.ss
http://www.w3.org/2001/XMLSchema	org.w3.www._2001.xmlschema
http://schemas.xmlsoap.org/wsdl/soap/	org.xmlsoap.schemas.wsdl.soap
http://schemas.xmlsoap.org/wsdl/	org.xmlsoap.schemas.wsdl

Then tell it to put the code into your SimpleService project. This time, no need to copy the Axis2 jar files again:

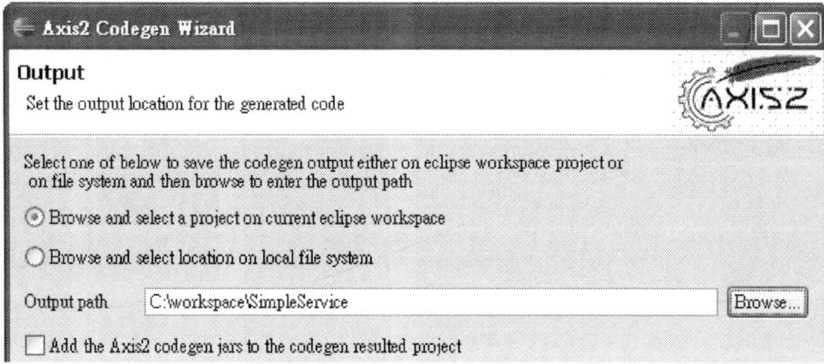

Click "Finish" and then refresh the project. You'll see a couple of new Java

source files:

Among them, SimpleServiceStub.java is the client stub. As you're simulating someone else calling your web service, they should not be mixed with the code implementing the web service. Therefore, move them into another package such as com.ttdev.ss.client.

Next, create a SimpleClient.java file in the com.ttdev.ss.client package:

LOOK OUT! There is a ConcatRequest class defined inside the SimpleServiceStub class. There is another one in the com.ttdev.ss package for the service implementation. You must use the former as you're writing a client. You should have no access to the server side code.

```
package com.ttdev.ss.client;

import java.rmi.RemoteException;
import com.ttdev.ss.client.SimpleServiceStub.ConcatRequest;
import com.ttdev.ss.client.SimpleServiceStub.ConcatResponse;

public class SimpleClient {
  public static void main(String[] args) throws RemoteException {
    SimpleServiceStub service = new SimpleServiceStub();
    ConcatRequest request = new ConcatRequest();
    request.setS1("abc");
    request.setS2("123");
    ConcatResponse response = service.concat(request);
    System.out.println(response.getConcatResponse());
  }
}
```

The same is true for the ConcatResponse class

Call the web service and get the response

Run it and it should work:

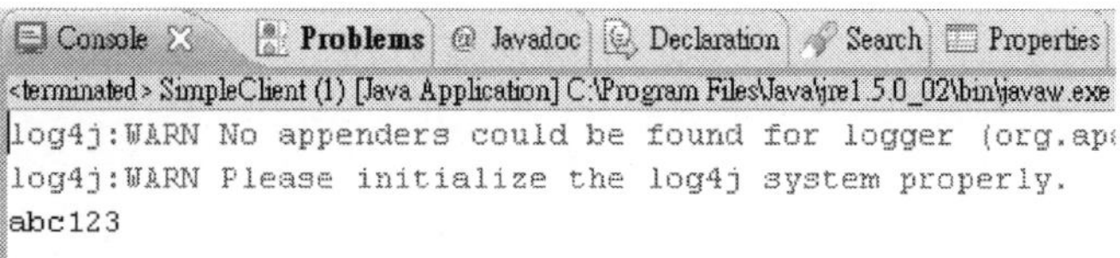

Undeploying a web service

If you'd like to undeploy a web service, all you need to do is to delete the SimpleService folder:

```
c:
└ axis
   └ repository
      └ services
         └ SimpleService
            ├ META-INF
            │  ├ services.xml
            │  └ SimpleService.wsdl
            └ com
               └ ttdev
                  └ ss
                     ├ ...
                     └ ...
```

Delete this folder

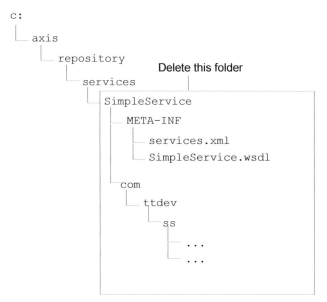

This works even when the Axis2 server is running. It will note the removal of the folder and undeploy the service:

```
Using JAVA_HOME    C:\Program Files\Java\jdk1.5.0_02
Using AXIS2_HOME   c:\axis2-1.3\bin\..
[INFO] [SimpleAxisServer] Starting
[INFO] [SimpleAxisServer] Using the Axis2 Repositoryc:\axis2-1.3\
ry
[SimpleAxisServer] Using the Axis2 Repositoryc:\axis2-1.3\bin\..\
[SimpleAxisServer] Using the Axis2 Configuration Filec:\axis2-1.3
is2.xml
[INFO] Deploying module: addressing-1.3
[INFO] Deploying module: metadataExchange-1.3
[INFO] Deploying module: ping-1.3
[INFO] Deploying module: script-1.3
[INFO] Deploying module: soapmonitor-1.3
[INFO] script module activated
[INFO] Deploying Web service: SimpleService
[INFO] Deploying Web service: version.aar
[INFO] [SimpleAxisServer] Started
[SimpleAxisServer] Started
[INFO] Listening on port 8080
[INFO] Undeploying Web service: SimpleService
```

If you put the folder back, it will be deployed again:

```
Using JAVA_HOME    C:\Program Files\Java\jdk1.5.0_02
Using AXIS2_HOME   c:\axis2-1.3\bin\..
[INFO] [SimpleAxisServer] Starting
[INFO] [SimpleAxisServer] Using the Axis2 Repositoryc:\axis2-
ry
[SimpleAxisServer] Using the Axis2 Repositoryc:\axis2-1.3\bin
[SimpleAxisServer] Using the Axis2 Configuration Filec:\axis2-
is2.xml
[INFO] Deploying module: addressing-1.3
[INFO] Deploying module: metadataExchange-1.3
[INFO] Deploying module: ping-1.3
[INFO] Deploying module: script-1.3
[INFO] Deploying module: soapmonitor-1.3
[INFO] script module activated
[INFO] Deploying Web service: SimpleService
[INFO] Deploying Web service: version.aar
[INFO] [SimpleAxisServer] Started
[SimpleAxisServer] Started
[INFO] Listening on port 8080
[INFO] Undeploying Web service: SimpleService
[INFO] Deploying Web service: SimpleService
```

This is called "hot deployment".

Summary

Tomcat hosts one or more web applications. The Axis server is installed as one of the web applications. It in turn hosts one or more web services.

Most usually your input message or output message is sent in a SOAP message. A SOAP message is always an <Envelope> element. It may contain a <Header> which contains one or more header entries/elements. The <Envelope> must contain a <Body> which may contain one or more body entries/elements. For a document style web service, the one and only input message part is usually the single body entry. For a RPC style web service, the element named after the operation will usually contain all message parts and is then included as the single body entry.

To create a web service, you first create a WSDL file describing its interface. This can be done manually or using a tool like Eclipse. Then use the Axis Code Generator Wizard on the WSDL file to generate a service stub. Then fill in the code in the service skeleton. The service stub will convert the XML elements in a request message into Java data/objects, call your skeleton and convert the Java objects returned into XML elements and put them into the response message.

To deploy a web service, copy the class files and the services.xml file to the Axis2 server according to a specific folder structure. To undeploy a web service, just delete that folder. The Axis2 server supports hot deployment. It means you can deploy or undeploy a service while it is running.

The endpoint of the deployed web service is http://localhost:8080/axis2/services/<name-of-your-service>.

To call a web service, run the Axis Code Generator Wizard on the WSDL file to generate a client stub. Then, in your code create an instance of the client stub and call its methods as if it were the web service. The client stub will convert the Java data/objects into XML elements, create the request message in the right format, send it to the right endpoint using the right transport protocol and convert the XML elements in the response message back into Java data/objects.

Chapter 3

Optimizing the development environment

What's in this chapter?

In this chapter you'll learn how to optimize the development environment.

Placing the class files into Axis directly

At the moment, whenever you make changes to say your web service Java code (SimpleServiceSkeleton.java), you will have to copy the class file into the Axis server again. This is troublesome. To solve this problem, you can tell Eclipse to put the class files directly into the Axis repository:

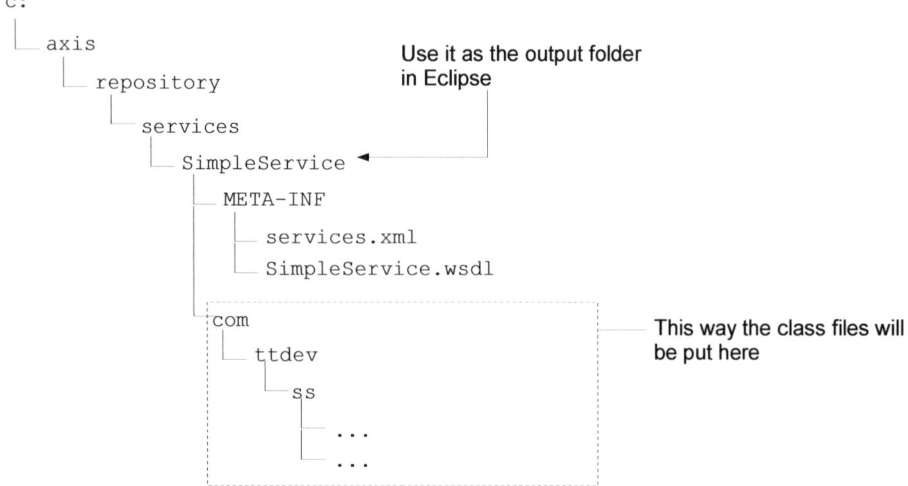

However, there is a problem: Eclipse can only use a folder inside the project as the output folder. To allow you to work around this restriction, fortunately Eclipse allows you to link such a folder to an outside folder:

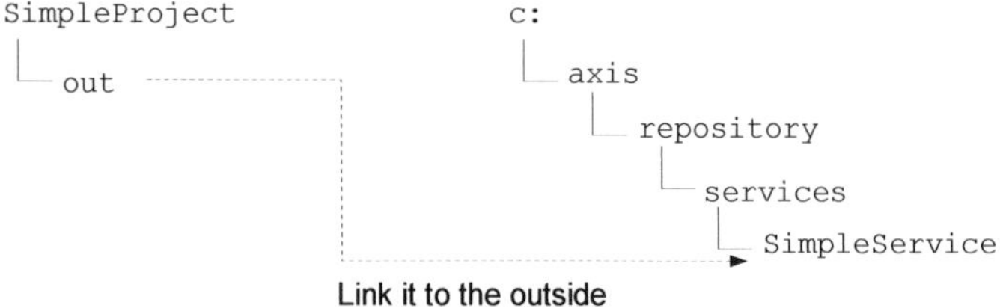

To implement this idea, right click the project and choose "New | Folder". Enter the information as shown below:

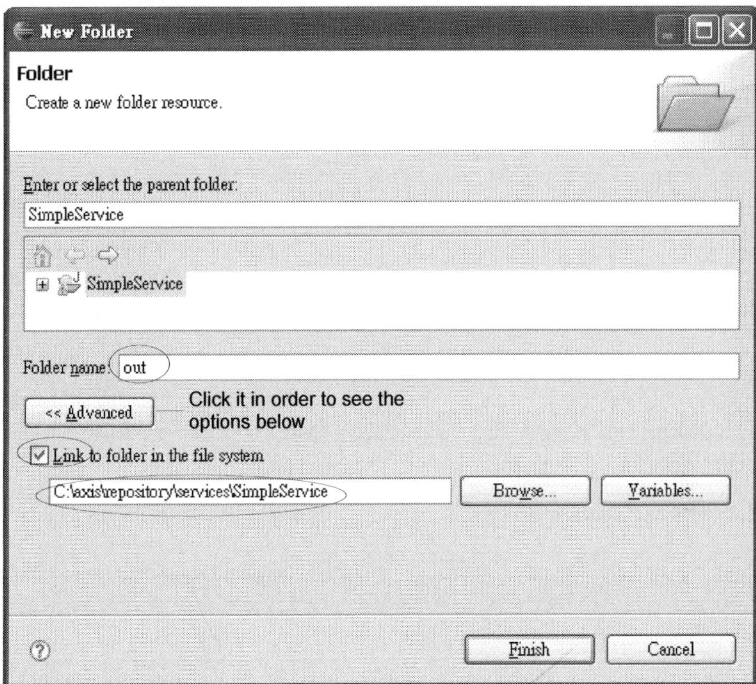

To set the output folder, right click the project in Eclipse and choose "Properties", then choose "Java Build Path" and choose the "Source" tab:

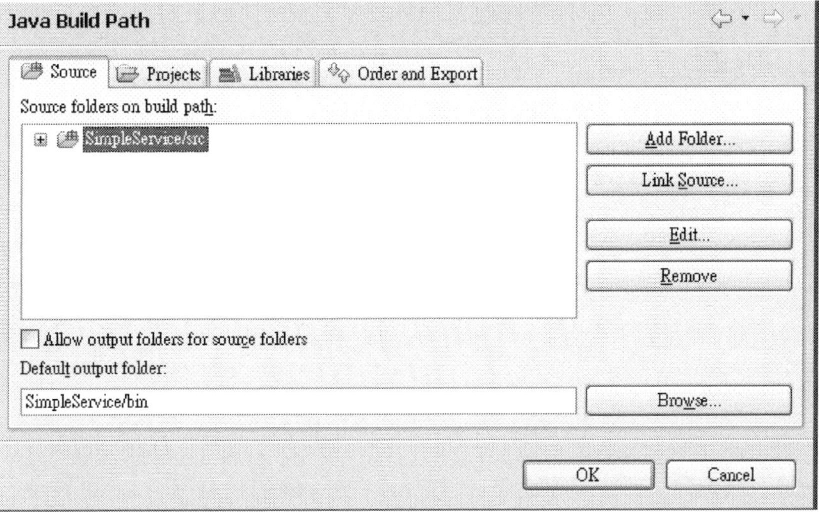

Click "Browse" and choose the "out" folder. Then confirm to delete the existing "bin" folder as it is no longer used.

Now the class files are in the right place. The next step is to make the META-INF folder appear in the service folder. To do that, you need to have such a folder in the "src" folder:

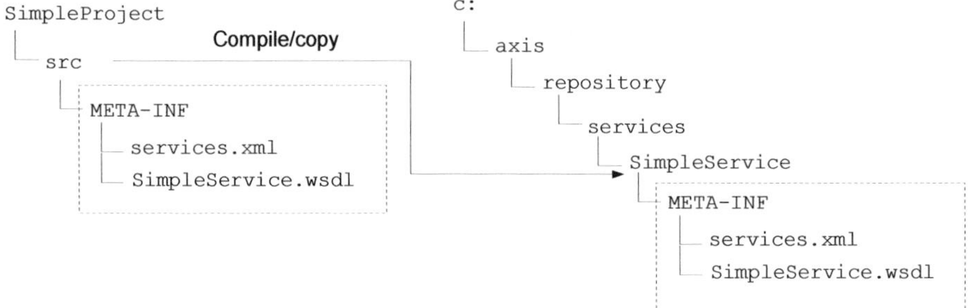

Therefore, rename your "resources" folder as META-INF and move it into "src". To verify that this setup is working, modify the code to turn the result string into upper case:

```
public class SimpleServiceSkeleton implements SimpleServiceSkeletonInterface {
  public com.ttdev.ss.ConcatResponse concat(
      com.ttdev.ss.ConcatRequest concatRequest0) {
    String result = concatRequest0.getS1()+concatRequest0.getS2();
    ConcatResponse response = new ConcatResponse();
    response.setConcatResponse(result.toUpperCase());
    return response;
  }
}
```

Now start the Axis2 server. Run the client and the output should be in upper case:

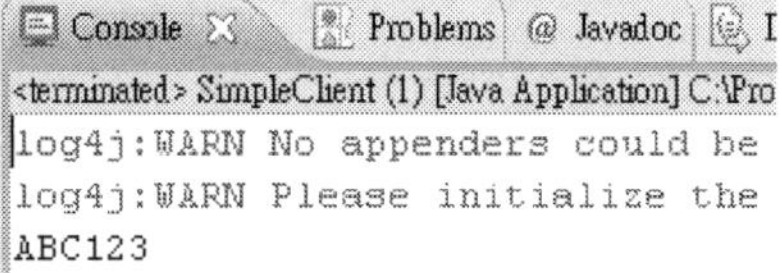

Making changes take effect immediately

Let's restore the code now:

```
public class SimpleServiceSkeleton implements SimpleServiceSkeletonInterface {
  public com.ttdev.ss.ConcatResponse concat(
      com.ttdev.ss.ConcatRequest concatRequest0) {
    String result = concatRequest0.getS1()+concatRequest0.getS2();
    ConcatResponse response = new ConcatResponse();
    response.setConcatResponse(result~~.toUpperCase()~~);
    return response;
  }
}
```

Will it take effect while the Axis server is running? No. It will still output ABC123. This is because by default once the Axis server loads a web service, it will not monitor changes to its file any more. To change this behavior, modify c:\axis\conf\axis2.xml:

```
<axisconfig name="AxisJava2.0">
  <parameter name="hotdeployment">true</parameter>
  <parameter name="hotupdate">false true</parameter>
  <parameter name="enableMTOM">false</parameter>
  <parameter name="enableSwA">false</parameter>
  ...
</axisconfig>
```

Enable hot update

You may have noticed that there is also a hot deployment option in addition to the hot update option. What's the difference? It is explained in the diagram:

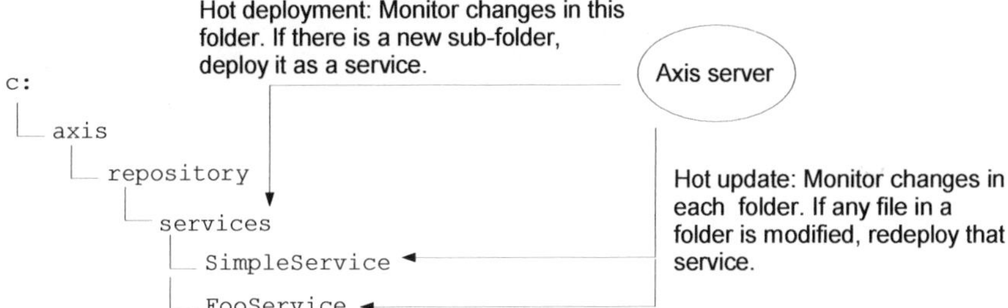

You need to restart the Axis server so that this hot update option takes effect. Then modify the Java code:

```
public class SimpleServiceSkeleton implements SimpleServiceSkeletonInterface {
  public com.ttdev.ss.ConcatResponse concat(
      com.ttdev.ss.ConcatRequest concatRequest0) {
    String result = concatRequest0.getS1()+concatRequest0.getS2();
    ConcatResponse response = new ConcatResponse();
    response.setConcatResponse("hello: "+result);
    return response;
  }
}
```

Save the code. Then you should see that the Axis server redeploying your service:

```
Using JAVA_HOME    C:\Program Files\Java\jdk1.5.0_02
Using AXIS2_HOME   c:\axis2-1.3\bin\..
[INFO] [SimpleAxisServer] Starting
[INFO] [SimpleAxisServer] Using the Axis2 Repositoryc:\axis2-1.3\bi
ry
[SimpleAxisServer] Using the Axis2 Repositoryc:\axis2-1.3\bin\..\re
[SimpleAxisServer] Using the Axis2 Configuration Filec:\axis2-1.3\b
is2.xml
[INFO] Deploying module: addressing-1.3
[INFO] Deploying module: metadataExchange-1.3
[INFO] Deploying module: ping-1.3
[INFO] Deploying module: script-1.3
[INFO] Deploying module: soapmonitor-1.3
[INFO] script module activated
[INFO] Deploying Web service: SimpleService
[INFO] Deploying Web service: version.aar
[INFO] [SimpleAxisServer] Started
[SimpleAxisServer] Started
[INFO] Listening on port 8080
[INFO] Undeploying Web service: SimpleService
[INFO] Deploying Web service: SimpleService
```

Run the client and it should work:

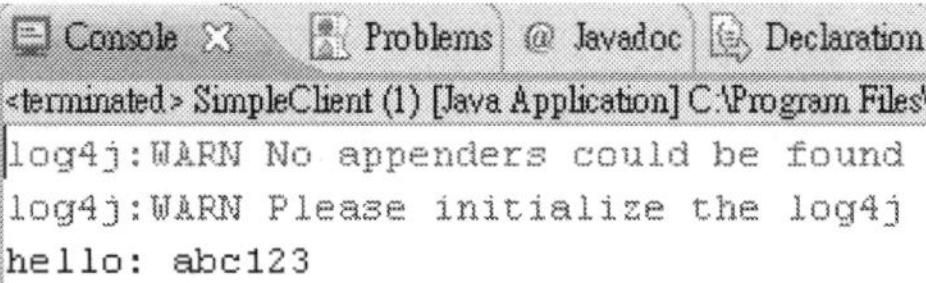
Console
Problems
Javadoc
Declaration
<terminated> SimpleClient (1) [Java Application] C:\Program Files\
log4j:WARN No appenders could be found
log4j:WARN Please initialize the log4j
hello: abc123

Note that the Axis server looks for changes every 10 seconds. So it may take some time before the web service is redeployed.

Debugging a web service

To debug your web service in Eclipse, you need to set an environment variable before launching the Axis server (shut it down first if it's running):

Type it all on one line

```
C:\axis\bin>set JAVA_OPTS=-Xdebug -Xrunjdwp:transport=dt_socket,add
ress=8000,server=y,suspend=n

C:\axis\bin>axis2server.bat
```

Launch it as usual

This way the Axis server will run the JVM in debug mode so that the JVM will listen for connections on port 8000. Later you'll tell Eclipse to connect to this port. Now, set a breakpoint here:

```
public class SimpleServiceSkeleton implements SimpleServiceSkeletonInt
    public com.ttdev.ss.ConcatResponse concat(
            com.ttdev.ss.ConcatRequest concatRequest0) {
        String result = concatRequest0.getS1()+concatRequest0.getS2();
        ConcatResponse response = new ConcatResponse();
        response.setConcatResponse("hello: "+result);
        return response;
    }
}
```

Choose "Open Debug Dialog":

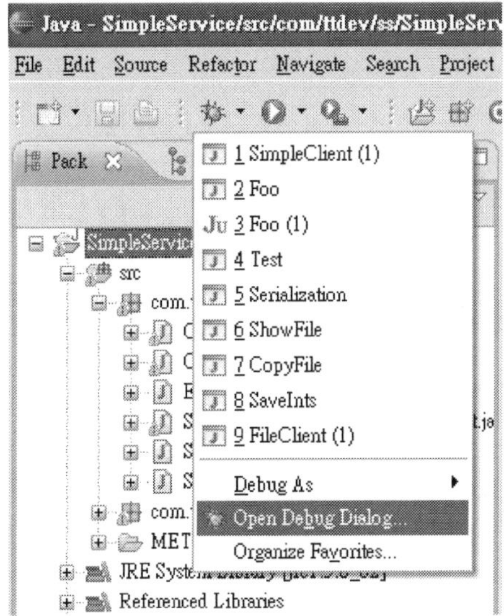

The following window will appear:

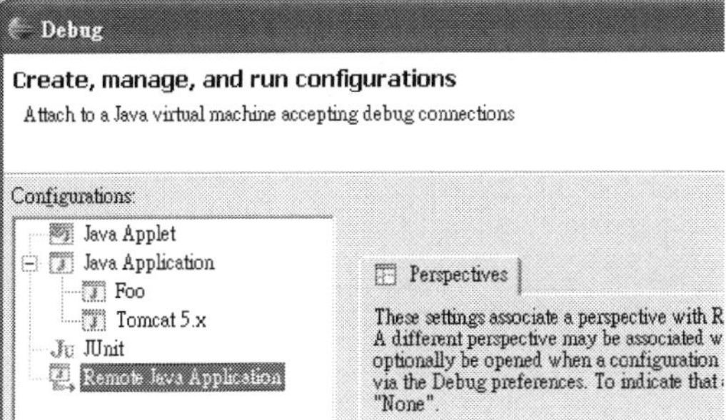

Right click "Remote Java Application" and choose "New". Name this configuration "Debug Axis" (it doesn't really matter). Make sure your SimpleService project is selected and make sure the port is 8000:

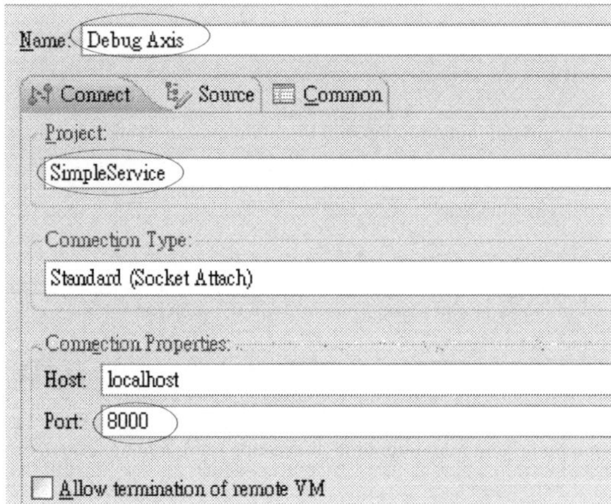

Click "Debug" to connect to the JVM running the Axis server. Now run the client to call the web service. Eclipse will stop at the breakpoint:

Debug Hierarchy
Debug Axis [Remote Java Application]
Java HotSpot(TM) Client VM[localhost:8000]
Thread [DestroyJavaVM] (Running)
Thread [HttpListener-8080-1] (Running)
Daemon Thread [Timer-1] (Running)
Daemon Thread [Timer-0] (Running)
Thread [HttpConnection-8080-1] (Suspended (breakpoint at line 15 in SimpleServiceSkeleton))
SimpleServiceSkeleton.concat(ConcatRequest) line: 15
SimpleServiceMessageReceiverInOut.invokeBusinessLogic(MessageContext, MessageContext) line: 53
SimpleServiceMessageReceiverInOut(AbstractInOutSyncMessageReceiver).invokeBusinessLogic(Message

SimpleServiceSkeleton.java

```
 * SimpleServiceSkeleton.java
package com.ttdev.ss;

/**
 * SimpleServiceSkeleton java skeleton for the axisService
 */
public class SimpleServiceSkeleton implements SimpleServiceSkeletonInte
    public com.ttdev.ss.ConcatResponse concat(
            com.ttdev.ss.ConcatRequest concatRequest0) {
        String result = concatRequest0.getS1()+concatRequest0.getS2();
        ConcatResponse response = new ConcatResponse();
        response.setConcatResponse("hello: "+result);
        return response;
    }
}
```

Then you can step through the program, check the variables and whatever. To stop the debug session, choose the SimpleService in the Debug window and click the Stop icon:

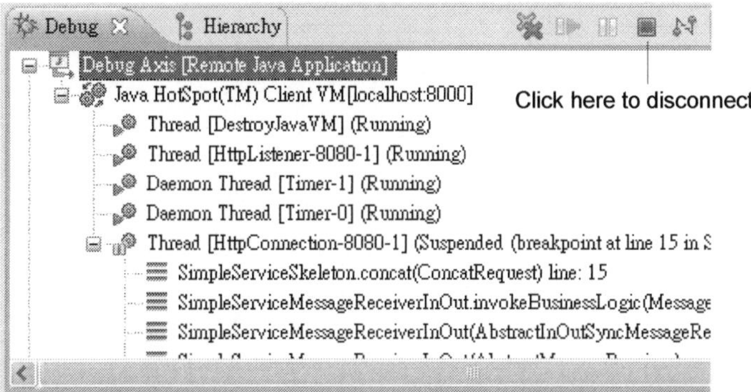

Having to set this environment variable every time is not fun. So, you may create a batch file c:\axis\bin\debug.bat:

debug.bat

```
set JAVA_OPTS=-Xdebug -Xrunjdwp:transport=dt_socket,address=8000,server=y,suspend=n
axis2server.bat
```

Then in the future you can just run it to start the Axis server in debug mode.

Generating code automatically

For the moment you're using the Code Generator Wizard to generate the code from the WSDL file. If you modify the WSDL file, you'll have to do it once again. This is troublesome. You need an automated process to generate the code. To do that, you'll edit the build.xml file that was generated by the Code Generator Wizard. But first, you need to understand the structure of the build.xml (see below). A build.xml file contains a project, which is like a class in a Java file. A project contains one or more targets. A target is like a method in a Java class. A target contains one or more tasks. A task is like a statement in a Java method:

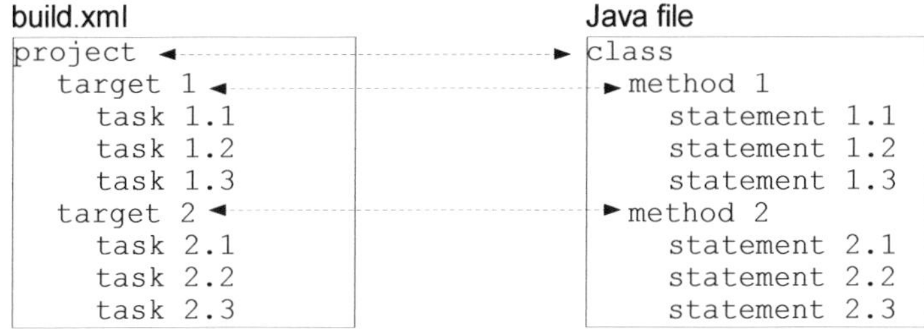

Now, let's edit the build.xml file:

The project
Here is a target named "generate-service". Later you can say, for example, "let's run the generate-service" target.
This target contains only one task here (<wsdl2code>). This task will generate Java code from a WSDL file.
<?xml version="1.0" encoding="UTF-8"?>
<project ...>
...
<target name="generate-service">
<wsdl2code
wsdlfilename="SimpleService.wsdl"
serverside="true"
generateservicexml="true"
skipbuildxml="true"
serversideinterface="true"
namespacetopackages="http://ttdev.com/ss=com.ttdev.ss"
targetsourcefolderlocation="src"
targetresourcesfolderlocation="src/META-INF"/>
</target>
</project>
The path to the WSDL file. Here you are using a relative path. It is relative to the build.xml file (project root).
Generate code for the service. Otherwise it will generate code for the client.
Generate the services.xml file
Don't generate the build.xml. Otherwise it will overwrite this file!
Generate an interface in addition to the skeleton:
Map the http://ttdev.com/ss namespace to the com.ttdev.ss package. This is not really needed here as it is the default. It is here just to show you the syntax.
Put the Java files into the "src" folder which is a relative path to the project root.
Put the "resources files" (e.g., services.xml) into the "src/META-INF" folder which is a relative path to the project root.
public interface SimpleServiceSkeletonInterface {
public ConcatResponse concat(...);
}
public class SimpleServiceSkeleton
implements SimpleServiceSkeletonInterface {
public ConcatResponse concat(...) {
...
}
}

Next, you are about to run this build.xml file using a program called "Ant". However, the <wsdl2code> task is not a built-in task in Ant and therefore Ant doesn't know how to execute it. It is implemented by a Java class named AntCodegenTask in c:\axis\lib\axis2-ant-plugin-1.3.jar. To tell Ant how the <wsdl2code> task is implemented, modify build.xml:

Ultimately it depends on an environment variable AXIS2_HOME pointing to the home of Axis

```
<project ...>
  ...
  <property name="axis2.home" value="${env.AXIS2_HOME}"/>
  ...
  <path id="axis2.class.path">
    ...
    <fileset dir="${axis2.home}">
      <include name="lib/*.jar"/>
    </fileset>
  </path>
  ...
  <taskdef
    name="wsdl2code"
    classname="org.apache.axis2.tool.ant.AntCodegenTask"
    classpathref="axis2.class.path" />
  <target name="generate-service">
    <wsdl2code
      wsdlfilename="SimpleService.wsdl"
      serverside="true"
      generateservicexml="true"
      skipbuildxml="true"
      serversideinterface="true"
      namespacetopackages="http://ttdev.com/ss=com.ttdev.ss"
      targetsourcefolderlocation="src"
      targetresourcesfolderlocation="src/META-INF"/>
  </target>
</project>
```

Paths to the Axis jar files have been defined

Define a task <wsdl2code>

It is implemented by this Java class

To define an environment variable AXIS2_HOME, you can either do it in Windows or in Eclipse. Let's do it in Eclipse. Choose "Window | Preferences | Ant | Runtime", choose the "Properties" tab:

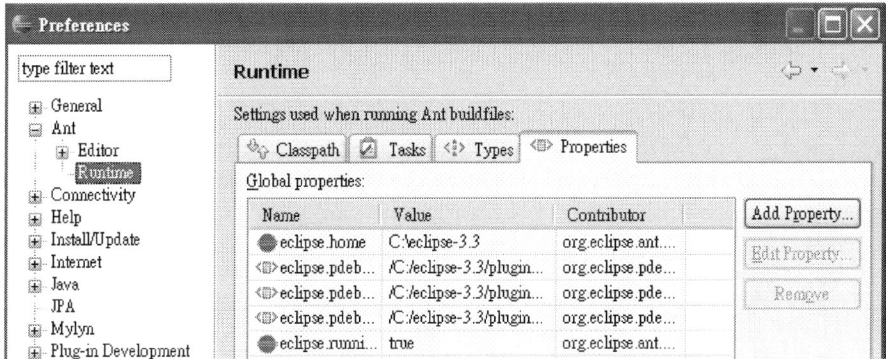

Click "Add Property" and enter the data as shown below:

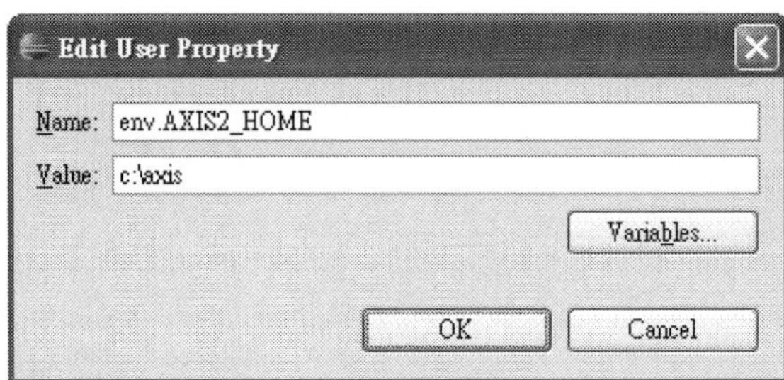

Now you're about to run Ant. To verify that it is really working, rename your SimpleServiceSkeleton.java file as SimpleServiceImpl file. Then delete all the other Java files in the package. Delete the files in the META-INF folder too.

BUG ALERT: In Axis2 1.3 there is a bug in the Code Generator Wizard. After installing it, you'll be unable to run Ant in Eclipse. To workaround the problem, in the Ant Runtime window above, choose the "Classpath" tab and click "Ant Home" and browse to choose the org.apache.ant folder in c:\eclipse\plugins:

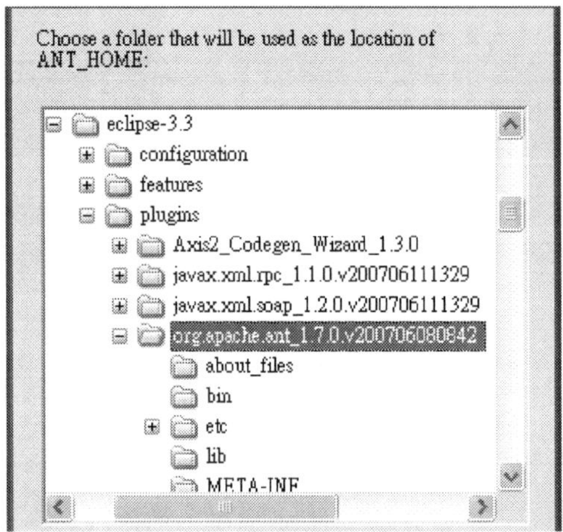

To run Ant, right click the build.xml file and then choose "Run As | Ant Build..." as shown below:

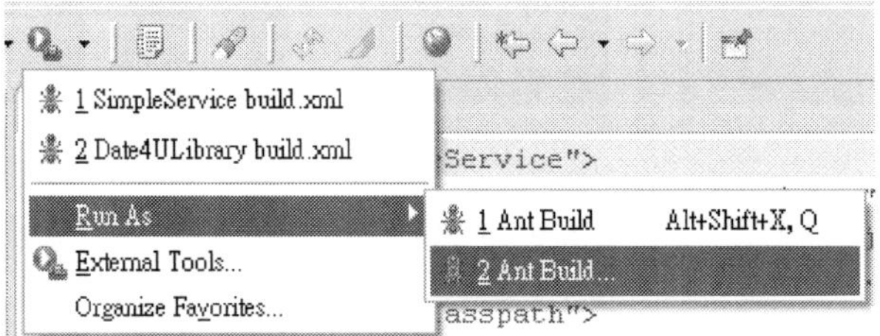

Then choose the "generate-service" target and click "Run":

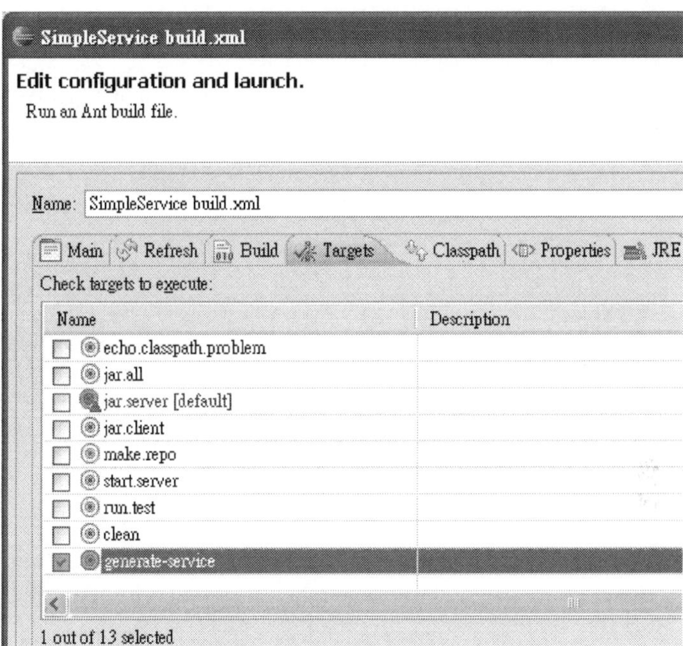

You should see that it is working in the console:

```
Console  Problems  @ Javadoc  Declaration  Search  Properties
<terminated> SimpleService build.xml [Ant Build] C:\Program Files\Java\jre1.5.0_02\bin\javaw.exe (Nov 4, 2
Buildfile: C:\Books\DWSAA\v20\workspace\SimpleService\build.xml
generate-service:
[wsdl2code] log4j:WARN No appenders could be found for logger (c
[wsdl2code] log4j:WARN Please initialize the log4j system proper
BUILD SUCCESSFUL
Total time: 5 seconds
```

Then refresh the project and you'll see that the Java files and the files in META-INF have been recreated. Now, ideally if your WSDL file is modified, all you need to do is to run the build.xml file again. However, this is not the default behavior. By default, the <wsdl2code> task will not overwrite any existing file! To tell it to do so, set an option:

```
<project ...>
  ...
  <target name="generate-service">
    <wsdl2code
      wsdlfilename="SimpleService.wsdl"
      serverside="true"
      generateservicexml="true"
      skipbuildxml="true"
      serversideinterface="true"
      namespacetopackages="http://ttdev.com/ss=com.ttdev.ss"
      targetsourcefolderlocation="src"
      targetresourcesfolderlocation="src/META-INF"
      overwrite="true"/>
```

```
    </target>
  </project>
```

But this introduces another problem: If you fill your code into SimpleServiceSkeleton, when you run build.xml, the file will be overwritten and your code will be lost! The idea is not to use SimpleServiceSkeleton any more. Instead, create your own SimpleServiceImpl that implements the same interface:

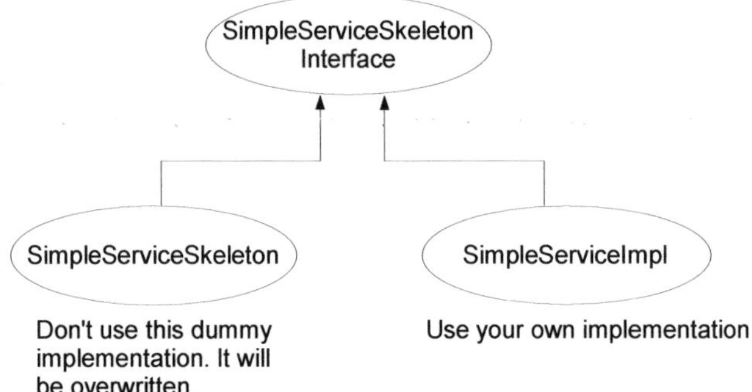
SimpleServiceSkeleton Interface
SimpleServiceSkeleton
SimpleServiceImpl
Don't use this dummy implementation. It will be overwritten.
Use your own implementation

In order to use your SimpleServiceImpl to implement the web service, you need to know how the Axis server knows which Java class implements your web service. It looks up the class name in the services.xml file:

```
<serviceGroup>
  <service name="SimpleService">
    <messageReceivers>
      <messageReceiver
        mep="http://www.w3.org/ns/wsdl/in-out"
        class="com.ttdev.ss.SimpleServiceMessageReceiverInOut" />
    </messageReceivers>
    <parameter name="ServiceClass">com.ttdev.ss.SimpleServiceSkeleton</parameter>
    <parameter name="useOriginalwsdl">true</parameter>
    <parameter name="modifyUserWSDLPortAddress">true</parameter>
    <operation name="concat"
      mep="http://www.w3.org/ns/wsdl/in-out">
      <actionMapping>
        http://ttdev.com/ss/NewOperation
      </actionMapping>
      <outputActionMapping>
        http://ttdev.com/ss/SimpleService/concatResponse
      </outputActionMapping>
    </operation>
  </service>
</serviceGroup>
```

The Axis server will look up the class name and then create instances to serve the requests.

So, you need to change it to SimpleServiceImpl.

You could modify this services.xml file every time it is generated, but it is too troublesome and easy to forget. A much better way is to let Ant do it for you automatically:

```
<project ...>
  ...
  <target name="generate-service">
    <wsdl2code
      wsdlfilename="SimpleService.wsdl"
      serverside="true"
      generateservicexml="true"
      skipbuildxml="true"
      serversideinterface="true"
      namespacetopackages="http://ttdev.com/ss=com.ttdev.ss"
      targetsourcefolderlocation="src"
      targetresourcesfolderlocation="src/META-INF"
      overwrite="true"/>
    <replaceregexp
      file="src/META-INF/services.xml"
      match="SimpleServiceSkeleton"
      replace="SimpleServiceImpl"/>
  </target>
</project>
```

Replace regular expression. That is, perform search and replace in a text file using a regular expression.

Add a task after the <wsdl2code> task

Search for strings that match the regular expression "SimpleServiceSkeleton"

Search & replace in the services.xml file

Replace each match with the string "SimpleServiceImpl"

Run it and refresh the project. Check the services.xml file and it should be using your SimpleServiceImpl:

```
<serviceGroup>
  <service name="SimpleService">
    <messageReceivers>
      <messageReceiver mep="http://www.w3.org/ns/wsdl/in-out"
        class="com.ttdev.ss.SimpleServiceMessageReceiverInOut" />
    </messageReceivers>
    <parameter name="ServiceClass">com.ttdev.ss.SimpleServiceImpl</parameter>
    <parameter name="useOriginalwsdl">true</parameter>
    <parameter name="modifyUserWSDLPortAddress">true</parameter>
    <operation name="concat"
      mep="http://www.w3.org/ns/wsdl/in-out">
      <actionMapping>
        http://ttdev.com/ss/NewOperation
      </actionMapping>
      <outputActionMapping>
        http://ttdev.com/ss/SimpleService/concatResponse
      </outputActionMapping>
    </operation>
  </service>
</serviceGroup>
```

Generating client code automatically

To generate the client code, it is very similar:

```
<project ...>
  ...
  <target name="generate-service">
    <wsdl2code
      wsdlfilename="SimpleService.wsdl"
      serverside="true"
      generateservicexml="true"
      skipbuildxml="true"
      serversideinterface="true"
      namespacetopackages="http://ttdev.com/ss=com.ttdev.ss"
      targetsourcefolderlocation="src"
      targetresourcesfolderlocation="src/META-INF"
      overwrite="true"/>
    <replaceregexp
      file="src/META-INF/services.xml"
      match="SimpleServiceSkeleton"
      replace="SimpleServiceImpl"/>
  </target>
  <target name="generate-client">
    <wsdl2code
      wsdlfilename="SimpleService.wsdl"
      skipbuildxml="true"
      namespacetopackages="http://ttdev.com/ss=com.ttdev.ss.client"
      targetsourcefolderlocation="src"
      overwrite="true"/>
  </target>
</project>
```

Add another target. The main difference is that the serverside option is not set (the default is false).

Map to the client package

Delete the files in the client package except SimpleClient.java which was created by you. Run build.xml and choose the "generate-client" target. Refresh the project and you'll see the Java files in the client package again.

To make sure everything is working, start the Axis server and run the client. It should continue to work.

Summary

You can set the output folder in Eclipse so that you don't need to copy the files into the service folder in Axis manually.

To make sure the changes to your Java code take effect immediately, you can enable hot update in the Axis server.

To debug a web service, tell the Axis server to run the JVM in debug mode, set a breakpoint in the Java code and make a Debug configuration in Eclipse to connect to that JVM.

To automate the process of generating Java code from a WSDL file, you can use the <wsdl2code> Ant task. In general you'll want it to overwrite existing files. To prevent from overwriting your own code, you should never modify the code generated. Instead, create your own service implementation class that implements the service interface and modify services.xml to tell the Axis server to use that class.

Chapter 4

Understanding the calling process

What's in this chapter?

In this chapter you'll learn what is happening internally when you call a web service.

Calling a web service without a client stub

Suppose that you'd like to call a web service without a client stub. To do that, in the SimpleService project in Eclipse, create a file LowLevelClient.java in a new com.ttdev.ss.lowlevel package:

```
import org.apache.axiom.om.OMElement;
import org.apache.axis2.AxisFault;
import org.apache.axis2.addressing.EndpointReference;
import org.apache.axis2.client.Options;
import org.apache.axis2.client.ServiceClient;

public class LowLevelClient {
   public static void main(String[] args) throws AxisFault {
      ServiceClient client = new ServiceClient();
      Options options = new Options();
      options.setTo(new EndpointReference(
            "http://localhost:8080/axis2/services/SimpleService"));
      client.setOptions(options);
      OMElement request = makeRequest();
      OMElement response = client.sendReceive(request);
      System.out.println(response.toString());
   }
}
```

Create a service client object. You will use it to call the web service.

Set the options. Here you only set the endpoint.

Convert the response to a string and print it out

Send the request and get the response

An OMElement is just an XML element. OM means "object model".

You'll write this method yourself which will create a <concatRequest> element.

Define the makeRequest() method:

```
import javax.xml.namespace.QName;
import org.apache.axiom.om.OMAbstractFactory;
import org.apache.axiom.om.OMFactory;
import org.apache.axis2.addressing.EndpointReference;

public class LowLevelClient {
   ...
   private static OMElement makeRequest() {
      OMFactory factory = OMAbstractFactory.getOMFactory();
      OMElement request = factory.createOMElement(new QName(
            "http://ttdev.com/ss", "concatRequest"));
      OMElement s1 = factory.createOMElement(new QName("s1"));
      s1.setText("abc");
      OMElement s2 = factory.createOMElement(new QName("s2"));
      s2.setText("def");
      request.addChild(s1);
      request.addChild(s2);
      return request;
   }
}
```

Get the default OMFactory. You'll use it to create XML elements.

Note that the <s1> element has no namespace, just the local name.

Create <s1>

Create the <concatRequest> element

Add <s1> to <concatRequest> as a child

```
<foo:concatRequest xmlns:foo="http://ttdev.com/ss">
   <s1>abc</s1>
   <s2>def</s2>
</foo:concatRequest>
```

Set the body text to "abc"

Now run it and it should work. This low level API is called AXIOM (**Axi**s2 **O**bject **M**odel). Usually it is far easier to use the generated stub. However, if you need to do some special customizations, you may have to use AXIOM.

Seeing the SOAP messages

Next, let's see the actual SOAP messages. To do that, you'll use a program called "TCP Monitor". It works like this (see the diagram below). You tell the client to treat the TCP Monitor as the destination. Then when the client needs to send the request message, it will send it to the TCP Monitor. Then TCP Monitor will print it to the console and then forward it to the real destination (the web service). When the web service returns a response message, it will return it to the TCP Monitor. It will print it to the console and then forward it to the client:

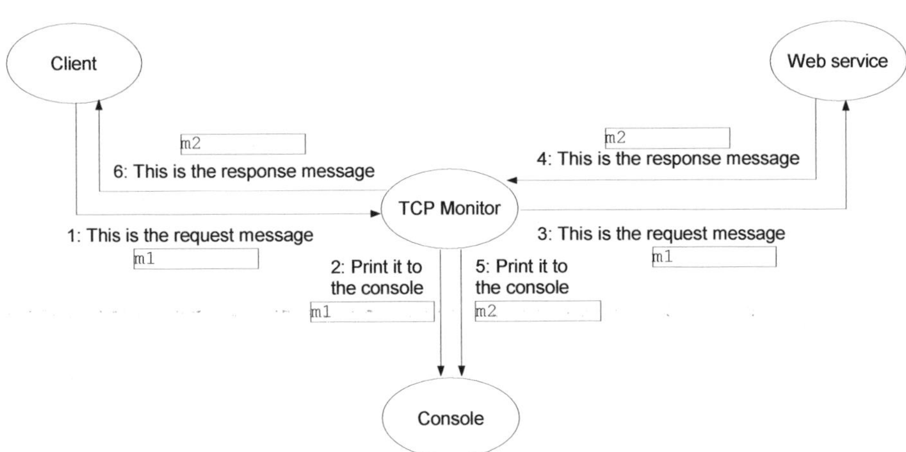

To implement this idea, go to http://ws.apache.org/commons/tcpmon to download the binary distribution of TCP Monitor. Suppose that it is tcpmon-1.0-bin.zip. Unzip it into say c:\tcpmon. Then change into the c:\tcpmon\build folder and run tcpmon.bat:

```
C:\>cd tcpmon\build

C:\tcpmon\build>tcpmon.bat
```

Note that directly running c:\tcpmon\build\tcpmon.bat will NOT work; it requires the current folder to be c:\tcpmon\build. Next, you'll see a window. Enter the data as shown below:

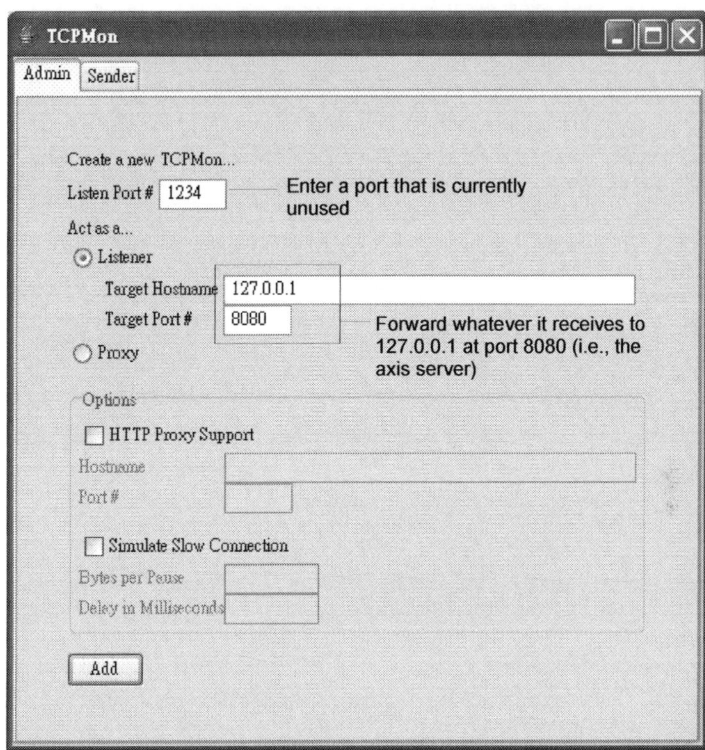

Click "Add". This will open a new tab (shown below). Then it will listen on port 1234. Check the "XML Format" option. This way it will format the content of the TCP connection (an HTTP request containing a SOAP request, but it doesn't know that) nicely as XML:

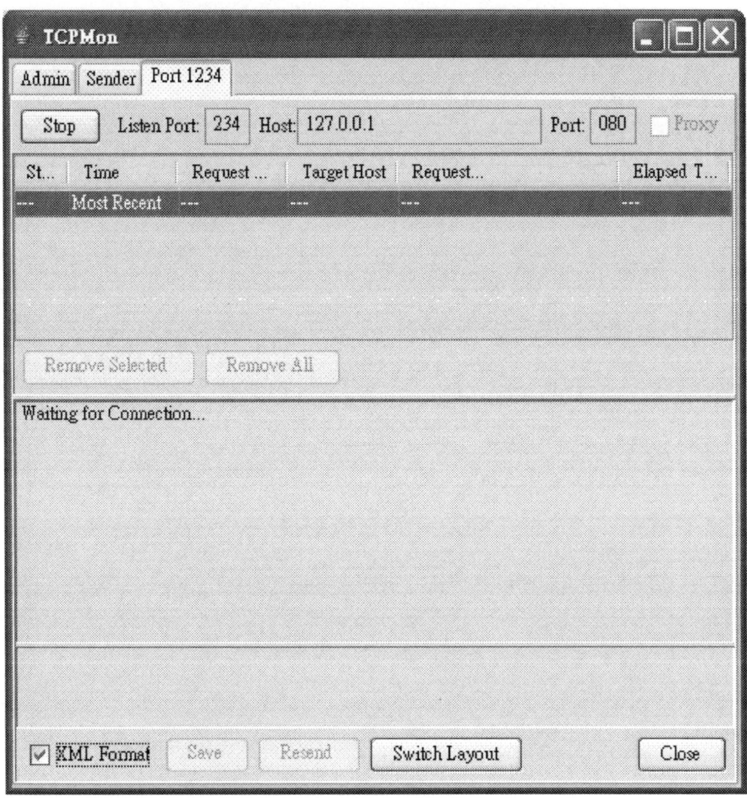

For the client, you need to tell it to use localhost:1234 as the endpoint. For example, in LowLevelClient.java:

```
public class LowLevelClient {
  public static void main(String[] args) throws AxisFault {
    ServiceClient client = new ServiceClient();
    Options options = new Options();
    options.setTo(new EndpointReference(
        "http://localhost:~~8080~~**1234**/axis2/services/SimpleService"));
    client.setOptions(options);
    OMElement request = makeRequest();
    OMElement response = client.sendReceive(request);
    System.out.println(response.toString());
  }
  ...
}
```

Run it and you will see the messages in TCP Monitor:

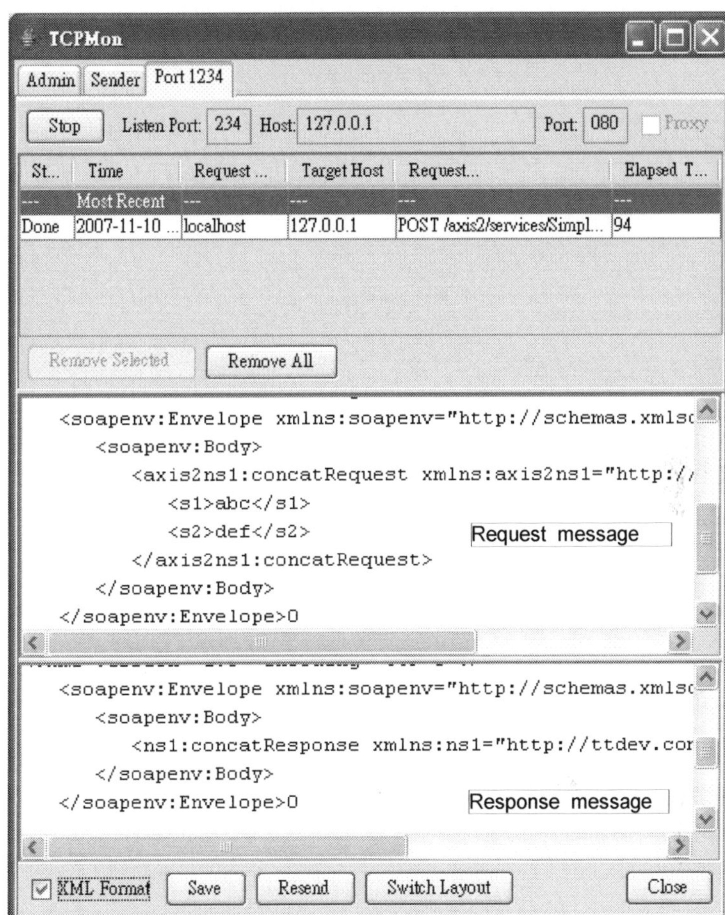

Similarly, for the SimpleClient that is using the generated client stub, you can specify the endpoint address to override the default:

```
public class SimpleClient {
    public static void main(String[] args) throws RemoteException {
        SimpleServiceStub service = new SimpleServiceStub(
          "http://localhost:1234/axis2/services/SimpleService");
        ConcatRequest request = new ConcatRequest();
        request.setS1("abc");
        request.setS2("123");
        ConcatResponse response = service.concat(request);
        System.out.println(response.getConcatResponse());
    }
}
```

Summary

To call a web service without using a generated stub, you may use the AXIOM interface. It is a lower level interface and thus is harder to use, but it provides a lot of flexibility.

To check the SOAP messages, you can use the TCP Monitor.

Chapter 5

Accepting multiple parameters

What's in this chapter?

In this chapter you'll learn how to accept multiple parameters in your implementation class.

Accepting multiple parameters

Consider the SimpleServiceImpl class:

```
public class SimpleServiceImpl implements SimpleServiceSkeletonInterface {
    public ConcatResponse concat(ConcatRequest concatRequest0) {
        String result = concatRequest0.getS1() + concatRequest0.getS2();
        ConcatResponse response = new ConcatResponse();
        response.setConcatResponse(result);
        return response;
    }
}
```

Because it's a document style web service, you can have a single part in the input message. Therefore, you have a single parameter only. The same is true for the output message. It would be nice if you could write:

```
public class SimpleServiceImpl implements SimpleServiceSkeletonInterface {
    public String concat(String s1, String s2) {
      return s1+s2;
    }
}
```

while still accepting a single part (<concatRequest>) in the message. To do that, you just need to make two changes to the WSDL file:

```
<?xml version="1.0" encoding="UTF-8"?>
<wsdl:definitions ...>
  <wsdl:types>
    <xsd:schema ...>
      <xsd:element name="concatRequest concat">
        <xsd:complexType>
          <xsd:sequence>
            <xsd:element name="s1" type="xsd:string" />
            <xsd:element name="s2" type="xsd:string" />
          </xsd:sequence>
        </xsd:complexType>
      </xsd:element>
      <xsd:element name="concatResponse" type="xsd:string" />
    </xsd:schema>
  </wsdl:types>
  <wsdl:message name="concatRequest">
    <wsdl:part name="parameters" element="tns:concatRequest concat" />
  </wsdl:message>
  <wsdl:message name="concatResponse">
    <wsdl:part name="parameters" element="tns:concatResponse" />
  </wsdl:message>
  <wsdl:portType name="SimpleService">
    <wsdl:operation name="concat">
      <wsdl:input message="tns:concatRequest" />
      <wsdl:output message="tns:concatResponse" />
    </wsdl:operation>
  </wsdl:portType>
  ...
</wsdl:definitions>
```

The element must be a sequence, which is indeed the case here.

Make sure the element name of that single part in the input message is the same as that of the operation.

Similarly, for the output message, the element name must be the name of the operation with the word "Response" appended and it must be a sequence (containing a single child element):

```
<?xml version="1.0" encoding="UTF-8"?>
<wsdl:definitions ...>
  <wsdl:types>
    <xsd:schema ...>
      <xsd:element name="concat">
        <xsd:complexType>
          <xsd:sequence>
            <xsd:element name="s1" type="xsd:string" />
            <xsd:element name="s2" type="xsd:string" />
          </xsd:sequence>
        </xsd:complexType>
      </xsd:element>
      <xsd:element name="concatResponse" type="xsd:string" >
        <xsd:complexType>
          <xsd:sequence>
            <xsd:element name="r" type="xsd:string" />
          </xsd:sequence>
        </xsd:complexType>
      </xsd:element>
    </xsd:schema>
  </wsdl:types>
  <wsdl:message name="concatRequest">
    <wsdl:part name="parameters" element="tns:concat" />
  </wsdl:message>
  <wsdl:message name="concatResponse">
    <wsdl:part name="parameters" element="tns:concatResponse" />
  </wsdl:message>
  <wsdl:portType name="SimpleService">
    <wsdl:operation name="concat">
      <wsdl:input message="tns:concatRequest" />
      <wsdl:output message="tns:concatResponse" />
    </wsdl:operation>
  </wsdl:portType>
  ...
</wsdl:definitions>
```

It must not be a simple type such as string. It must be a sequence.

The sequence must contain a single element. The element name (<r> here) is unimportant.

The element name must be "concat" + "Response", which happens to be the case already.

To test it, copy the SimpleService project and paste it as WrappedService. Delete all the Java files. The "out" folder is still linking to the old location (c:\axis\repository\services\SimpleService). So go to the Navigator view in Eclipse and open the .project file:

Choose the Navigator view

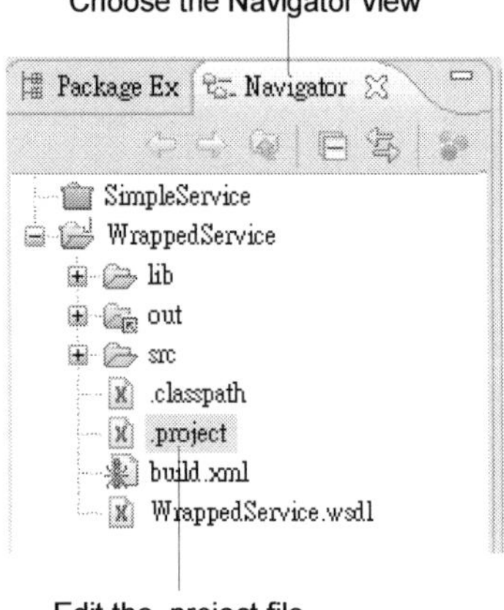

Edit the .project file

Then change the path to c:\axis\repository\services\WrappedService:

```
*project
<?xml version="1.0" encoding="UTF-8"?>
<projectDescription>
    <name>WrappedService</name>
    <comment></comment>
    <projects>
    </projects>
    <buildSpec>
        <buildCommand>
            <name>org.eclipse.jdt.core.javabuilder</name>
            <arguments>
            </arguments>
        </buildCommand>
    </buildSpec>
    <natures>
        <nature>org.eclipse.jdt.core.javanature</nature>
    </natures>
    <linkedResources>
        <link>
            <name>out</name>
            <type>2</type>
            <location>C:/axis/repository/services/WrappedService<
        </link>
    </linkedResources>
</projectDescription>
```

Set the path

Rename SimpleService.wsdl to WrappedService.wsdl and modify it:

```
<?xml version="1.0" encoding="UTF-8"?>
<wsdl:definitions xmlns:wsdl="http://schemas.xmlsoap.org/wsdl/"
  xmlns:soap="http://schemas.xmlsoap.org/wsdl/soap/"
  xmlns:tns="http://ttdev.com/ss"
  xmlns:xsd="http://www.w3.org/2001/XMLSchema" name="WrappedService"
  targetNamespace="http://ttdev.com/ss">
  <wsdl:types>
    <xsd:schema targetNamespace="http://ttdev.com/ss"
      xmlns:xsd="http://www.w3.org/2001/XMLSchema">
      <xsd:element name="concat">
        <xsd:complexType>
          <xsd:sequence>
            <xsd:element name="s1" type="xsd:string" />
            <xsd:element name="s2" type="xsd:string" />
          </xsd:sequence>
        </xsd:complexType>
      </xsd:element>
      <xsd:element name="concatResponse">
        <xsd:complexType>
          <xsd:sequence>
            <xsd:element name="r" type="xsd:string" />
          </xsd:sequence>
        </xsd:complexType>
      </xsd:element>
    </xsd:schema>
  </wsdl:types>
  <wsdl:message name="concatRequest">
    <wsdl:part name="parameters" element="tns:concat" />
  </wsdl:message>
  <wsdl:message name="concatResponse">
    <wsdl:part name="parameters" element="tns:concatResponse" />
```

```
    </wsdl:message>
    <wsdl:portType name="WrappedService">
      <wsdl:operation name="concat">
        <wsdl:input message="tns:concatRequest" />
        <wsdl:output message="tns:concatResponse" />
      </wsdl:operation>
    </wsdl:portType>
    <wsdl:binding name="WrappedServiceSOAP" type="tns:WrappedService">
      <soap:binding style="document"
        transport="http://schemas.xmlsoap.org/soap/http" />
      <wsdl:operation name="concat">
        <soap:operation
          soapAction="http://ttdev.com/ss/NewOperation" />
        <wsdl:input>
          <soap:body use="literal" />
        </wsdl:input>
        <wsdl:output>
          <soap:body use="literal" />
        </wsdl:output>
      </wsdl:operation>
    </wsdl:binding>
    <wsdl:service name="WrappedService">
      <wsdl:port binding="tns:WrappedServiceSOAP"
        name="WrappedServiceSOAP">
        <soap:address
          location="http://localhost:8080/axis2/services/WrappedService" />
      </wsdl:port>
    </wsdl:service>
  </wsdl:definitions>
```

Modify build.xml:

```
<?xml version="1.0" encoding="UTF-8"?>
<project basedir="." default="jar.server">
  ...
  <property name="name" value="~~SimpleService~~WrappedService" />
  ...
  <target name="generate-service">
    <wsdl2code
      wsdlfilename="~~SimpleService~~${name}.wsdl"
      serverside="true"
      generateservicexml="true"
      skipbuildxml="true"
      serversideinterface="true"
      namespacetopackages="http://ttdev.com/ss=com.ttdev.wrap"
      targetsourcefolderlocation="src"
      targetresourcesfolderlocation="src/META-INF"
      overwrite="true" />
    <replaceregexp
      file="src/META-INF/services.xml"
      match="~~SimpleService~~${name}Skeleton"
      replace="~~SimpleService~~${name}Impl" />
  </target>
  <target name="generate-client">
    <wsdl2code
      wsdlfilename="~~SimpleService~~${name}.wsdl"
      skipbuildxml="true"
      namespacetopackages="http://ttdev.com/ss=com.ttdev.wrap.client"
      targetsourcefolderlocation="src"
      overwrite="true" />
  </target>
</project>
```

There is a property telling the name of the project
Refer to the property
Put the code into another package
Refer to the property

Next is an important step: You need a service stub that performs some special processing (see the diagram below). When an incoming <concat> element arrives, the service stub will extract the <s1> and <s2> elements from the <concat> element and use them as values for the two parameters ("unwrapping"). When the service implementation returns a string, the stub will use it as the value for the <r> element and put the <r> element into a <concatResponse> element ("wrapping"):

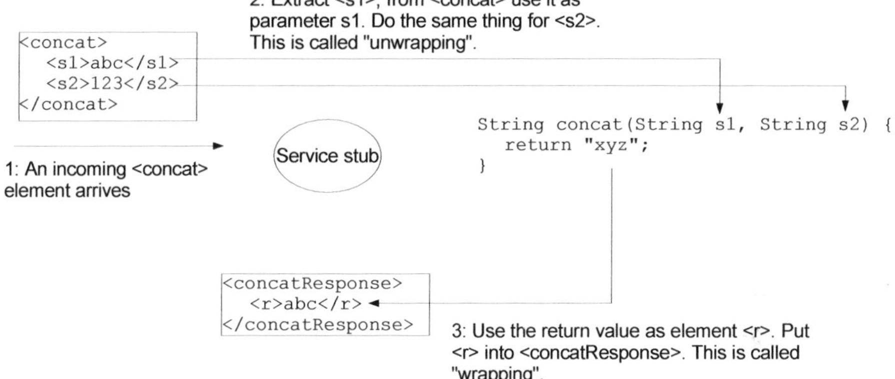

Note that this service is still a 100% document style service. The clients can still call it the same way (except that <concatRequest> is changed to <concat>). The difference is how the service stub calls your implementation and how it handles your return value. There is no difference seen by the client. To generate such a service stub, add an option to the <wsdl2code> Ant task:

```
<?xml version="1.0" encoding="UTF-8"?>
<project basedir="." default="jar.server">
  ...
  <target name="generate-service">
    <wsdl2code
      wsdlfilename="${name}.wsdl"
      serverside="true"
      generateservicexml="true"
      skipbuildxml="true"
      serversideinterface="true"
      namespacetopackages="http://ttdev.com/ss=com.ttdev.wrap"
      targetsourcefolderlocation="src"
      targetresourcesfolderlocation="src/META-INF"
      overwrite="true"
      unwrap="true" />
    <replaceregexp
      file="src/META-INF/services.xml"
      match="${name}Skeleton"
      replace="${name}Impl" />
  </target>
  <target name="generate-client">
    <wsdl2code
      wsdlfilename="${name}.wsdl"
      skipbuildxml="true"
      namespacetopackages="http://ttdev.com/ss=com.ttdev.wrap.client"
      targetsourcefolderlocation="src"
      overwrite="true"
      unwrap="true" />
  </target>
</project>
```

Generate a service stub that performs wrapping and unwrapping

Generate a client stub that performs wrapping and unwrapping

Run build.xml to generate the service stub and client stub. BUG ALERT: In Axis2 1.3 there is a bug preventing <wsdl2code> to overwrite the services.xml file. So, delete it first before running build.xml. Refresh the project. Check the WrappedServiceSkeleton.java:

```
public class WrappedServiceSkeleton implements WrappedServiceSkeletonInterface {
    public String concat(String s11, String s22) {
      ...
    }
}
```

To see it working, create a WrappedServiceImpl class:

```
public class WrappedServiceImpl implements WrappedServiceSkeletonInterface {
  public String concat(String s1, String s2) {
    return s1 + s2;
  }
}
```

Start the Axis server. Create a WrappedClient.java in the client package:

```
public class WrappedClient {
  public static void main(String[] args) throws RemoteException {
    WrappedServiceStub wrappedService = new WrappedServiceStub();
    String result = wrappedService.concat("xyz", "111");
    System.out.println(result);
  }
}
```

The client stub will perform wrapping and unwrapping

Run it and it should work.

Interoperability

The wrapped convention is a good idea. It is the only kind of web service supported by the .NET framework. Obviously Axis has also implemented this convention. The good news is, from the viewpoint of the caller, it is just a document+literal style service. So if the caller doesn't understand the wrapped convention, it can still access it as a regular document style service.

Summary

You can use the wrapped convention support in <wsdl2code> so that your back end Java method can have multiple parameters. The clients understanding this convention can also call it using multiple parameters. For those not understanding it, they can still call it as a regular document style service.

To ensure interoperability with .NET, you should use this convention.

Chapter 6

Sending and receiving complex data structures

What's in this chapter?

In this chapter you'll learn how to send and receive complex data structures to and from a web service.

Product query

Suppose that your company would like to use web service to let your customers query the product availability and place orders with you. For this you need to discuss with them to decide on the interface. It doesn't make sense to say that "When doing query, please send me an object of such a Java class. In this class there are this and that fields..." because perhaps the people involved aren't programmers or don't use Java. Instead, XML is what is designed for this. It is platform neutral and programming language neutral. So, suppose that you all agree on the following schema:

Use the XML schema namespace as the default namespace. It defines elements such as <element>, <complexType> needed for you to define new elements.
Put your elements and types into this namespace
A <productQuery> contains one or more <queryItem> elements. Here is an example:
Define an element <productQuery>
A <queryItem> must appear at least once (1). There is no upper limit of its occurrence.
The string type and int type are defined in the XML schema. They are usually shown as xsd:string and xsd:int, but the XML schema namespace here is the default namespace, so no prefix is needed.
A <productQuery> has two attributes named "productId" and "qty" respectively.


```
<?xml version="1.0"?>
<schema
  xmlns="http://www.w3.org/2001/XMLSchema"
  targetNamespace="http://foo.com">
  <element name="productQuery">
    <complexType>
      <sequence>
        <element name="queryItem" minOccurs="1" maxOccurs="unbounded">
          <complexType>
            <attribute name="productId" type="string"/>
            <attribute name="qty" type="int"/>
          </complexType>
        </element>
      </sequence>
    </complexType>
  </element>
</schema>
```

```
<?xml version="1.0"?>
<foo:productQuery xmlns:foo="http://foo.com">
  <queryItem productId="p01" qty="100"/>
  <queryItem productId="p02" qty="200"/>
  <queryItem productId="p03" qty="500"/>
</foo:productQuery>
```

That is, when they need to find out the availability of some products, they will send you a <productQuery> element. For example if they'd like to check if you have 100 pieces of p01, 200 pieces of p02 and 500 pieces of p03, they may send you a request like this:

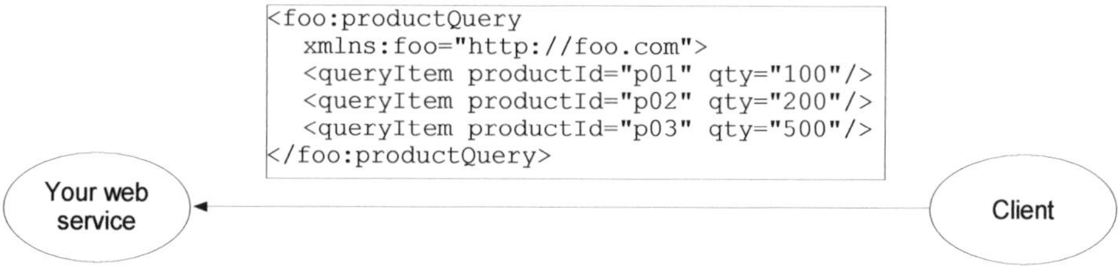

```
<foo:productQuery
  xmlns:foo="http://foo.com">
  <queryItem productId="p01" qty="100"/>
  <queryItem productId="p02" qty="200"/>
  <queryItem productId="p03" qty="500"/>
</foo:productQuery>
```

Your web service ◄—— Client

How does your web service reply? Use an XML element of course. So, in the schema you may have:

```
<?xml version="1.0"?>
<schema
  xmlns="http://www.w3.org/2001/XMLSchema"
  targetNamespace="http://foo.com">
  <element name="productQuery">
    ...
  </element>
  <element name="productQueryResult">
    <complexType>
      <sequence>
        <element name="resultItem" minOccurs="1" maxOccurs="unbounded">
          <complexType>
            <attribute name="productId" type="string"/>
            <attribute name="price" type="int"/>
          </complexType>
        </element>
      </sequence>
    </complexType>
  </element>
</schema>
```

For each <queryItem>, if the product is available, create a <resultItem> telling the unit price.

So, for the sample query above, if you have over 100 pieces of p01 and 500 pieces of p03 but only 150 pieces of p02, and you're willing to sell p01 at 5 dollars each and p03 at 8 dollars each, you may reply:

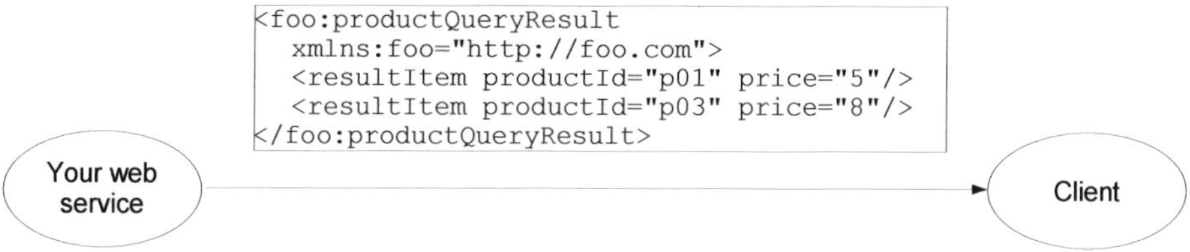

```
<foo:productQueryResult
  xmlns:foo="http://foo.com">
  <resultItem productId="p01" price="5"/>
  <resultItem productId="p03" price="8"/>
</foo:productQueryResult>
```

Your web service ——► Client

To implement this idea, create a new project named BizService as usual (You may copy an old one). Make sure the "out" folder links to c:\axis\repository\services\BizService. Delete the existing WSDL file and create a BizService.wsdl file (use Eclipse or manually):

```
<?xml version="1.0" encoding="UTF-8"?>
<wsdl:definitions xmlns:wsdl="http://schemas.xmlsoap.org/wsdl/"
  xmlns:soap="http://schemas.xmlsoap.org/wsdl/soap/"
  xmlns:tns="http://foo.com"
  xmlns:xsd="http://www.w3.org/2001/XMLSchema" name="BizService"
```

```
  targetNamespace="http://foo.com">
  <wsdl:types>
    <xsd:schema targetNamespace="http://foo.com"
      xmlns:xsd="http://www.w3.org/2001/XMLSchema">
      <xsd:element name="productQuery">
        <xsd:complexType>
          <xsd:sequence>
            <xsd:element name="queryItem" maxOccurs="unbounded" minOccurs="1">
              <xsd:complexType>
                <xsd:attribute name="productId" type="xsd:string">
                </xsd:attribute>
                <xsd:attribute name="qty" type="xsd:int">
                </xsd:attribute>
              </xsd:complexType>
            </xsd:element>
          </xsd:sequence>
        </xsd:complexType>
      </xsd:element>
      <xsd:element name="productQueryResult">
        <xsd:complexType>
          <xsd:sequence>
            <xsd:element name="resultItem" maxOccurs="unbounded" minOccurs="1">
              <xsd:complexType>
                <xsd:attribute name="productId" type="xsd:string">
                </xsd:attribute>
                <xsd:attribute name="price" type="xsd:int">
                </xsd:attribute>
              </xsd:complexType>
            </xsd:element>
          </xsd:sequence>
        </xsd:complexType>
      </xsd:element>
    </xsd:schema>
  </wsdl:types>
  <wsdl:message name="queryRequest">
    <wsdl:part name="parameters" element="tns:productQuery" />
  </wsdl:message>
  <wsdl:message name="queryResponse">
    <wsdl:part name="parameters" element="tns:productQueryResult" />
  </wsdl:message>
  <wsdl:portType name="BizService">
    <wsdl:operation name="query">
      <wsdl:input message="tns:queryRequest" />
      <wsdl:output message="tns:queryResponse" />
    </wsdl:operation>
  </wsdl:portType>
  <wsdl:binding name="BizServiceSOAP" type="tns:BizService">
    <soap:binding style="document"
      transport="http://schemas.xmlsoap.org/soap/http" />
    <wsdl:operation name="query">
      <soap:operation soapAction="http://foo.com/NewOperation" />
      <wsdl:input>
        <soap:body use="literal" />
      </wsdl:input>
      <wsdl:output>
        <soap:body use="literal" />
      </wsdl:output>
    </wsdl:operation>
  </wsdl:binding>
  <wsdl:service name="BizService">
    <wsdl:port binding="tns:BizServiceSOAP" name="BizServiceSOAP">
      <soap:address
        location="http://localhost:8080/axis2/services/BizService" />
    </wsdl:port>
  </wsdl:service>
</wsdl:definitions>
```

If you edit it visually, here are the key steps: First, rename the operation to "query". The input element is automatically renamed to <query>. Double click on the arrow to right of the <query> element in order to edit it. Then right click on it and choose "Refactor | Rename":

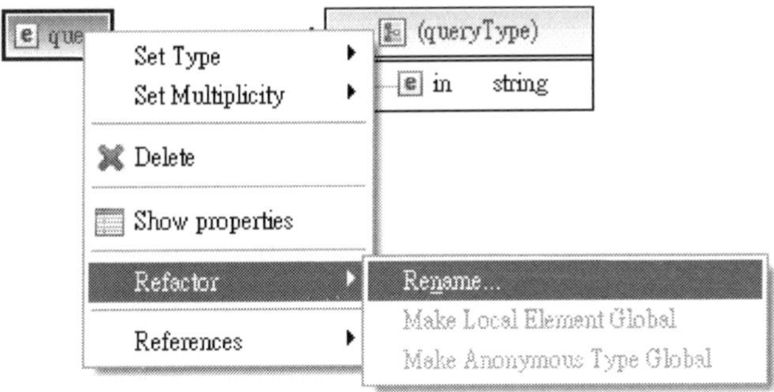

Rename it to "productQuery":

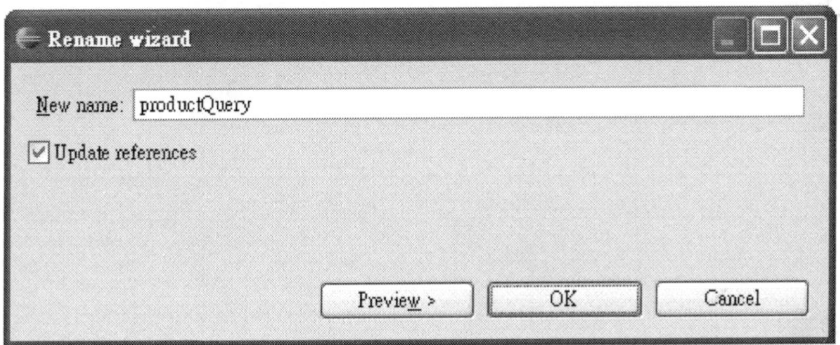

Rename the "in" element to "queryItem":

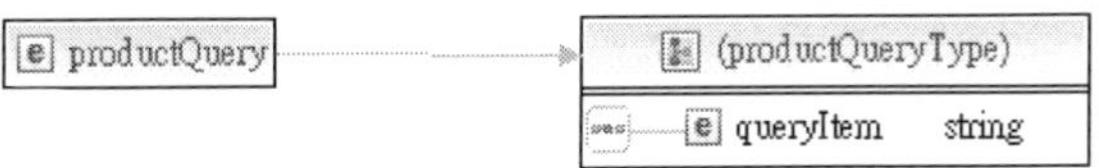

For the moment it is a string. Right click on it and choose "Set Type | New":

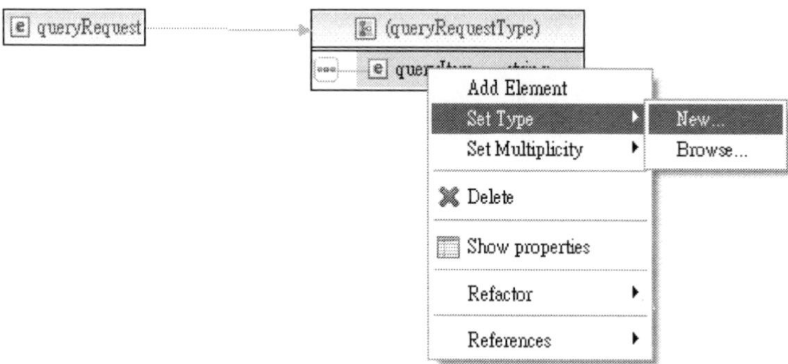

Choose to create an anonymous local complex type:

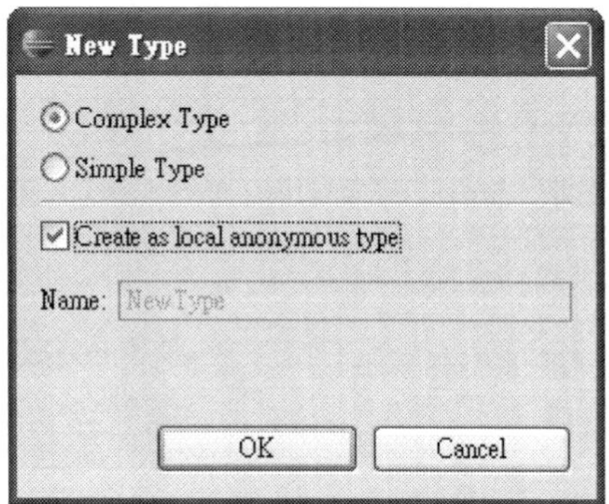

It will be like:

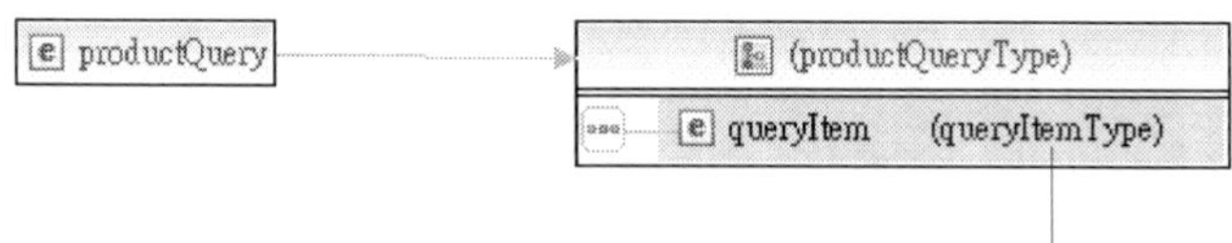

Next, you'd like to edit the (queryItemType). But clicking on it will NOT allow you to edit it. Instead, it will only let you choose another type for <queryItem>:

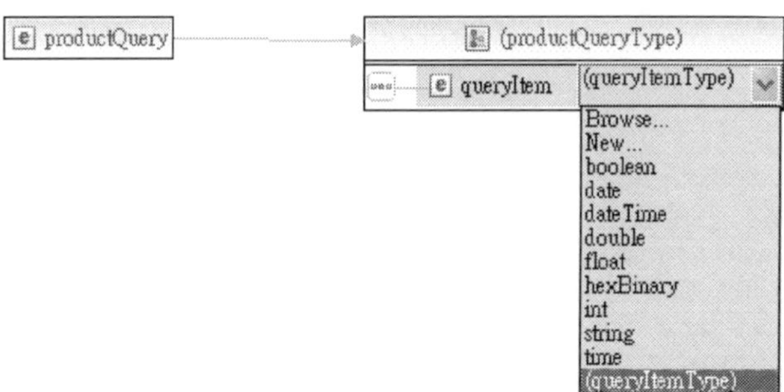

This is because Eclipse will not allow you to directly edit something too deep. Instead, it requires you to drill down by one level. So, double click on (productQueryType) [Note: NOT (queryItemType)] to drill down. You'll see that the (queryitemType) is available for editing:

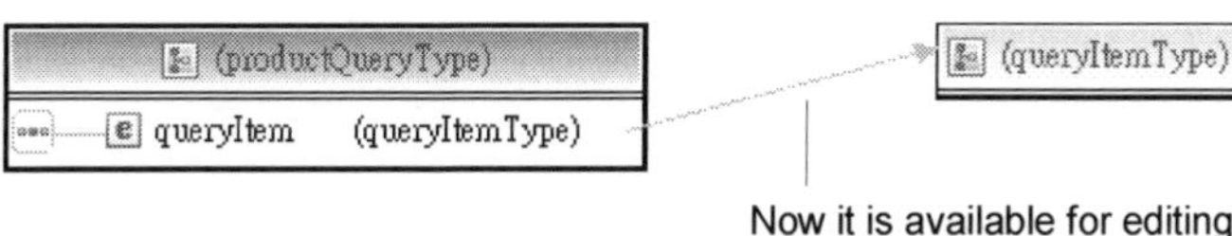

Right click on (queryItemType) and choose "Add Attribute":

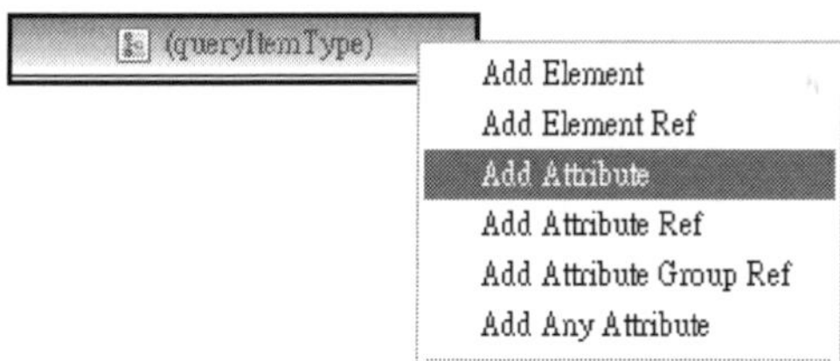

Rename the attribute to "productId". The type is by default string which is what you want:

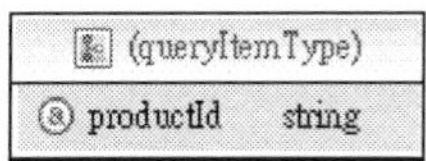

Similarly, add another attribute "qty" and set its type to int:

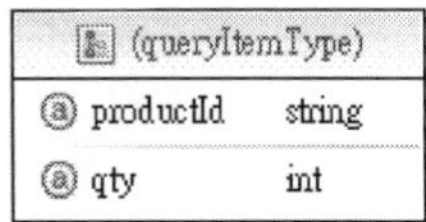

To tell that there can be 1 to many <queryItem> elements, right click the <queryItem> element and choose "Set Multiplicity | 1..*":

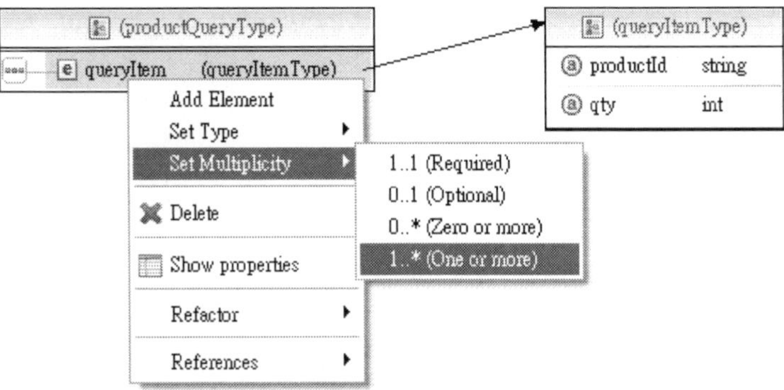

You'll see:

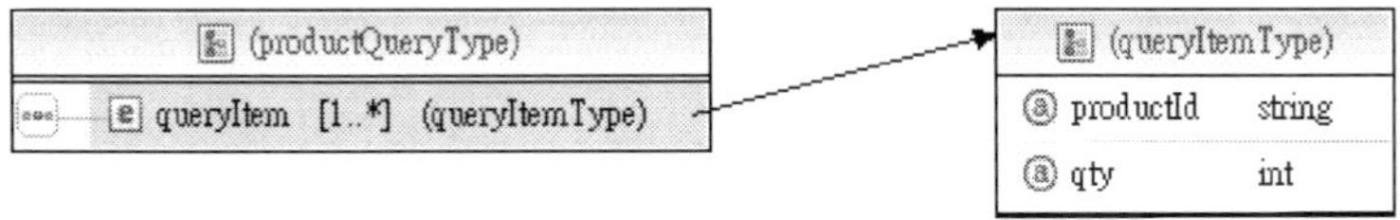

Now, it is done. To return to one level up, click the left arrow icon as if it were a browser:

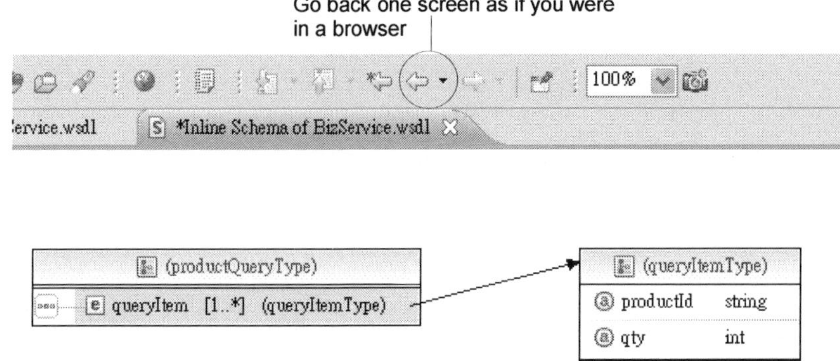

Similarly, create the <productQueryResult> element. As usual, validate it when you're done.

Next, update the build.xml file:

```
<?xml version="1.0" encoding="UTF-8"?>
<project basedir="." default="jar.server">
    ...
    <property name="name" value="WrappedBizService"/>
  ...
  <target name="generate-service">
    <wsdl2code
      wsdlfilename="${name}.wsdl"
      serverside="true"
      generateservicexml="true"
      skipbuildxml="true"
      serversideinterface="true"
      namespacetopackages="http://ttdev.com/ss=com.ttdev.wrapped"
      namespacetopackages="http://foo.com=com.ttdev.biz"
      targetsourcefolderlocation="src"
      targetresourcesfolderlocation="src/META-INF"
      overwrite="true"
      unwrap="true"/>
    <replaceregexp
      file="src/META-INF/services.xml"
      match="${name}Skeleton"
      replace="${name}Impl"/>
  </target>
  <target name="generate-client">
    <wsdl2code
      wsdlfilename="${name}.wsdl"
      skipbuildxml="true"
      namespacetopackages="http://ttdev.com/ss=com.ttdev.wrapped.client"
      namespacetopackages="http://foo.com=com.ttdev.biz.client"
      targetsourcefolderlocation="src"
      overwrite="true"
      unwrap="true"/>
  </target>
</project>
```

Generate the service stub and client stub. BUG ALERT: In Axis2 1.3 there is a bug preventing <wsdl2code> to overwrite the services.xml file. So, delete it first before running build.xml. Then create a BizServiceImpl class in the com.ttdev.biz package:

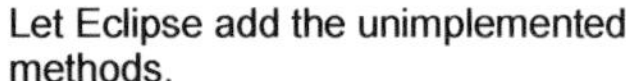


```
public class BizServiceImpl implements BizServiceSkeletonInterface {
    public ProductQueryResult query(ProductQuery productQuery) {

    }
}
```

XML elements are mapped to Java classes

```
<xsd:schema ...>
  <xsd:element name="productQuery">
    ...
  </xsd:element>
  <xsd:element name="productQueryResult">
    ...
  </xsd:element>
</xsd:schema>
```

If you inspect the ProductQuery class and the ProductQueryResult class, you'll note the mapping is like this:

Each element in a sequence is mapped to a field in the class

An element that can occur multiple times (i.e., maxOccurs > 1) is mapped to a Java array

```
class ProductQuery {
  QueryItem_type0[] queryItem;
}
class QueryItem_type0 {
  String productId;
  int qty;
}
class ProductQueryResult {
  ProductQueryItem_type0[] resultItem;
}
class ResultItem_type0 {
  String productId;
  int price;
}
```

```
<xsd:element name="productQuery">
  <xsd:complexType>
    <xsd:sequence>
      <xsd:element
        name="queryItem"
        maxOccurs="unbounded"
        minOccurs="1">
        ...attr productId, qty...
      </xsd:element>
    </xsd:sequence>
  </xsd:complexType>
</xsd:element>
<xsd:element name="productQueryResult">
  ...
</xsd:element>
```

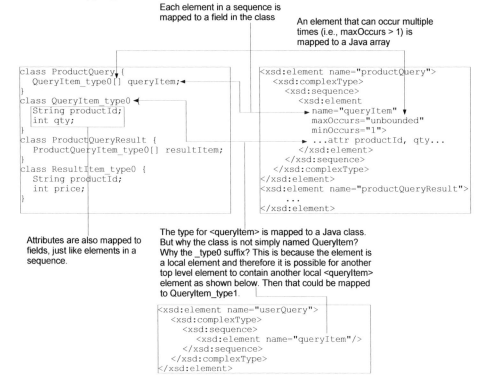

Attributes are also mapped to fields, just like elements in a sequence.

The type for <queryItem> is mapped to a Java class. But why the class is not simply named QueryItem? Why the _type0 suffix? This is because the element is a local element and therefore it is possible for another top level element to contain another local <queryItem> element as shown below. Then that could be mapped to QueryItem_type1.

```
<xsd:element name="userQuery">
  <xsd:complexType>
    <xsd:sequence>
      <xsd:element name="queryItem"/>
    </xsd:sequence>
  </xsd:complexType>
</xsd:element>
```

Then fill in the code to complete the implementation:

```
public class BizServiceImpl implements BizServiceSkeletonInterface {
  public ProductQueryResult query(ProductQuery productQuery) {
    ProductQueryResult result = new ProductQueryResult();
    QueryItem_type0[] queryItems = productQuery.getQueryItem();
    for (int i = 0; i < queryItems.length; i++) {
      QueryItem_type0 queryItem = queryItems[i];
      if (queryItem.getQty() <= 200) {
        ResultItem_type0 resultItem = new ResultItem_type0();
        resultItem.setProductId(queryItem.getProductId());
        resultItem.setPrice(20);
        result.addResultItem(resultItem);
      }
    }
    return result;
  }
}
```

Loop through each query item. Assume it's available if qty is <= 200.

Assume the unit price is always 20

Deploy it. Create a BizClient.java in the com.ttdev.biz.client package:

```
public class BizClient {
  public static void main(String[] args) throws RemoteException {
    BizServiceStub bizService = new BizServiceStub();
    ProductQuery query = new ProductQuery();
    QueryItem_type0 queryItem = new QueryItem_type0();
    queryItem.setProductId("p01");
    queryItem.setQty(100);
    query.addQueryItem(queryItem);
    queryItem = new QueryItem_type0();
    queryItem.setProductId("p02");
    queryItem.setQty(200);
    query.addQueryItem(queryItem);
    queryItem = new QueryItem_type0();
    queryItem.setProductId("p03");
    queryItem.setQty(500);
    query.addQueryItem(queryItem);
    ProductQueryResult result = bizService.query(query);
    for (ResultItem_type0 resultItem : result.getResultItem()) {
      System.out.println(resultItem.getProductId() + ": "
          + resultItem.getPrice());
    }
  }
}
```

Run the client and it should work:

```
Console  Problems  @ Javadoc  Declaration
<terminated> BizClient [Java Application] C:\Program Files\Java\jr
log4j:WARN No appenders could be found
log4j:WARN Please initialize the log4j
p01: 20
p02: 20
```

Avoiding the type suffix

If you don't like the type suffixes like _type0, you can turn the type for <queryItem> into a top level type. To do that, right click (queryItemType) and choose "Refactor | Make Anonymous Type Global":

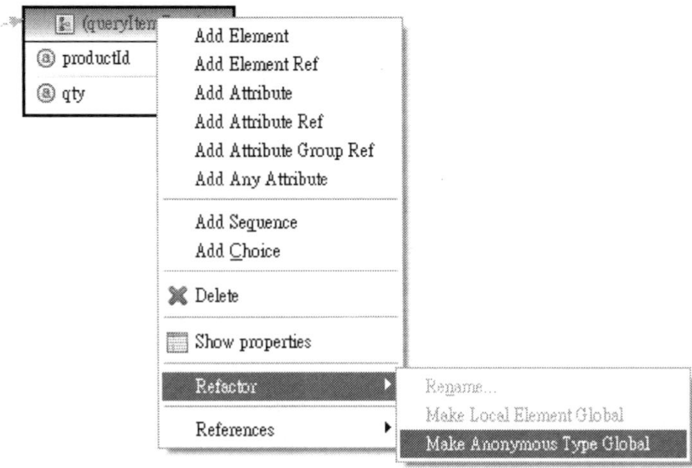

The WSDL code will become:

```
<xsd:schema ...>
  <xsd:element name="productQuery">
    <xsd:complexType>
      <xsd:sequence>
        <xsd:element name="queryItem"
          minOccurs="1"
          maxOccurs="unbounded"
          type="tns:queryItemComplexType">
        </xsd:element>
      </xsd:sequence>
    </xsd:complexType>
  </xsd:element>
  <xsd:complexType name="queryItemComplexType">
    <xsd:attribute name="productId" type="xsd:string"/>
    <xsd:attribute name="qty" type="xsd:int"/>
  </xsd:complexType>
</xsd:schema>
```

"type" means that this element conforms to an existing type

Rename the type from queryItemComplexType to queryItemType:

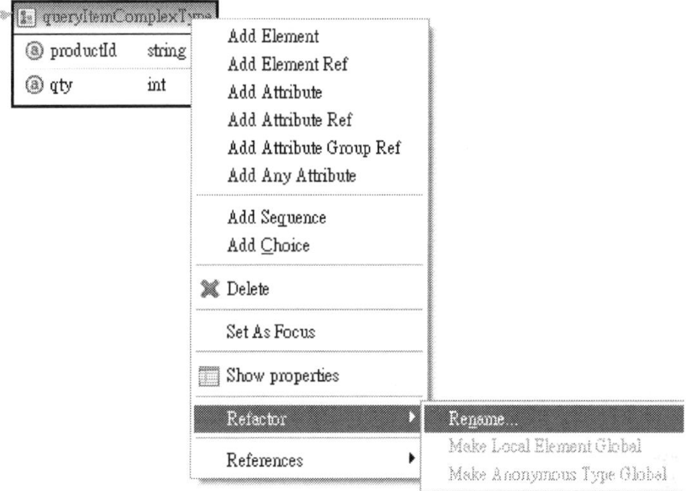

Generate the service code and client code again. The QueryItem_type0 class will be gone and you'll have a QueryItemType class instead. You'll need to update your code accordingly:

```
public class BizServiceImpl implements BizServiceSkeletonInterface {
    public ProductQueryResult query(ProductQuery productQuery) {
        ProductQueryResult result = new ProductQueryResult();
        QueryItem_type0 QueryItemType[] queryItems = productQuery.getQueryItem();
        for (int i = 0; i < queryItems.length; i++) {
            QueryItem_type0 QueryItemType queryItem = queryItems[i];
            if (queryItem.getQty() <= 200) {
                ResultItem_type0 resultItem = new ResultItem_type0();
                resultItem.setProductId(queryItem.getProductId());
                resultItem.setPrice(20);
                result.addResultItem(resultItem);
            }
        }
        return result;
    }
}
```

Make similar changes to the BizClient class. Run it and it should continue to work.

Sending more data in a message

By the way, this query operation demonstrates a good practice in web services: You generally hope to send more data in a message. For example, you may be sending many query items in a single response message. This is more efficient than sending a single query item object in a message. This is because there is a certain overhead involved in sending a message, even if it contains no data:

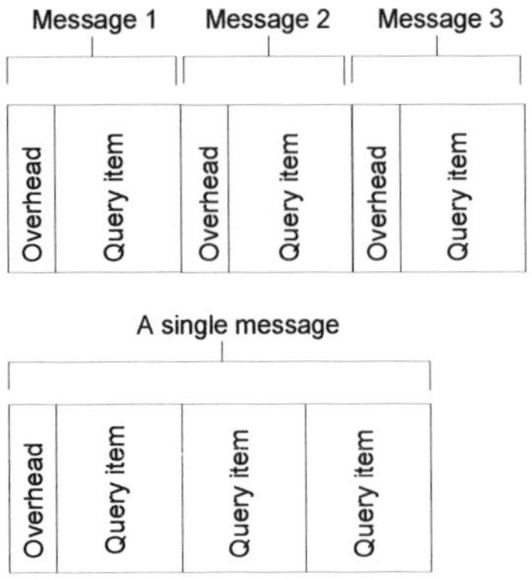

Returning faults

Suppose that a client is calling your query operation but a product id is invalid (not just out of stock, but absolutely unknown) or the quantity is zero or negative. You may want to throw an exception. To return an exception to the client, you send a "fault message", which is very much like an output message. To do that, modify the WSDL file:

```
<?xml version="1.0" encoding="UTF-8"?>
<wsdl:definitions ...>
  <wsdl:types>
    <xsd:schema ...>
      <xsd:element name="productQuery">
        ...
      </xsd:element>
      <xsd:element name="productQueryResult">
        ...
      </xsd:element>
      <xsd:complexType name="queryItemType">
        ...
      </xsd:complexType>
      <xsd:element name="invalidProductId" type="xsd:string" />
      <xsd:element name="invalidQty" type="xsd:int "/>
    </xsd:schema>
  </wsdl:types>
  <wsdl:message name="queryRequest">
    <wsdl:part name="parameters" element="tns:productQuery" />
  </wsdl:message>
  <wsdl:message name="queryResponse">
    <wsdl:part name="parameters" element="tns:productQueryResult" />
  </wsdl:message>
  <wsdl:message name="queryInvalidProductId">
    <wsdl:part name="parameters" element="tns:invalidProductId" />
  </wsdl:message>
  <wsdl:message name="queryInvalidQty">
    <wsdl:part name="parameters" element="tns:invalidQty" />
  </wsdl:message>
  <wsdl:portType name="BizService">
    <wsdl:operation name="query">
      <wsdl:input message="tns:queryRequest" />
      <wsdl:output message="tns:queryResponse" />
      <wsdl:fault name="f01" message="tns:queryInvalidProductId" />
      <wsdl:fault name="f02" message="tns:queryInvalidQty" />
    </wsdl:operation>
  </wsdl:portType>
  ...
</wsdl:definitions>
```

The one and only part is a well defined element in the schema

A fault message is like an output message, but it indicates an error.

Unlike an input or output message which doesn't need a name, a fault needs a unique name because there can be multiple fault messages (here you have 2). Later you'll refer to a fault using its name.

How to include the fault message in a SOAP message? It is included in the SOAP body, but not directly:

```
<wsdl:definitions ...>
  ...
  <wsdl:portType name="BizService">
    <wsdl:operation name="query">
      <wsdl:input message="tns:queryRequest" />
      <wsdl:output message="tns:queryResponse" />
      <wsdl:fault name="f01" message="tns:queryInvalidProductId" />
      <wsdl:fault name="f02" message="tns:queryInvalidQty" />
    </wsdl:operation>
  </wsdl:portType>
  <wsdl:binding name="BizServiceSOAP" type="tns:BizService">
    <soap:binding style="document"
      transport="http://schemas.xmlsoap.org/soap/http" />
    <wsdl:operation name="query">
      <soap:operation soapAction="http://foo.com/NewOperation" />
      <wsdl:input>
        <soap:body use="literal" />
      </wsdl:input>
      <wsdl:output>
        <soap:body use="literal" />
      </wsdl:output>
      <wsdl:fault name="f01" >
        <soap:fault name="f01" use="literal"/>
      </wsdl:fault>
      <wsdl:fault name="f02" >
        <soap:fault name="f02" use="literal"/>
      </wsdl:fault>
    </wsdl:operation>
  </wsdl:binding>
  ...
</wsdl:definitions>
```

How to store this fault message in a binding?

In SOAP, include the fault message into the SOAP <Fault>:

The message part is already in XML

```
<soap-env:Envelope
  xmlns:soap-env="http://http://schemas.xmlsoap.org/soap/envelope/">
  <soap-env:Header>
    ...
  </soap-env:Header>
  <soap-env:Body>
    <soap-env:Fault>
      <soap-env:faultcode>...</soap-env:faultcode>
      <soap-env:faultstring>...</soap-env:faultstring>
      <soap-env:detail>
        <foo:invalidProductId xmlns:foo="http://foo.com">
          p1000
        </foo:invalidProductId>
      </soap-env:detail>
    </soap-env:Fault>
  </soap-env:Body>
<soap-env:Envelope>
```

The SOAP <Fault> element tells the caller that something is wrong. The <faultcode> is a QName acting as an error code. The <faultstring> is an error message for human reading. The <detail> will contain any information that both sides agree on. In this case, it contains your fault message part.

To make the above changes to the WSDL file visually, right click the query operation and choose "Add Fault":

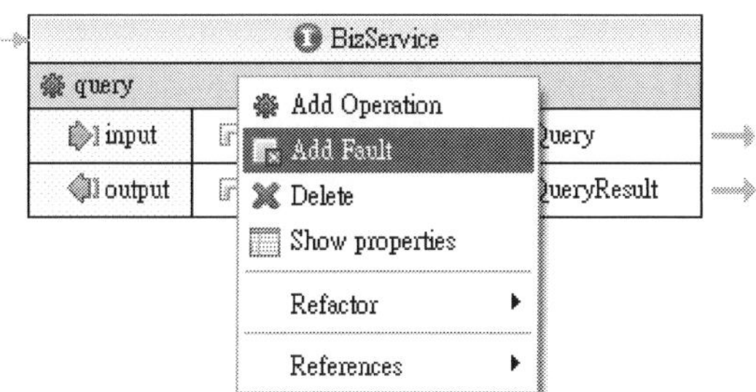

Choose the fault, in the Properties window, set its name to f01:

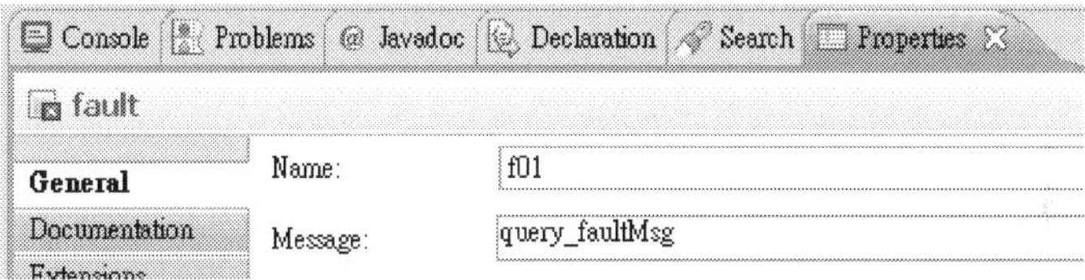

Choose to create a new message:

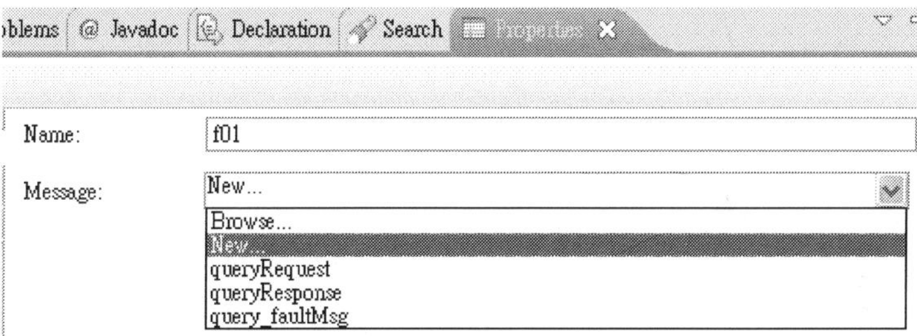

Enter the name for the message:

Set the one and only part to a new XML element <invalidProductId>. By default it should be of type xsd:string which is what you want here. Create the second fault similarly. Set the message name to queryInvalidQty, set the XML element to <invalidQty> whose type is xsd:int. Finally it should be like:

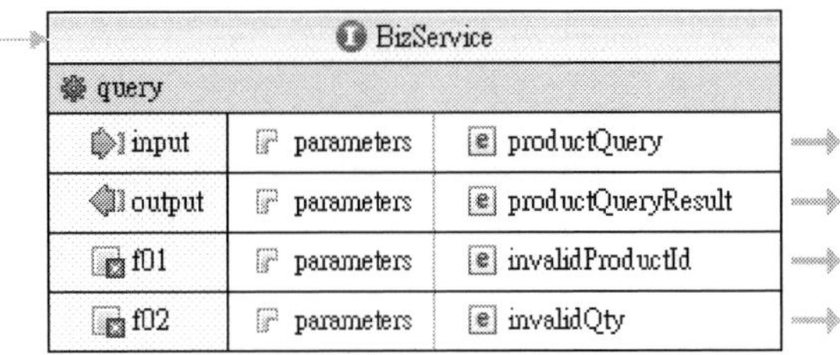

Next, create the binding for the two faults. Choose the binding and click "Generate Binding Content" in the Properties window:

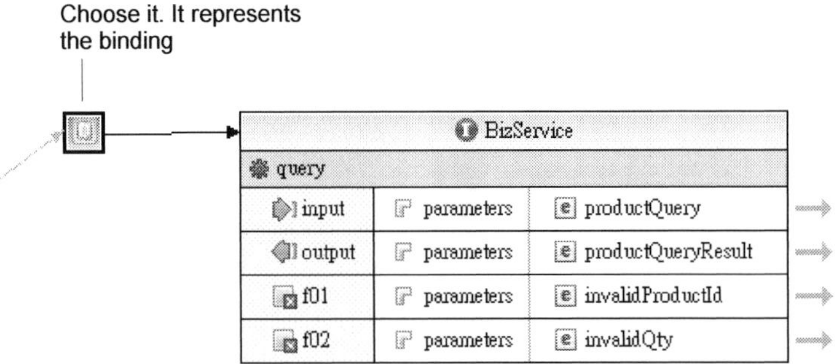

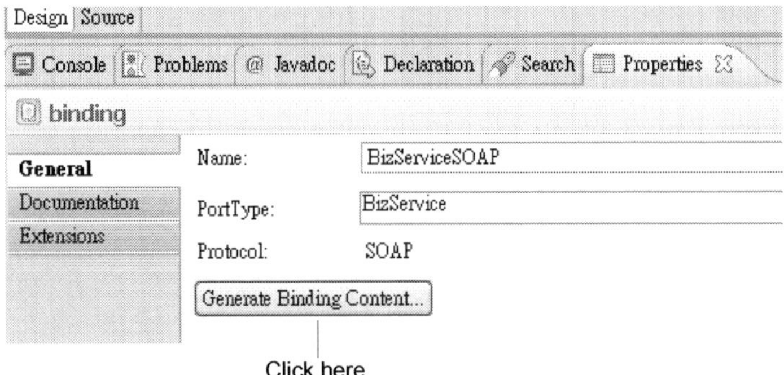

Check "Overwrite existing binding information" and then click "Finish":

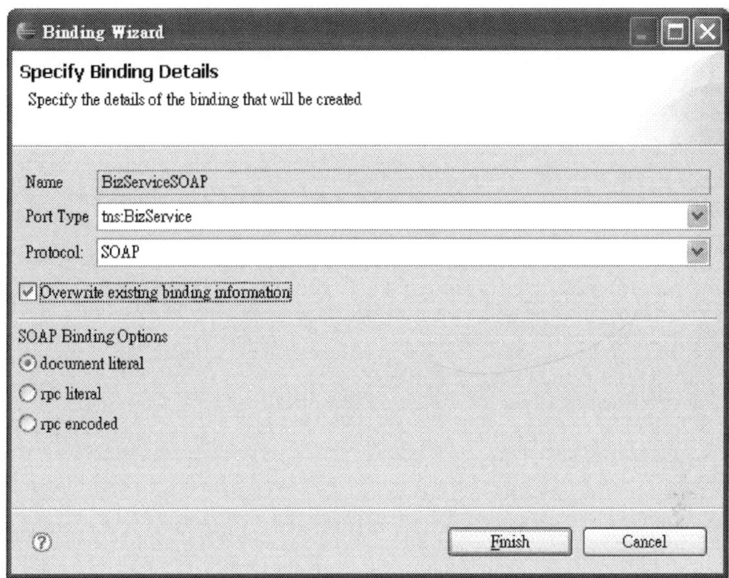

This will generate the binding portion:

```
<wsdl:binding name="BizServiceSOAP" type="tns:BizService">
  <soap:binding style="document"
    transport="http://schemas.xmlsoap.org/soap/http" />
  <wsdl:operation name="query">
    <soap:operation soapAction="http://foo.com/query" />
    <wsdl:input>
      <soap:body use="literal" />
    </wsdl:input>
    <wsdl:output>
      <soap:body use="literal" />
    </wsdl:output>
    <wsdl:fault name="f01">
      <soap:fault use="literal" name="f01" />
    </wsdl:fault>
    <wsdl:fault name="f02">
      <soap:fault use="literal" name="f02" />
    </wsdl:fault>
  </wsdl:operation>
</wsdl:binding>
```

Finally go into the schema index to delete the unused elements created by Eclipse:

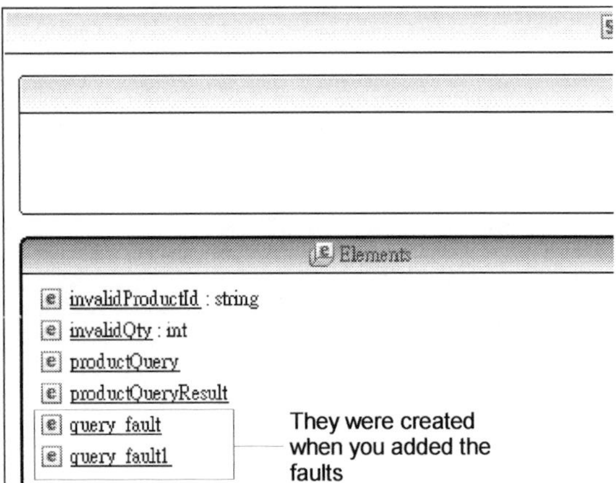

Similarly, choose "Window | Show View | Outline" to show the outline of the WSDL file as shown below. Right click and delete the unused messages such as query_faultMsg and query_faultMsg1:

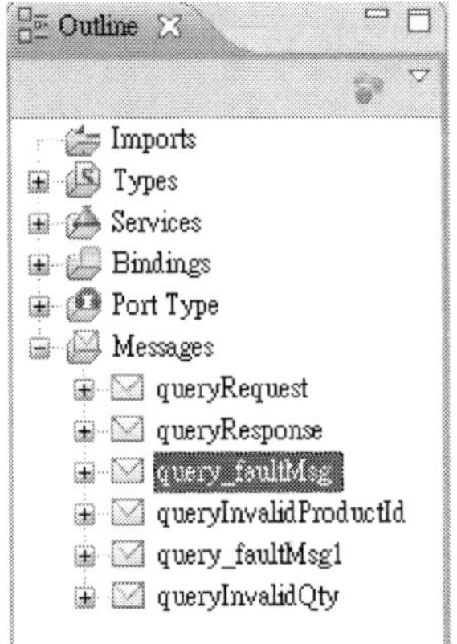

Now, generate the service and client stubs and refresh the files in Eclipse. You will find some new Java classes:

```
class QueryInvalidProductId extends Exception {
  InvalidProductId faultMessage;
  ...
}
```

A fault message is mapped to a Java exception. Its one and only part (an XML element) is mapped to a field.

```
class InvalidProductId {
  String invalidProductId;
  ...
}
```

As usual, an XML element such as the <invalidProductId> element is mapped to a Java class. It wanted to extend String, but String is a final class. So the string is mapped to a field.

```
class QueryInvalidQty extends Exception {
  InvalidQty faultMessage;
  ...
}
```

```
class InvalidQty {
  int invalidQty;
  ...
}
```

The method signature in BizServiceSkeletonInterface has also been updated to throw such exceptions:

```
public interface BizServiceSkeletonInterface {
    public ProductQueryResult query(ProductQuery productQuery)
    throws QueryInvalidProductId, QueryInvalidQty;
}
```

Now modify your implementation code:

```
public class BizServiceImpl implements BizServiceSkeletonInterface {
  public ProductQueryResult query(ProductQuery productQuery)
      throws QueryInvalidProductId, QueryInvalidQty {
    ProductQueryResult result = new ProductQueryResult();
    QueryItemType[] queryItems = productQuery.getQueryItem();
    for (int i = 0; i < queryItems.length; i++) {
      QueryItemType queryItem = queryItems[i];
      if (!queryItem.getProductId().startsWith("p")) {
        QueryInvalidProductId fault = new QueryInvalidProductId();
        InvalidProductId part = new InvalidProductId();
        part.setInvalidProductId(queryItem.getProductId());
        fault.setFaultMessage(part);
        throw fault;
      }
      if (queryItem.getQty() <= 0) {
        QueryInvalidQty fault = new QueryInvalidQty();
        InvalidQty part = new InvalidQty();
        part.setInvalidQty(queryItem.getQty());
        fault.setFaultMessage(part);
        throw fault;
      }
      if (queryItem.getQty() <= 200) {
        ResultItem_type0 resultItem = new ResultItem_type0();
        resultItem.setProductId(queryItem.getProductId());
        resultItem.setPrice(20);
        result.addResultItem(resultItem);
      }
    }
    return result;
  }
}
```

To see if it's working, modify BizClient.java:

```
public class BizClient {
```

```
    public static void main(String[] args) throws RemoteException {
        BizServiceStub bizService = new BizServiceStub();
        ProductQuery query = new ProductQuery();
        QueryItemType queryItem = new QueryItemType();
        queryItem.setProductId("p01");
        queryItem.setQty(100);
        query.addQueryItem(queryItem);
        queryItem = new QueryItemType();
        queryItem.setProductId("p02");
        queryItem.setQty(-200);
        query.addQueryItem(queryItem);
        queryItem = new QueryItemType();
        queryItem.setProductId("p03");
        queryItem.setQty(500);
        query.addQueryItem(queryItem);
    try {
      ProductQueryResult result = bizService.query(query);
          for (ResultItem_type0 resultItem : result.getResultItem()) {
              System.out.println(resultItem.getProductId() + ": " +
                  resultItem.getPrice());
          }
    } catch (QueryInvalidProductId e) {
      System.out.println("Invalid product id: "
              + e.getFaultMessage().getInvalidProductId());
    } catch (QueryInvalidQty e) {
      System.out.println("Invalid qty: "
              + e.getFaultMessage().getInvalidQty());
    }
  }
}
```

Start the Axis server, then run the BizClient and it should work:

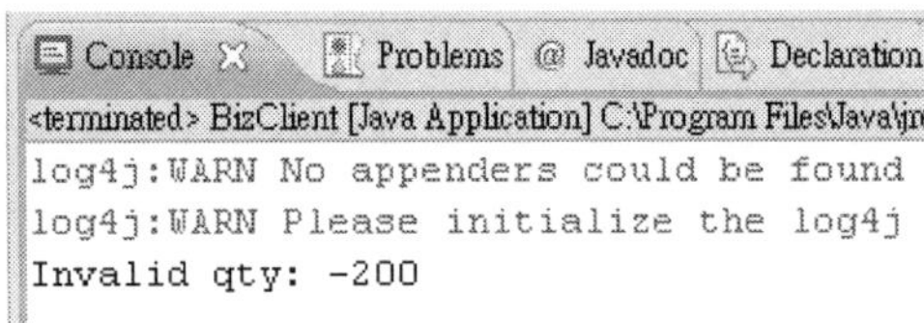
Console
Problems
Javadoc
Declaration
<terminated> BizClient [Java Application] C:\Program Files\Java\jr
log4j:WARN No appenders could be found
log4j:WARN Please initialize the log4j
Invalid qty: -200

If you'd like, you can see the messages in TCP Monitor:

```
<?xml version='1.0' encoding='UTF-8'?>
  <soapenv:Envelope xmlns:soapenv="http://schemas.xmlsoap.org/soap/envelope/">
    <soapenv:Body>
      <soapenv:Fault>
        <faultcode>soapenv:Server</faultcode>
        <faultstring>QueryInvalidQty</faultstring>
        <detail>
          <ns1:invalidQty xmlns:ns1="http://foo.com">-200</ns1:invalidQty>
        </detail>
      </soapenv:Fault>
    </soapenv:Body>
  </soapenv:Envelope>
```

Using encoded

You have been writing document style services. In addition, the parts are sent as "literal":

```
...
<wsdl:binding name="BizServiceSOAP" type="tns:BizService">
  <soap:binding style="document"
```

```
      transport="http://schemas.xmlsoap.org/soap/http" />
    <wsdl:operation name="query">
      <soap:operation soapAction="http://foo.com/query" />
      <wsdl:input>
        <soap:body use="literal" />
      </wsdl:input>
      <wsdl:output>
        <soap:body use="literal" />
      </wsdl:output>
      <wsdl:fault name="f01">
        <soap:fault name="f01" use="literal" />
      </wsdl:fault>
      <wsdl:fault name="f02">
        <soap:fault name="f02" use="literal" />
      </wsdl:fault>
    </wsdl:operation>
  </wsdl:binding>
```

What does literal means? If you don't use literal, you may set it to "encoded". Then Axis will perform some extra encoding of the data in order to convert it into XML. For example, it will be able to handle multi-dimension arrays and data structures containing loops (e.g., a circular linked-list). These kind of data structures don't have direct counter-parts in XML. In fact, if you start from a WSDL, you will never get these data types from the <wsdl2code> Ant task. So, "encoded" is useful only when you have some legacy code that uses such data structures and you'd like to expose it as a web service.

The resulting XML is XML but can't be validated by any schema. This is prohibited in document style services. Therefore, in order to use "encoded", you must use the RPC style.

To use RPC+encoded, in theory you only need to change the WSDL and then generate the stubs again. However, as of Axis2 1.3, Axis2 doesn't support the encoded use as it is not good for interoperability and is getting phased out (in the next version of WSDL, namely WSDL 2.0, only document+literal is supported).

Referring to existing XML elements

For the moment you're defining XML elements such as <productQuery> directly in the WSDL file. However, in practice, most likely such elements are defined by a 3rd party such as an industrial consortium or neutral association. Suppose that they are provided in a file purchasing.xsd such as this:

The root element is <schema>

The default namespace is the XML schema namespace, so you don't need to use the xsd prefix below.

As they are defined by a 3rd party, it should use a different target namespace. Let's assume that it is http://bar.com/purchasing.

Everything else remains unchanged

```
<?xml version="1.0" encoding="UTF-8"?>
<schema xmlns="http://www.w3.org/2001/XMLSchema"
   targetNamespace="http://bar.org/purchasing"
   xmlns:tns="http://bar.org/purchasing">
   <element name="productQuery">
      <complexType>
         <sequence>
            <element name="queryItem" minOccurs="1"
               maxOccurs="unbounded" type="tns:queryItemType">
            </element>
         </sequence>
      </complexType>
   </element>
   <element name="productQueryResult">
      <complexType>
         <sequence>
            <element name="resultItem" maxOccurs="unbounded"
               minOccurs="1">
               <complexType>
                  <attribute name="productId"
                     type="string">
                  </attribute>
                  <attribute name="price" type="int">
                  </attribute>
               </complexType>
            </element>
         </sequence>
      </complexType>
   </element>
   <complexType name="queryItemType">
      <attribute name="productId" type="string"></attribute>
      <attribute name="qty" type="int"></attribute>
   </complexType>
   <element name="invalidProductId" type="string"></element>
   <element name="invalidQty" type="int"></element>
</schema>
```

How to refer to those XML elements in your WSDL file? First, put the purchasing.xsd file into the same folder as the WSDL file (i.e., the project root). Then modify the WSDL file:

You're saying: I'd like to refer to the XML elements defined in the http://bar.org/purchasing namespace. Then the XML elements will be visible to this WSDL file. This is like the import statement in Java used to import a package or a class.

How can the WSDL parser find out the XML elements defined there? It will work if the person parsing the WSDL have set up a table like below. Such a table is called an XML catalog.

Namespace	Path to its xsd file
http://bar.org/purchasing	c:\schema\f1.xsd
http://...	c:\...
http://...	c:\...

You don't need to define your own elements anymore

```
<?xml version="1.0" encoding="UTF-8"?>
<wsdl:definitions xmlns:wsdl="http://schemas.xmlsoap.org/wsdl/"
  xmlns:soap="http://schemas.xmlsoap.org/wsdl/soap/"
  xmlns:tns="http://foo.com"
  xmlns:p="http://bar.org/purchasing"
  xmlns:xsd="http://www.w3.org/2001/XMLSchema"
  name="BizService"
  targetNamespace="http://foo.com">
  <wsdl:types>
    <xsd:schema targetNamespace="http://foo.com"
      xmlns:xsd="http://www.w3.org/2001/XMLSchema">
      <xsd:import
        namespace="http://bar.org/purchasing"
        schemaLocation="purchasing.xsd">
      </xsd:import>
      <xsd:element name="productQuery">
        ...
      </xsd:element>
      ...
    </xsd:schema>
  </wsdl:types>
  <wsdl:message name="queryRequest">
    <wsdl:part name="parameters" element="p:productQuery" />
  </wsdl:message>
  <wsdl:message name="queryResponse">
    <wsdl:part name="parameters" element="p:productQueryResult" />
  </wsdl:message>
  <wsdl:message name="queryInvalidProductId">
    <wsdl:part name="NewPart" element="p:invalidProductId" />
  </wsdl:message>
  <wsdl:message name="queryInvalidQty">
    <wsdl:part name="NewPart" element="p:invalidQty" />
  </wsdl:message>
  <wsdl:portType name="BizService">
    ...
  </wsdl:portType>
  <wsdl:binding name="BizServiceSOAP" type="tns:BizService">
    ...
  </wsdl:binding>
  <wsdl:service name="BizService">
    ...
  </wsdl:service>
</wsdl:definitions>
```

As you'll be giving away this WSDL to many people, it may be too difficult to ask everyone to set up the XML catalog. So you may simply distribute the XSD file and make sure it is in the same folder as the WSDL file and specify the relative path here. In addition to the XML catalog, their WSDL processor will follow this path to find the XSD file.

The elements are now defined in another namespace

Modify build.xml:

```
<project ...>
  ...
  <target name="generate-service">
    <wsdl2code
      wsdlfilename="${name}.wsdl"
      serverside="true"
      generateservicexml="true"
      skipbuildxml="true"
      serversideinterface="true"
      namespacetopackages=
        "http://foo.com=com.ttdev.biz,http://bar.org/purchasing=com.ttdev.biz.purchasing"
      targetsourcefolderlocation="src"
      targetresourcesfolderlocation="src/META-INF"
      overwrite="true"/>
    <replaceregexp
      file="src/META-INF/services.xml"
      match="${name}Skeleton"
      replace="${name}Impl"/>
  </target>
  <target name="generate-client">
    <wsdl2code
      wsdlfilename="${name}.wsdl"
      skipbuildxml="true"
      namespacetopackages="http://foo.com=com.ttdev.biz.client"
      targetsourcefolderlocation="src"
      overwrite="true"/>
  </target>
</project>
```

As the XML elements are in the http://bar.org/purchasing namespace, you may want to map it to a Java package.

Separate them by a comma

You could do the same thing for the client, but by default the XML elements will be mapped to inner classes of the client stub. So you don't need to specify a package for them.

Delete all the Java files generated. That is, all files except your BizServiceImpl and BizClient. Also delete all the files in META-INF. Run build.xml. You should see the following output in the console:

```
Buildfile: C:\workspace\BizService\build.xml
generate-service:
[wsdl2code] Retrieving schema at 'purchasing.xsd', relative to
'file:/C:/workspace/BizService/'.
generate-client:
[wsdl2code] Retrieving schema at 'purchasing.xsd', relative to
'file:/C:/workspace/BizService/'.
BUILD SUCCESSFUL
Total time: 10 seconds
```

Refresh the project. Note that the XSD file will have been copied into the META-INF folder to be accessed by potential clients:

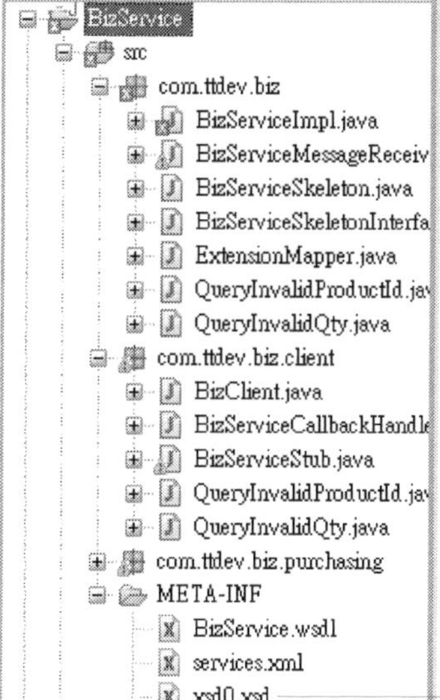

The BizServiceImpl class should still be in error as the XML element classes are now in a different package. Fix this. For example, in Eclipse, open the BizServiceImpl file and press Ctrl-Shift-O and then choose the classes in the com.ttdev.biz.purchasing package (do NOT choose those inner classes in the com.ttdev.biz.client.BizServiceStub):

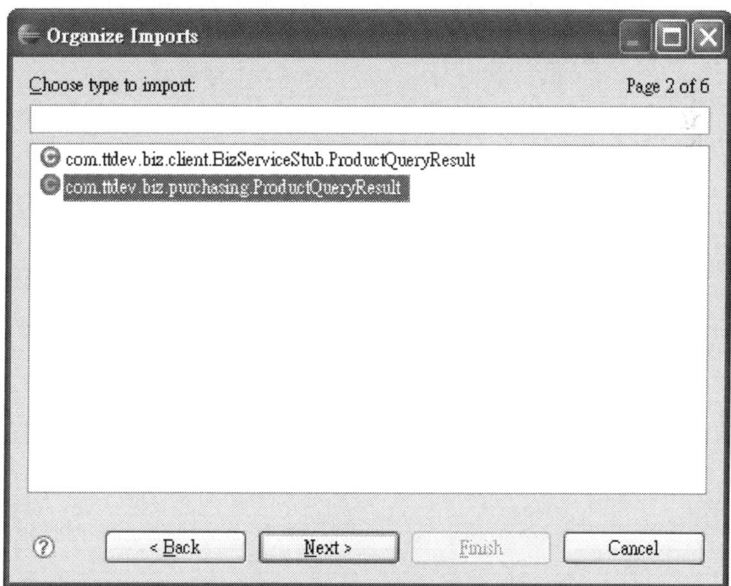

Run the BizClient and it should continue to work.

Retrieving WSDL files using HTTP

To really simulate the client side, it should retrieve the WSDL file using http://localhost:8080/axis2/services/BizService?wsdl instead of a local file. It should also be able to retrieve the XSD file automatically. To verify that, modify build.xml:

```
<project ...>
  ...
  <target name="generate-client">
    <wsdl2code
      wsdlfilename="http://localhost:8080/axis2/services/BizService?wsdl"
      skipbuildxml="true"
      namespacetopackages="http://foo.com=com.ttdev.biz.client"
      targetsourcefolderlocation="src"
      overwrite="true"/>
  </target>
</project>
```

Make sure the Axis server is running. Then run build.xml to generate the client stub again. It should work and display something like that in the console:

```
Buildfile: C:\workspace\BizService\build.xml
generate-client:
[wsdl2code] Retrieving schema at 'BizService?xsd=xsd0.xsd', relative to
'http://localhost:8080/axis2/services/'.
BUILD SUCCESSFUL
Total time: 7 seconds
```

Run the client and it should continue to work.

Summary

You can freely use XML schema elements to express complex data structures. The <wsdl2code> Ant task will translate them into Java types.

For better performance, you should design the interfaces of your web service operations so that more data is sent in a message.

To report an error from your operation, define a message in the WSDL file and use it as a fault message in the operation. Then add a corresponding child element in the SOAP binding to store it into the SOAP Fault element. The fault message should contain one and only one part which is an XML element describing the fault. The <wsdl2code> Ant task will map a fault message to a Java exception class and the part as a field. The operation will be mapped to a Java method throwing that exception.

If you need to send weird data structures, you can use RPC+encoded but interoperability will be affected. The encoded use is not supported by Axis2 as of 1.3.

If you have existing XML elements in an XSD file that you'd like to use in a WSDL file, you can use <import> to import them. You can specify the relative path to the XSD file so that the WSDL parser can find it.

Chapter 7

Sending binary files

What's in this chapter?

In this chapter you'll learn how to receive and return binary files in your web service.

Providing the image of a product

Suppose that you'd like to have a web service to allow people to upload the image (jpeg) of a product (identified by a product id). The SOAP message may be like:

```
<Envelope>
  <Body>
    <uploadImage>
      <productId>p01</productId>
      <image>kdubn87kamlndy...</image>
    </uploadImage>
  </Body>
</Envelope>
```

Typically binary data such as the image is encoded using the base64 encoding

The problem is that the base64 encoded data will be much larger than the binary version. This wastes processing time, network bandwidth and transmission time. In fact, if the image is huge, then many XML parsers may not be able to handle it properly. To solve this problem, instead of always representing an XML document as text, people state that it can be represented as a MIME message. For example, the above XML document (SOAP envelope) can be represented as below without changing its meaning:

To implement this idea, create a new project named ImageService as usual (You may copy an old one. If so, change the linked folder). Modify the WSDL file:

Use a urn as the target namespace

```
<?xml version="1.0" encoding="UTF-8"?>
<wsdl:definitions xmlns:wsdl="http://schemas.xmlsoap.org/wsdl/"
  xmlns:soap="http://schemas.xmlsoap.org/wsdl/soap/"
  xmlns:tns="urn:ttdev.com:service/img"
  xmlns:xsd="http://www.w3.org/2001/XMLSchema" name="ImageService"
  targetNamespace="urn:ttdev.com:service/img">
  <wsdl:types>
    <xsd:schema targetNamespace="urn:ttdev.com:service/img"
      xmlns:xsd="http://www.w3.org/2001/XMLSchema">
      <xsd:element name="uploadImage">
        <xsd:complexType>
          <xsd:sequence>
            <xsd:element name="productId" type="xsd:string" />
            <xsd:element name="image" type="xsd:base64Binary" />
          </xsd:sequence>
        </xsd:complexType>
      </xsd:element>
    </xsd:schema>
  </wsdl:types>
  <wsdl:message name="uploadImageRequest">
    <wsdl:part name="parameters" element="tns:uploadImage" />
  </wsdl:message>
  <wsdl:portType name="ImageService">
    <wsdl:operation name="uploadImage">
      <wsdl:input message="tns:uploadImageRequest" />
    </wsdl:operation>
  </wsdl:portType>
  <wsdl:binding name="ImageServiceSOAP" type="tns:ImageService">
    <soap:binding style="document"
      transport="http://schemas.xmlsoap.org/soap/http" />
    <wsdl:operation name="uploadImage">
      <soap:operation
        soapAction="urn:ttdev.com:service/img/uploadImage" />
      <wsdl:input>
        <soap:body use="literal" />
      </wsdl:input>
    </wsdl:operation>
  </wsdl:binding>
  <wsdl:service name="ImageService">
    <wsdl:port binding="tns:ImageServiceSOAP"
      name="ImageServiceSOAP">
      <soap:address
        location="http://localhost:8080/axis2/services/ImageService" />
    </wsdl:port>
  </wsdl:service>
</wsdl:definitions>
```

It will contain binary data. It is basically to be encoded using base64. Later you will tell Axis to use XOP for it.

The operation doesn't return anything, so there is no output message.

Although this is not required, it uses the wrapped convention. Next, update build.xml:

```
<?xml version="1.0" encoding="UTF-8"?>
<project basedir="." default="jar.server">
  ...
  <property name="name" value="ImageService" />
  ...
  <target name="generate-service">
    <wsdl2code
      wsdlfilename="${name}.wsdl"
      serverside="true"
```

```
        generateservicexml="true"
        skipbuildxml="true"
        serversideinterface="true"
        namespacetopackages="urn:ttdev.com:service/img=com.ttdev.image"
        targetsourcefolderlocation="src"
        targetresourcesfolderlocation="src/META-INF"
        overwrite="true"
        unwrap="true" />
      <replaceregexp
        file="src/META-INF/services.xml"
        match="${name}Skeleton"
        replace="${name}Impl" />
    </target>
    <target name="generate-client">
      <wsdl2code
        wsdlfilename="${name}.wsdl"
        skipbuildxml="true"
        namespacetopackages="urn:ttdev.com:service/img=com.ttdev.image.client"
        targetsourcefolderlocation="src"
        overwrite="true"
        unwrap="true" />
    </target>
  </project>
```

Generate the service stub and client stub. Check the implementation class:

```
public class ImageServiceSkeleton implements ImageServiceSkeletonInterface {
    public void uploadImage(
        java.lang.String productId1,
        javax.activation.DataHandler image2) {
    }
}
```

Note that the binary image data is presented as a DataHandler object. To read the data from it, create an ImageServiceImpl class:

This is how you get the content type from a DataHandler

A DataHandler represents a MIME part above: It has a content type and some data (bytes).

```
public class ImageServiceImpl implements ImageServiceSkeletonInterface {

  public void uploadImage(String productId, DataHandler image) {
    System.out.println(image.getContentType());
    try {
      InputStream in = image.getInputStream();
      String imageDir = "c:/tmp";
      FileOutputStream out = new FileOutputStream(new File(imageDir,
            productId));
      try {
        byte buf[] = new byte[1024];
        for (;;) {
          int noBytesRead = in.read(buf);
          out.write(buf, 0, noBytesRead);
          if (noBytesRead < buf.length) {
            break;
          }
        }
      } finally {
        out.close();
      }
    } catch (IOException e) {
      throw new RuntimeException(e);
    }
  }
}
```

This is how you get the data from a DataHandler

Copy the jpeg file data into c:\tmp. The file is named after the product id (e.g., c:\tmp\p01).

Create an ImageClient.java file in the client package:

Start the Axis server (if it is not yet started). Create the c:\tmp folder. Run the

```
import javax.activation.DataHandler;
import javax.activation.DataSource;
import javax.activation.FileDataSource;

public class ImageClient {
  public static void main(String[] args) throws RemoteException {
    ImageServiceStub service = new ImageServiceStub();
    service._getServiceClient().getOptions().setProperty(
           Constants.Configuration.ENABLE_MTOM, "true");
    DataSource source = new FileDataSource("c:/axis/docs/xdocs/1_3/images/axis.jpg");
    DataHandler handler = new DataHandler(source);
    service.uploadImage("p01", handler);
    System.out.println("Done!");
  }
}
```

Critical point: Enable MTOM. MTOM stands for message transmission optimization mechanism. It means the same thing as XOP when it is applied to SOAP messages. The effect is, whenever it needs to send base64 encoded data, it will send it using XOP.

You need to make sure this file exists

Create a DataHandler object that reads that DataSource object

Create a DataSource object that will read the data from the file. It will also find out the MIME type (image/jpeg in this case) from the file extension (.jpg).

client. Then check c:\tmp and you should find a new file p01 there. You can verify that it's a copy of axis.jpg by opening it in a browser:

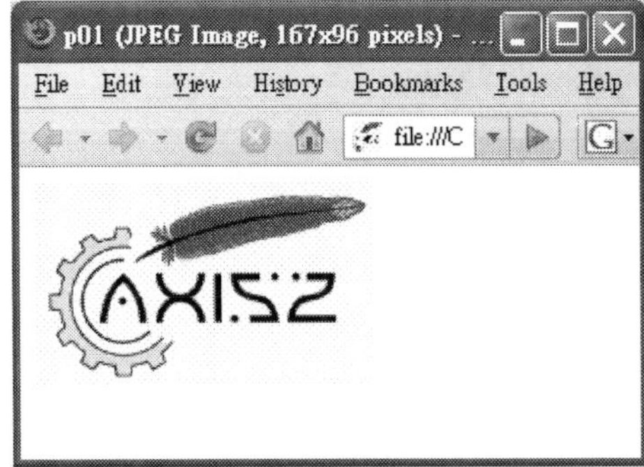

To be sure that it is using XOP, use the TCP Monitor. You should see:

```
Content-Type: multipart/related; boundary=MIMEBoundaryurn_uuid_6D8E7B2093DFD9FC5B1195966468539;
SOAPAction: "urn:ttdev.com:service/img/uploadImage"
User-Agent: Axis2
Host: 127.0.0.1:1234
Transfer-Encoding: chunked

2339
--MIMEBoundaryurn_uuid_6D8E7B2093DFD9FC5B1195966468539
Content-Type: application/xop+xml; charset=UTF-8; type="text/xml"
Content-Transfer-Encoding: binary
Content-ID: <0.urn:uuid:6D8E7B2093DFD9FC5B1195966468540@apache.org>
   <?xml version='1.0' encoding='UTF-8'?>
      <soapenv:Envelope xmlns:soapenv="http://schemas.xmlsoap.org/soap/envelope/">
         <soapenv:Body>
            <ns1:uploadImage xmlns:ns1="urn:ttdev.com:service/img">
               <productId>p01</productId>
               <image>
                  <xop:Include href="cid:1.urn:uuid:6D8E7B2093DFD9FC5B1195966468650@apache.org"
               </image>
            </ns1:uploadImage>
         </soapenv:Body>
      </soapenv:Envelope>
--MIMEBoundaryurn_uuid_6D8E7B2093DFD9FC5B1195966468539
Content-Type: image/jpeg
Content-Transfer-Encoding: binary
Content-ID: <1.urn:uuid:6D8E7B2093DFD9FC5B1195966468650@apache.org>
ÿØÿà  JFIF     H H  ÿÛ C                                                  ÿÛ C
 ÿÄ µ              }         !1A  Qa "q 2□'¡  #B±Á RÑð$3br,
```

MIME message (multipart/related)

Refer to the binary data using cid (content id)

The binary data

Enabling MTOM in the service

For the moment, it is your client that needs to send a file. If it was your web service that needed to do that, you would need to enable MTOM in the service. To do that, modify services.xml:

```
<?xml version="1.0" encoding="UTF-8"?>
<serviceGroup>
    <service name="ImageService">
        <messageReceivers>
            <messageReceiver mep="http://www.w3.org/ns/wsdl/in-only"... />
        </messageReceivers>
        <parameter name="ServiceClass">
          com.ttdev.image.ImageServiceImpl
        </parameter>
        <parameter name="useOriginalwsdl">true</parameter>
        <parameter name="modifyUserWSDLPortAddress">true</parameter>
        <parameter name="enableMTOM">true</parameter>
        <operation name="uploadImage" mep="http://www.w3.org/ns/wsdl/in-only">
            <actionMapping>urn:ttdev.com:service/img/uploadImage</actionMapping>
        </operation>
    </service>
</serviceGroup>
```

Note that no matter the setting is there or not, the service can always handle incoming messages using MTOM. This setting affects its outgoing messages only.

Interoperability

If you need to send binary files to others, make sure the other side supports

MTOM. For example, for .NET, MTOM is supported with WSE (Web Services Enhancements) 3.0 or later.

Summary

XOP stores XML elements that is of the type xsd:base64Binary as MIME parts and represents the whole XML document as a MIME message. When the XML document is a SOAP envelope, it is called MTOM.

To receive a binary file using MTOM, if the receiver is written with Axis2, for maximum interoperability, it can always handle incoming messages using MTOM without any configuration.

To send a binary file using MTOM, enable MTOM in the sender.

Chapter 8

Invoking lengthy operations

What's in this chapter?

What if your web service involves manual processing that could take days to finish? In this chapter you'll learn what the problems are and how to deal with them.

Providing lengthy operations

Suppose that you have a web service that processes business registration requests and that each request must be manually reviewed by a human being before it is approved. Then a business registration number is provided to the client. The problem is that this review process could take days and the web service client will be kept waiting for the HTTP response (assuming it is using SOAP over HTTP):

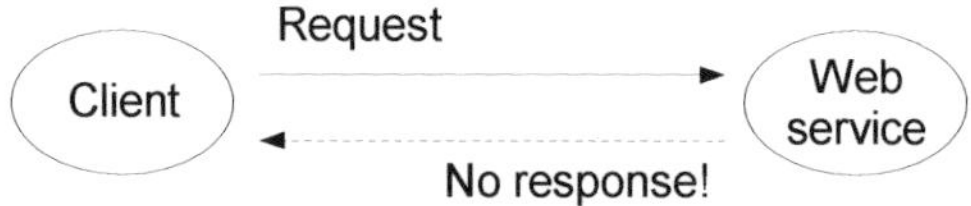

In that case, the HTTP client code in the client will think something may be wrong in the server. In order to avoid holding up the resources used by the connection, it will time out and terminate the connection. To solve this problem (see the diagram below), you can tell the client to send a request and then immediately listen on a port for incoming connection. On the server side, the web service will immediately return a short response saying that the request has been received for processing (not approved yet), then create a new thread to wait for the manual approval (so that the web service is free to serve other requests). When that thread gets the manual approval, it connects to the client and tells it that it has been approved and tells it the business registration number:

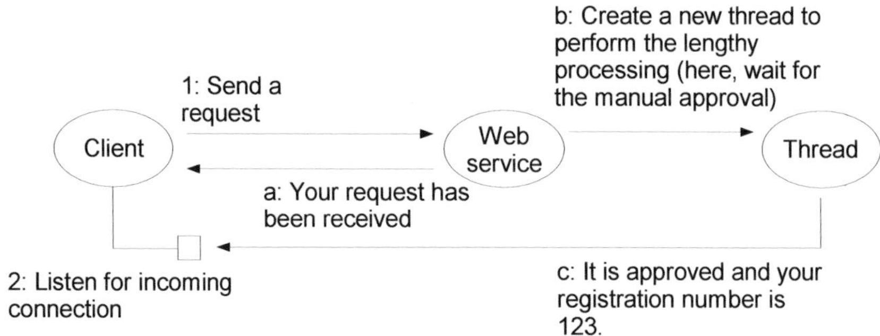

However, in step c above, how does it know the host name and port of the client? Therefore, when the client sends the request (see the diagram below), it could pick a random port and then include its host name and the port number in the reply-to URL and include that URL in a SOAP header entry. This way, the background thread created by the web service can send the result to that URL. This is very much like having a From address or Reply-To address in an email. This is called "WS-Addressing":

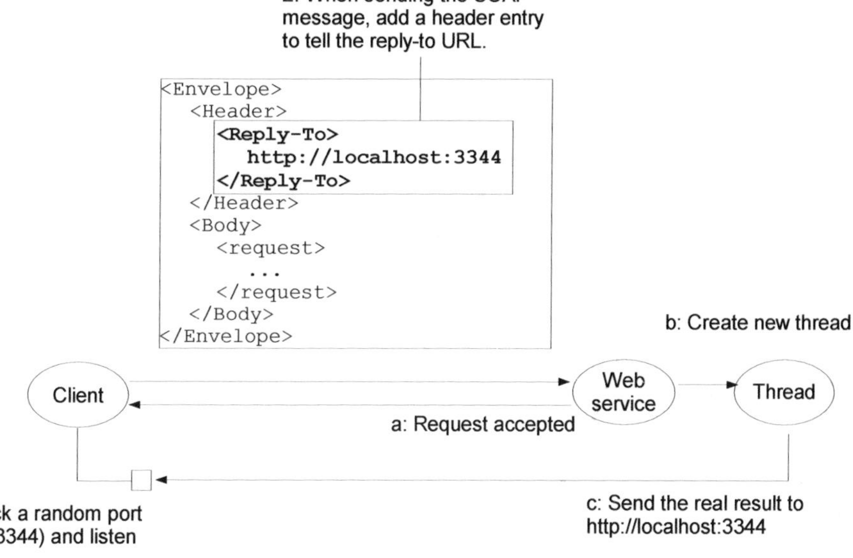

However, there is still a problem. If the client sends multiple requests to the web service or to different web services, if it opens a new port for each request, then it will use a lot of ports and will waste a lot of resources. Therefore, it will open a single port only and let a single background thread listening on it:

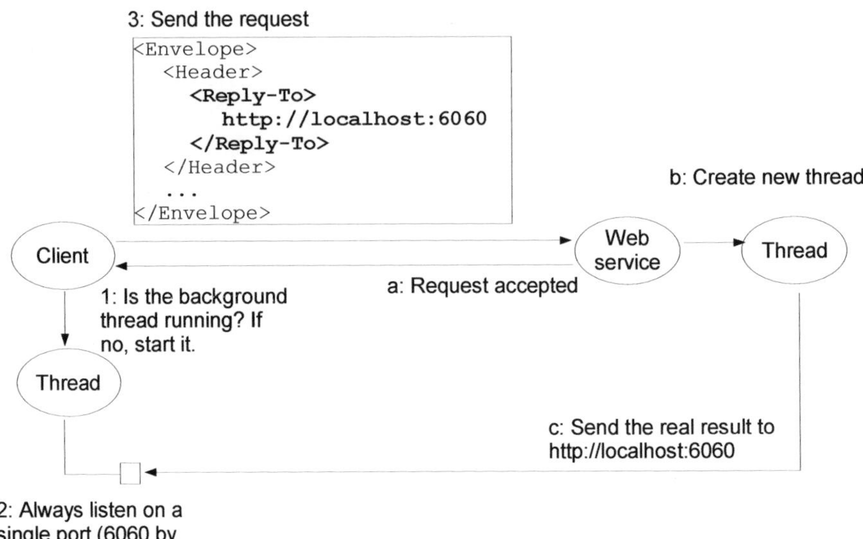

However, if multiple requests were sent, then multiple responses will arrive. Then in step c above, how can the background thread tell the response is for which request?

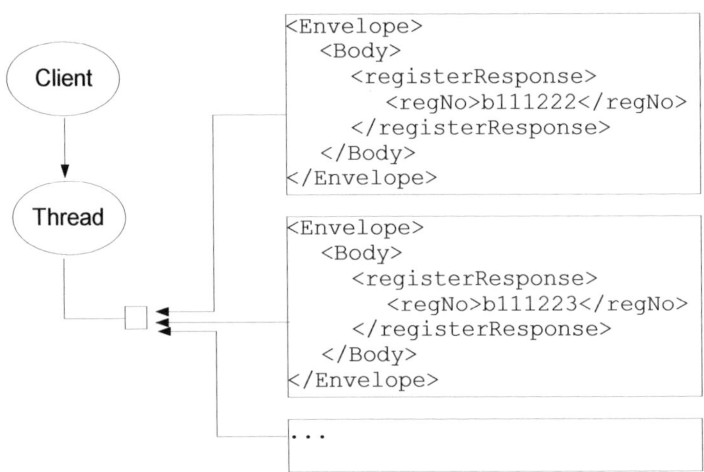

To solve this problem, when sending the request, the client will generate a unique message ID (e.g., m001) and include it in a header block (see the diagram below). When the web service generates the response message, it will copy the message ID m001 into the <Relates-To> header block. This way, when the background thread receives the response, it knows that it is the response for request m001:

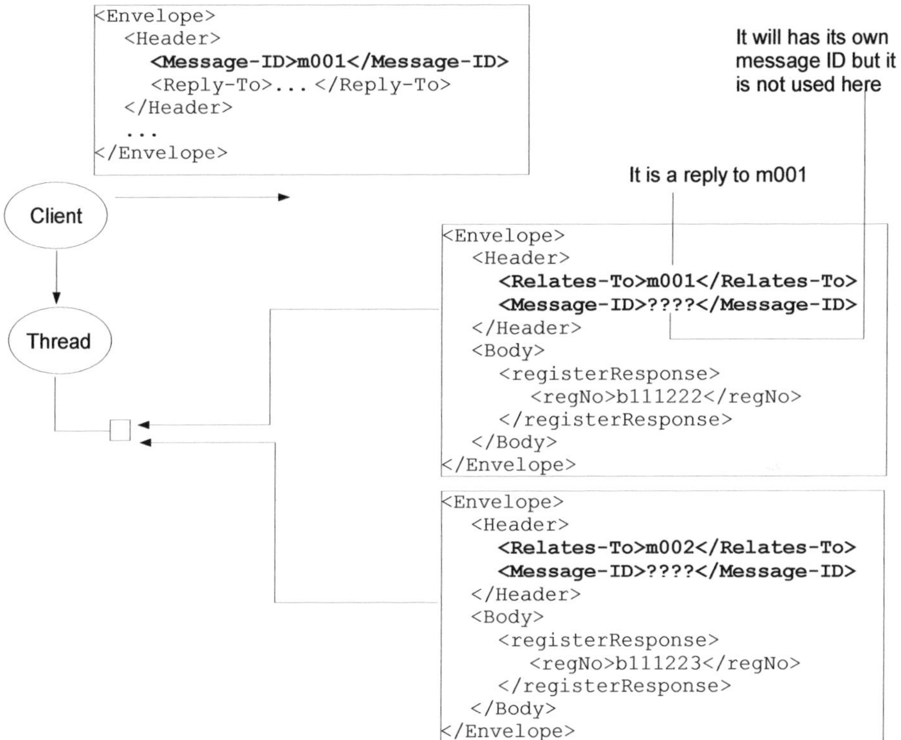

All these <Reply-To>, <Message-ID>, <Relates-To> header blocks are part of the WS-Addressing standard.

Creating the WSDL for business registrations

To implement this idea, create a new project named ManualService as usual (You may copy an old one. If so, change the linked folder). Modify the WSDL file:

Use this urn as the target namespace

```
<?xml version="1.0" encoding="UTF-8"?>
<wsdl:definitions xmlns:wsdl="http://schemas.xmlsoap.org/wsdl/"
  xmlns:soap="http://schemas.xmlsoap.org/wsdl/soap/"
  xmlns:tns="urn:fake.gov:biz/reg"
  xmlns:xsd="http://www.w3.org/2001/XMLSchema" name="ManualService"
  targetNamespace="urn:fake.gov:biz/reg">
  <wsdl:types>
    <xsd:schema
      targetNamespace="urn:fake.gov:biz/reg"
      xmlns:xsd="http://www.w3.org/2001/XMLSchema">
      <xsd:element name="register">
        <xsd:complexType>
          <xsd:sequence>
            <xsd:element name="bizName" type="xsd:string" />
            <xsd:element name="ownerId" type="xsd:string" />
          </xsd:sequence>
        </xsd:complexType>
      </xsd:element>
      <xsd:element name="registerResponse">
        <xsd:complexType>
          <xsd:choice>
            <xsd:element ref="tns:approved"></xsd:element>
            <xsd:element ref="tns:rejected"></xsd:element>
          </xsd:choice>
        </xsd:complexType>
      </xsd:element>
      <xsd:element name="approved" type="xsd:string"></xsd:element>
      <xsd:element name="rejected" type="xsd:string"></xsd:element>
    </xsd:schema>
  </wsdl:types>
  ...
</wsdl:definitions>
```

This is the request. It contains the business name and the id of the business owner.

This is the response. It contains either an <approved> or a <rejected> element.

<choice> says that one and only one element below will be there

Refers to this element

```
<registerResponse>
  <approved>123</approved>
</registerResponse>
```

```
<registerResponse>
  <rejected>business name in use</rejected>
</registerResponse>
```

To create the <choice> visually, right click the (registerResponseType) and choose "Add Choice":

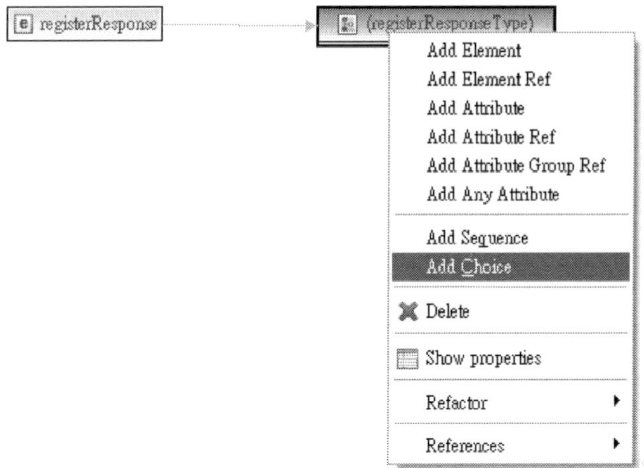

Then it will become:

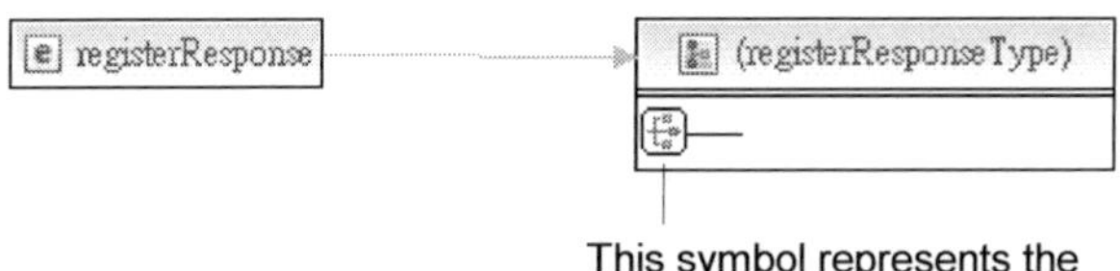

This symbol represents the <choice>

Right click the <choice> symbol and choose "Add Element Ref":

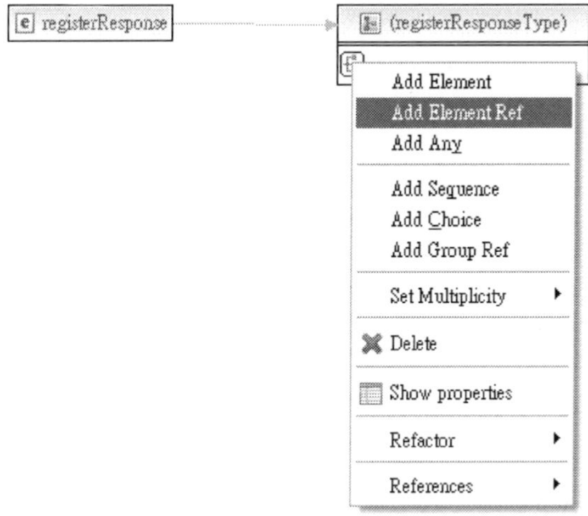

Then it will look like:

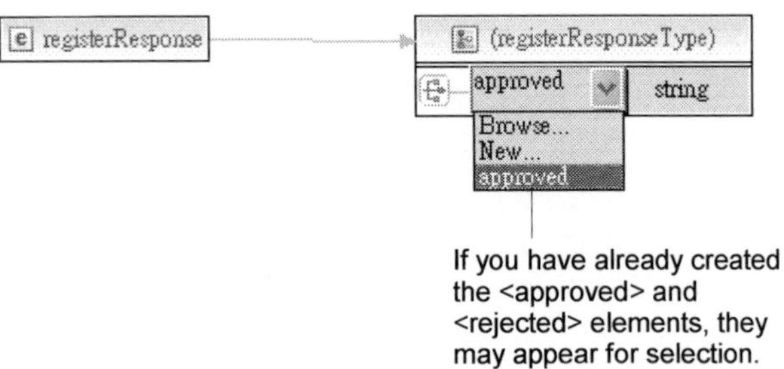

If you have created the <approved> and <rejected> elements,they may appear for selection, or you can choose "Browse" to select one of them. If you haven't created them yet, choose "New" to create them.

The rest of the WSDL file is as usual:

```
<?xml version="1.0" encoding="UTF-8"?>
<wsdl:definitions xmlns:wsdl="http://schemas.xmlsoap.org/wsdl/"
  xmlns:soap="http://schemas.xmlsoap.org/wsdl/soap/"
  xmlns:tns="urn:fake.gov:biz/reg"
  xmlns:xsd="http://www.w3.org/2001/XMLSchema" name="ManualService"
  targetNamespace="urn:fake.gov:biz/reg">
  <wsdl:types>
    <xsd:schema
      targetNamespace="urn:fake.gov:biz/reg"
      xmlns:xsd="http://www.w3.org/2001/XMLSchema">
      <xsd:element name="register">
        <xsd:complexType>
          <xsd:sequence>
            <xsd:element name="bizName" type="xsd:string" />
            <xsd:element name="ownerId"   type="xsd:string" />
          </xsd:sequence>
        </xsd:complexType>
      </xsd:element>
      <xsd:element name="registerResponse">
        <xsd:complexType>
          <xsd:choice>
            <xsd:element ref="tns:approved"></xsd:element>
            <xsd:element ref="tns:rejected"></xsd:element>
          </xsd:choice>
        </xsd:complexType>
      </xsd:element>
      <xsd:element name="approved" type="xsd:string"></xsd:element>
      <xsd:element name="rejected" type="xsd:string"></xsd:element>
    </xsd:schema>
  </wsdl:types>
  <wsdl:message name="registerRequest">
    <wsdl:part name="parameters" element="tns:register" />
  </wsdl:message>
  <wsdl:message name="registerResponse">
    <wsdl:part name="parameters" element="tns:registerResponse"></wsdl:part>
  </wsdl:message>
  <wsdl:portType name="ManualService">
    <wsdl:operation name="register">
      <wsdl:input message="tns:registerRequest" />
      <wsdl:output message="tns:registerResponse" />
    </wsdl:operation>
  </wsdl:portType>
  <wsdl:binding name="ManualServiceSOAP" type="tns:ManualService">
    <soap:binding style="document"
      transport="http://schemas.xmlsoap.org/soap/http" />
    <wsdl:operation name="register">
```

```
      <soap:operation soapAction="urn:fake.gov:biz/reg/register" />
      <wsdl:input>
        <soap:body use="literal" />
      </wsdl:input>
      <wsdl:output>
        <soap:body use="literal" />
      </wsdl:output>
    </wsdl:operation>
  </wsdl:binding>
  <wsdl:service name="ManualService">
    <wsdl:port binding="tns:ManualServiceSOAP"
      name="ManualServiceSOAP">
      <soap:address
        location="http://localhost:8080/axis2/services/ManualService" />
    </wsdl:port>
  </wsdl:service>
</wsdl:definitions>
```

Next, update build.xml:

```
<?xml version="1.0" encoding="UTF-8"?>
<project basedir="." default="jar.server">
  ...
  <property name="name" value="ManualService" />
  ...
  <target name="generate-service">
    <wsdl2code
      wsdlfilename="${name}.wsdl"
      serverside="true"
      generateservicexml="true"
      skipbuildxml="true"
      serversideinterface="true"
      namespacetopackages="urn:fake.gov:biz/reg=gov.fake.bizreg"
      targetsourcefolderlocation="src"
      targetresourcesfolderlocation="src/META-INF"
      overwrite="true"
      unwrap="true" />
    <replaceregexp
      file="src/META-INF/services.xml"
      match="${name}Skeleton"
      replace="${name}Impl" />
  </target>
  <target name="generate-client">
    <wsdl2code
      wsdlfilename="${name}.wsdl"
      skipbuildxml="true"
      namespacetopackages="urn:fake.gov:biz/reg=gov.fake.bizreg.client"
      targetsourcefolderlocation="src"
      overwrite="true"
      unwrap="true" />
  </target>
</project>
```

Because the response uses a <choice>, you can't use the wrap convention anymore. Then, generate the service stub and client stub. All these are pretty standard stuff. The next step is to make the web service create a new thread for lengthy processing.

Creating a new thread for lengthy processing

In order to let the web service create a new thread to do the lengthy processing, you need to understand the concept of message receiver in Axis. There is a message receiver for each web service. When a request for your web service arrives (see the diagram below), the message receiver will be handed the message. It will check your services.xml file to find out the implementation class name (gov.fake.bizreg.ManualServiceImpl here). Then it will create an instance of this class, convert XML to Java objects, pass them as parameters to the right method on that object instance. Finally, it converts the return value back to XML and return it in a response:

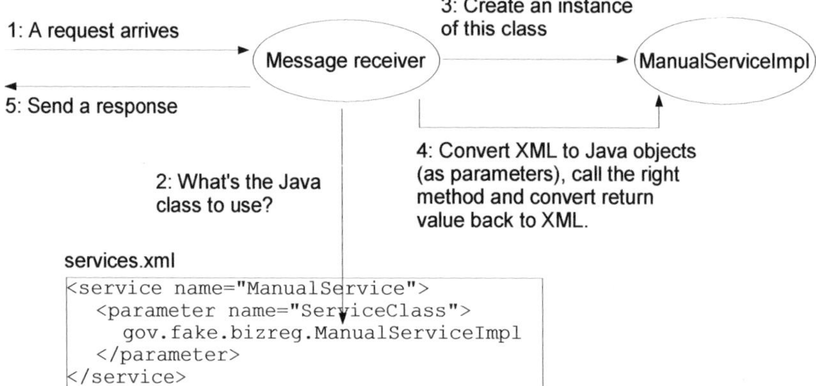


```
<service name="ManualService">
  <parameter name="ServiceClass">
    gov.fake.bizreg.ManualServiceImpl
  </parameter>
</service>
```

All these are happening in the same thread by default. Now, you will tell your message receiver to create a new thread to call your implementation class, while returning an "accepted" response at the same time. To do that, you can modify your message receiver, which is the ManualServiceMessageReceiverInOut class generated by the <wsdl2code> Ant task:

When a request (message) arrives, this method will be called. You're now overriding it.

```
import org.apache.axis2.AxisFault;
import org.apache.axis2.context.MessageContext;

public class ManualServiceMessageReceiverInOut extends
  AbstractInOutSyncMessageReceiver {
  public void receive(MessageContext messageCtx) throws AxisFault {
    messageCtx.setProperty(DO_ASYNC, "true");
    super.receive(messageCtx);
  }
  public void invokeBusinessLogic(
    ...
  }
}
```

Tell the parent class that the message should be handled asynchronously.

This method will perform data decoding and encoding and call your implementation class. Now it will be executed in a new thread.

Create ManualServiceImpl.java to implement your web service:

Return a hard-coded registration number for now

```
public class ManualServiceImpl implements ManualServiceSkeletonInterface {
   public RegisterResponse register(Register register) {
      System.out.println("Got request");
      String regNo = "123";
      try {
         Thread.sleep(5000);
      } catch (InterruptedException e) {
      }
      RegisterResponse response = new RegisterResponse();
      response.setApproved(regNo);
      return response;
   }
}
```

Sleep for five seconds to simulate human review

Now the message receiver will call your register() method in a new thread. The next step is to work on the client: It should kick start the background thread and include the <Reply-To> and <Message-ID> headers in the request.

Creating an asynchronous client

To create the client, create a BizRegClient.java file in the client package:

To encode the reply-to URL and message ID using the WS-Addressing standard, Axis provides a "module" to do that. This module is named "addressing". You can simply enable ("engage") it.

Internally the stub uses this object to call the web service

```
public class BizRegClient {
  public static void main(String[] args) throws RemoteException {
    ManualServiceStub stub = new ManualServiceStub();
    ServiceClient serviceClient = stub._getServiceClient();
    serviceClient.engageModule("addressing");
    Options options = serviceClient.getOptions();
    options.setUseSeparateListener(true);
    Register request = new Register();
    request.setBizName("Foo Ltd.");
    request.setOwnerId("Kent");
    ManualServiceCallbackHandler callback =
      new ManualServiceCallbackHandler() {
      public void receiveResultregister(RegisterResponse result) {
        System.out.println("Got result: " + result.getApproved());
      }
    };
    stub.startregister(request, callback);
    System.out.println("Request sent");
  }
}
```

The background thread will extract the response and pass it to your callback

Send the request and return immediately

This is the critical step. It causes the client to kick start the background thread to listen on port 6060 for the response. Conceptually, the background thread maintains an internal table like this:

Message ID	Callback
m001	→ Callback1
m002	→ Callback2
...	...

When it receives a response and finds that it is related to m001, it will call the callback for m001.

Note the difference between "using a callback" and "using a separate listener". Using a callback means the API is asynchronous, no matter one or two HTTP connections are used. For example, you can use a callback without using a separate listener:

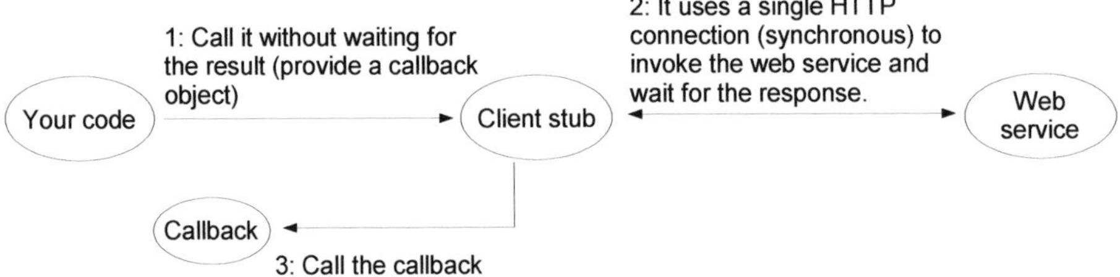
1: Call it without waiting for the result (provide a callback object)
2: It uses a single HTTP connection (synchronous) to invoke the web service and wait for the response.
Your code
Client stub
Web service
Callback
3: Call the callback

In this case, the API is asynchronous and your code seems to be asynchronous, but as only one HTTP connection is used, it is still subject to the timeout problem. So this is suitable when the processing is not too lengthy

(won't cause a timeout) and your client code really wants to proceed without getting the result immediately.

You've already seen the case of using a callback and a separate listener (business registration). This is the ultimate asynchronous situation. It is good for lengthy processing when your client code can proceed without getting the result.

You've also seen the case of not using a callback and not using a separate listener (the normal case). This is the ultimate synchronous situation. It is good for fast processing and your client code needs to wait for the result.

Finally, it is also possible to not use a callback while using a separate listener:

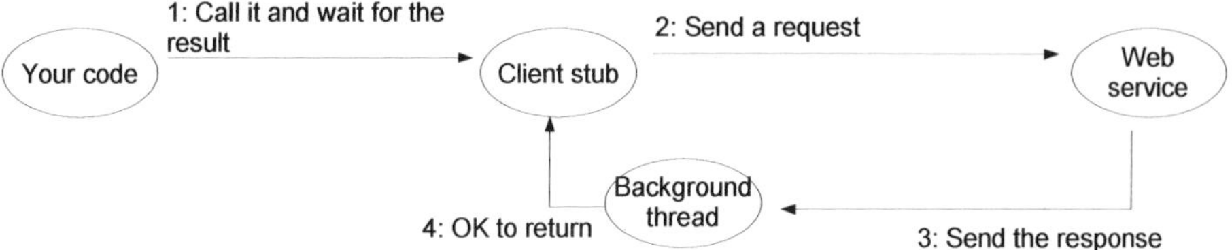

This is good for lengthy processing when your client code must wait for the result before proceeding.

Now the client is done. For the web service to decode the message ID and reply-to URL from the SOAP message, you need to engage the addressing module in the web service. This is the case by default. You can verify that in global configuration file for Axis, c:\axis\conf\axis2.xml:

```
<axisconfig name="AxisJava2.0">
  ...
  <module ref="addressing"/>
  ...
</axisconfig>
```

Start the Axis server (if it is not yet started). Run the client and it should work:

```
Console  Problems  Javadoc  Declaration  Search
BizRegClient [Java Application] C:\Program Files\Java\jre1.5.0_02\bin\ja
Request sent
log4j:WARN No appenders could be found for logger
log4j:WARN Please initialize the log4j system pro
Got result: 123
```

However, there are still two issues left. First, once started, the background thread will not terminate and will continue to listen on that port. So if you run it again, it will fail to grab the port and will fail to receive the response. Second, it will prevent your JVM from terminating. You can verify that with the red button in Eclipse in the above screen shot. Now, click that red button to terminate it. To fix these problems, modify the code:

```
public class BizRegClient {
  public static void main(String[] args) throws RemoteException {
    ManualServiceStub stub = new ManualServiceStub();
    final ServiceClient serviceClient = stub._getServiceClient();
    serviceClient.engageModule("addressing");
```

```
        Options options = serviceClient.getOptions();
        options.setUseSeparateListener(true);
        Register request = new Register();
        request.setBizName("Foo Ltd.");
        request.setOwnerId("Kent");
        ManualServiceCallbackHandler callback = new ManualServiceCallbackHandler() {
          public void receiveResultregister(RegisterResponse result) {
            System.out.println("Got result: " + result.getApproved());
            finished();
          }
          private void finished() {
            try {
              serviceClient.cleanup();
            } catch (AxisFault e) {
              throw new RuntimeException(e);
            } finally {
              System.exit(0);
            }
          }
        };
        stub.startregister(request, callback);
        System.out.println("Request sent");
    }
}
```

What if the web service returns an error? You can catch it this way:

```
public class BizRegClient {
  public static void main(String[] args) throws RemoteException {
    ManualServiceStub stub = new ManualServiceStub();
    final ServiceClient serviceClient = stub._getServiceClient();
    serviceClient.engageModule("addressing");
    Options options = serviceClient.getOptions();
    options.setUseSeparateListener(true);
    Register request = new Register();
    request.setBizName("Foo Ltd.");
    request.setOwnerId("Kent");
    ManualServiceCallbackHandler callback = new ManualServiceCallbackHandler() {
      public void receiveResultregister(RegisterResponse result) {
        System.out.println("Got result: " + result.getApproved());
        finished();
      }
      public void receiveErrorregister(Exception e) {
        ...
        finished();
      }
      private void finished() {
        try {
          serviceClient.cleanup();
        } catch (AxisFault e) {
          throw new RuntimeException(e);
        } finally {
          System.exit(0);
        }
      }
    };
    stub.startregister(request, callback);
    System.out.println("Request sent");
  }
}
```

Inspecting the WS-Addressing header blocks

You can also check the WS-Addressing header blocks using the TCP Monitor. The request should be like:

This is the target URL. Why is it needed? This allows routing the request message through intermediate hops because the target URL is maintained in the message.

The WS-Addressing namespace

As described before

```
<soapenv:Envelope
   xmlns:soapenv="http://schemas.xmlsoap.org/soap/envelope/"
   xmlns:wsa="http://www.w3.org/2005/08/addressing">
   <soapenv:Header>
      <wsa:To>
         http://localhost:1234/axis2/services/ManualService
      </wsa:To>
      <wsa:ReplyTo>
         <wsa:Address>
            http://192.168.0.146:6060/axis2/services/ManualService25107363
         </wsa:Address>
      </wsa:ReplyTo>
      <wsa:MessageID>
         urn:uuid:E8A307C115655F0CFC1197866807896
      </wsa:MessageID>
      <wsa:Action>urn:fake.gov:biz/reg/register</wsa:Action>
   </soapenv:Header>
   <soapenv:Body>
      <ns1:register xmlns:ns1="urn:fake.gov:biz/reg">
         <bizName>Foo Ltd.</bizName>
         <ownerId>Kent</ownerId>
      </ns1:register>
   </soapenv:Body>
</soapenv:Envelope>
```

It allows the client to uniquely specify the operation it wants to call. This is also specified by the WS-Addressing standard.

```
<wsdl:definitions ...>
   ...
   <wsdl:binding name="ManualServiceSOAP" type="tns:ManualService">
      <soap:binding style="document"
         transport="http://schemas.xmlsoap.org/soap/http" />
      <wsdl:operation name="register">
         <soap:operation soapAction="urn:fake.gov:biz/reg/register" />
         <wsdl:input>
            <soap:body use="literal" />
         </wsdl:input>
         <wsdl:output>
            <soap:body use="literal" />
         </wsdl:output>
      </wsdl:operation>
   </wsdl:binding>
   ...
</wsdl:definitions>
```

Note that TCP Monitor will get a dummy response as the real response is sent to port 6060.

Avoiding modifications to the message receiver

Currently you're modifying ManualServiceMessageReceiverInOut.java which is generated by <wsdl2code>. This is no good as it will be overwritten if you run <wsdl2code> again. Therefore, a better way is to extend it. For example, create ManualServiceReceiver.java and move the receive() method into there:

```
public class ManualServiceReceiver extends ManualServiceMessageReceiverInOut {
   public void receive(MessageContext messageCtx) throws AxisFault {
      messageCtx.setProperty(DO_ASYNC, "true");
```

```
      super.receive(messageCtx);
    }
  }
```

Then delete the receive() method from ManualServiceMessageReceiverInOut:

```
public class ManualServiceMessageReceiverInOut ... {
  public void receive(MessageContext messageCtx) throws AxisFault {
    messageCtx.setProperty(DO_ASYNC, "true");
    super.receive(messageCtx);
  }
  public void invokeBusinessLogic(...) {
    ...
  }
}
```

Modify build.xml to fix services.xml so that it uses ManualServiceReceiver as the message receiver:

```
<target name="generate-service">
  <wsdl2code
    wsdlfilename="${name}.wsdl"
    serverside="true"
    generateservicexml="true"
    skipbuildxml="true"
    serversideinterface="true"
    namespacetopackages="urn:fake.gov:biz/reg=gov.fake.bizreg"
    targetsourcefolderlocation="src"
    targetresourcesfolderlocation="src/META-INF"
    overwrite="true"/>
  <replaceregexp
    file="src/META-INF/services.xml"
    match="${name}Skeleton"
    replace="${name}Impl" />
  <replaceregexp
    file="src/META-INF/services.xml"
    match="${name}MessageReceiverInOut"
    replace="${name}Receiver" />
</target>
```

Delete the services.xml and run build.xml again. Everything should continue to work.

Summary

To support a lengthy operation in a web service, its message receiver needs to enable the DO_ASYNC flag so that it creates a new thread to call your business logic and return the response in that thread. For this to work, the client needs to kick start a background thread to listen on a certain port for the response and include a reply-to URL in a header block in the request SOAP message. To distinguish which response is for which request, the client also needs to include a unique message ID into the message and the web service needs to copy that into a relates-to header block. WS-Addressing supports the encoding and decoding of the message ID, relates-to and reply-to URL.

WS-Addressing is implemented by a module called "addressing" in Axis. A module is just some functionality that can be enabled or disabled. When it is enabled, it is said to be "engaged".

The client API can be synchronous or asynchronous, independent of whether the transport is synchronous or not. If your code can and should proceed without waiting for the result, use the asynchronous API. If it must wait for the result, use the synchronous API.

Chapter 9

Signing and encrypting SOAP messages

What's in this chapter?

In this chapter you'll learn how to sign and encrypt SOAP messages.

Private key and public key

Usually when you encrypt some text using a key, you need the same key to decrypt it:

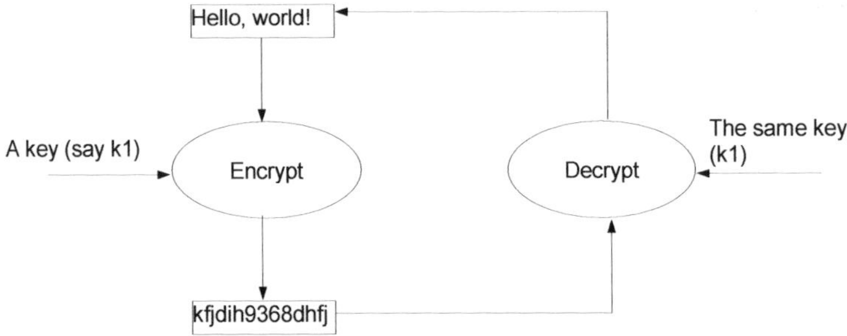

This is called "symmetric encryption". If you would like to send something to me in private, then we need to agree on a key. If you need to send something private to 100 individuals, then you'll need to negotiate with each such individual to agree on a key (so 100 keys in total). This is troublesome.

To solve the problem, an individual may use something called a "private key" and a "public key". First, he uses some software to generate a pair of keys: One is the private key and the other is the public key. There is an interesting relationship between these two keys: If you use the private key to encrypt something, then it can only be decrypted using the public key (using the private key won't work). The reverse is also true: If you use the public key to encrypt something, then it can only be decrypted using the private key:

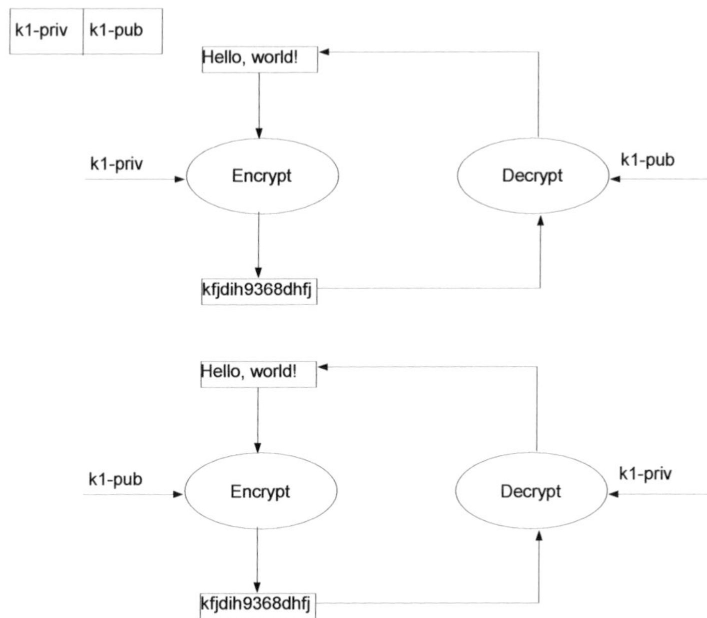

After generating the key pair, he will keep the private key really private (won't tell anyone), but he will tell everyone his public key. Can other people find out the private key from the public key? It is extremely difficult, so there is no worry about it. Now, suppose that you'd like to send something confidential to an individual Paul (see the diagram below), you can use his public key to encrypt it. Even though other people know his public key, they can't decrypt it (as it is encrypted using the public key, only the private key can decrypt it). Only Paul knows the private key and so only he can decrypt it:

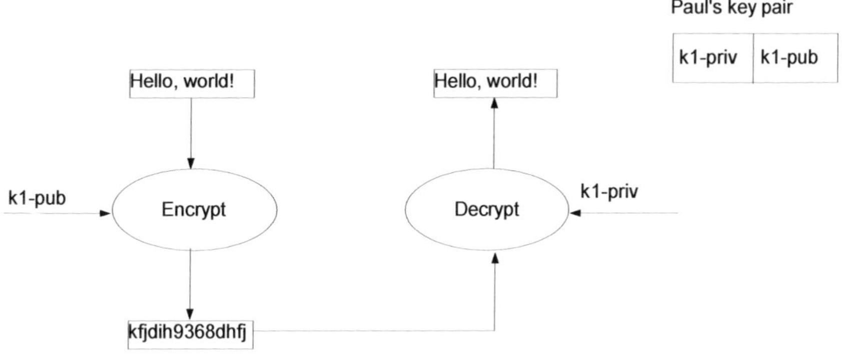

This kind of encryption is called "asymmetric encryption".

Digital signature

Suppose that the message you send to Paul is not confidential. However, Paul really needs to be sure that it is really from you. How to do that? You need to prove to Paul that the creator of the message knows your private key. If he does, then he must be you (remember, nobody else is supposed to know your private key). To prove that, you can use your private key to encrypt the message, then send it to Paul. Paul can try to decrypt it using your public key. If it works, then the creator of the message must know your private key and must be you.

However, this is not a good solution, because if the message is long, the encrypted message may double in size and the encryption takes a lot of time. To solve this problem, you can feed the message to a "one way hash function" (see the diagram below). No matter how long the input is, the output from the one way hash function is always the same small size (e.g., 128 bits). In addition, if two input messages are different (maybe just a single bit is different), then the output will be completely different. Therefore, the output message can be considered a small-sized snapshot of the input message. It is therefore called the "message digest" of the original message:

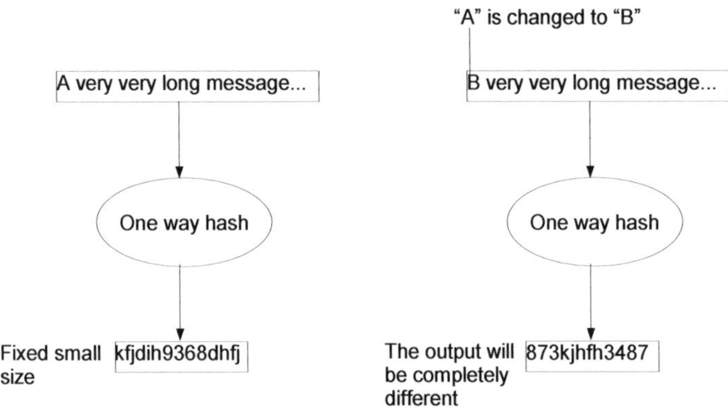

Another feature of the one way hash function is that it is very fast to calculate the digest of a given message, but it is extremely difficult to calculate a message given a digest. Otherwise people would find different messages for a given digest and it is no longer a good snapshot for the message:

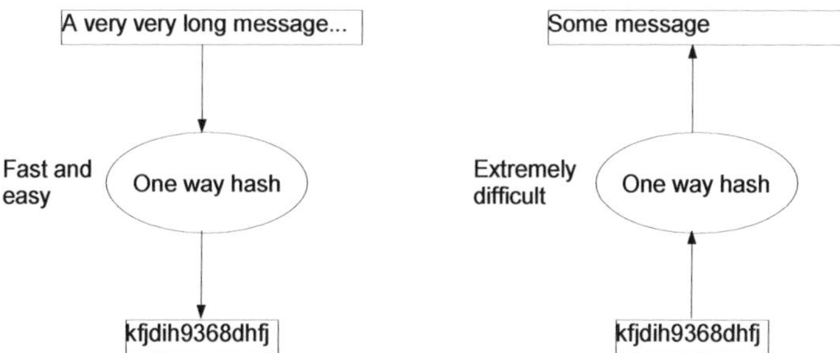

Now, to prove to Paul that you know your private key, you can use your private key to encrypt the message digest (because the digest is small, the result is also small and the encryption process will be fast), then send both the message and the message digest to Paul. He can try to decrypt the digest using your public key. Then he can calculate the digest from the message and compare the two. If the two match, then the person producing the encrypted digest must be you:

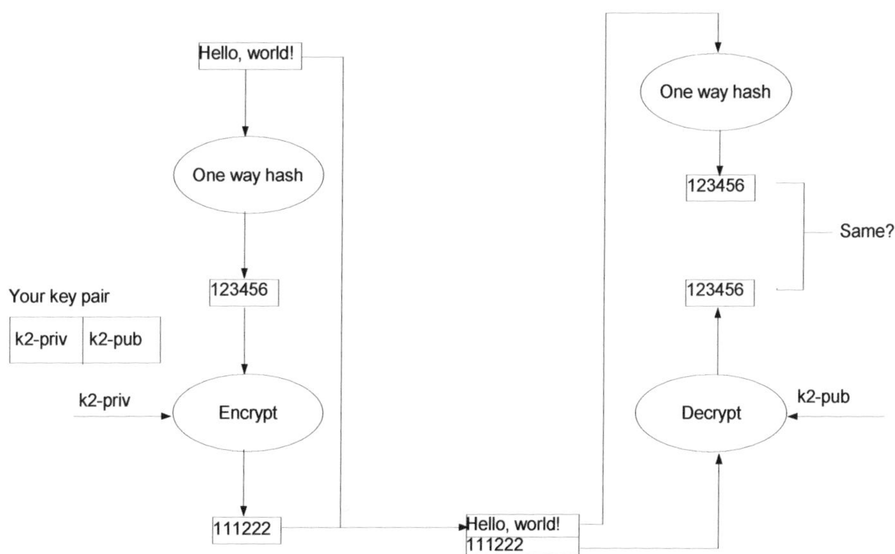

The encrypted digest is called the "digital signature". The whole process of calculating the digest and then encrypting it is called "signing the message".

Signing and encrypting

What if you'd like to sign the message, while keeping the message available to Paul only? Just sign it as usual (see the diagram below) and then encrypt the message and the digest using Paul's public key. When Paul receives it, he uses his private key to decrypt it and then go on to verify the signature as usual:

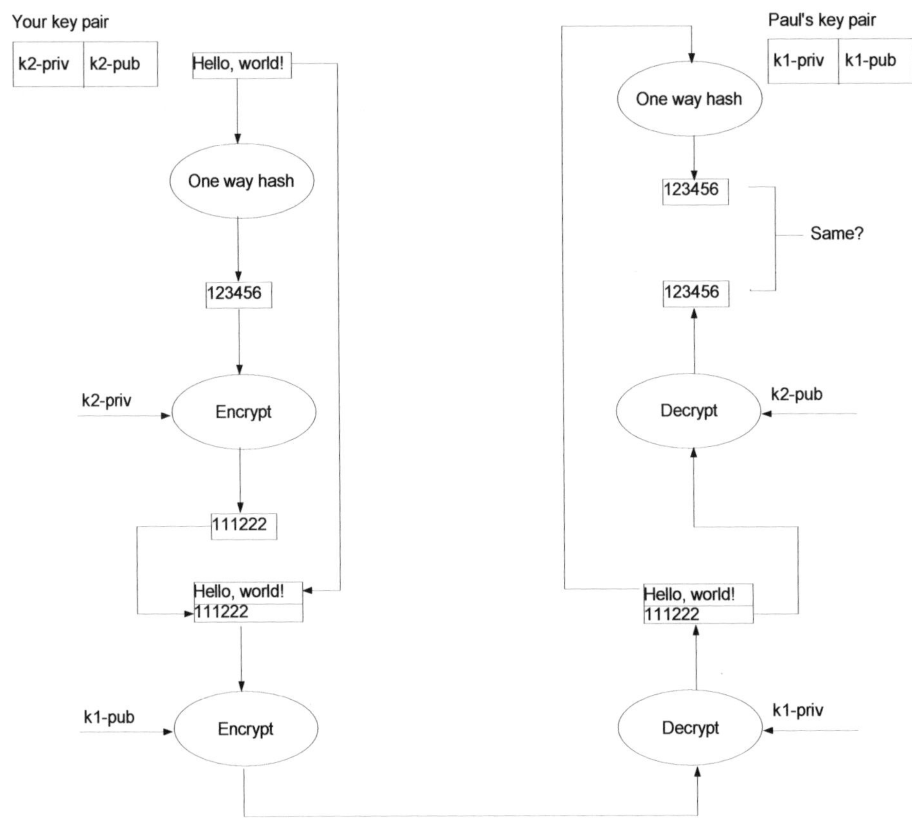

Certificate and CA

This seems to work very well. However, when you need to say send a confidential message to Paul, you'll need his public key. But how can you find out his public key? You can call him on the phone to ask him. But how can you be sure that the person on the phone is really Paul? If he is a hacker, he will tell you his public key. When you send the message to Paul using the hacker's public key, the hacker will be able to decrypt it using his private key.

If you need to communicate with many different individuals, this will get even more troublesome. To solve the problem, Paul may go to a government authority, show his ID card and etc and tell the authority his public key. Then the authority will generate an electronic message (like an email) stating Paul's public key. Finally, it signs that message using its own private key:

Name: Paul Public key: 666888
Signature

Such a signed message is called a "certificate". That authority is called a "certificate authority (CA)". Then Paul can put his certificate on his personal web site, email it to you directly or put it onto some 3rd party public web site. From where you get the certificate is unimportant. What is important is that if you can verify the signature of that CA and you trust what the CA says, then you can trust that public key in the certificate. In order to verify the signature, you will need the public key of that CA. What?! You're back to the origin of the problem. However, you only need to find out a single public key for a single entity (the CA), not a public key for everyone you need to communicate with. How to obtain that public key? Usually it is already configured in your browser or you can download it from a trusted web site, newspaper or other sources that you trust.

A CA doesn't really need to be a government authority. It can be well known commercial organizations such as VeriSign.

It means that in order to use asymmetric encryption and digital signature, people need private keys, public keys, a CA and certificates. All these elements combined together is called a “public key infrastructure (PKI)” because it provides a platform for us to use public keys.

Distinguished name

If you review the certificate:

Name: Paul Public key: 666888
Signature

you will see that it is not that useful because there are probably millions of people named “Paul” in the world. Therefore, in a real certificate, usually the country, city and the company of that individual are also included like:

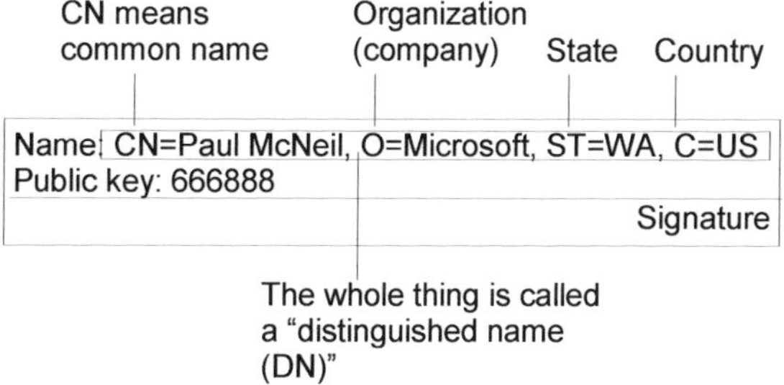

Now if you're looking for the public key of Paul McNeil who works at IBM, you know that the certificate above should NOT be used.

Performance issue with asymmetric encryption

Suppose that you'd like to send an encrypted message to Paul. You can use

Paul's public key to do that. However, in practice few people would do it this way, because asymmetric encryption is very slow. In contrast, symmetric encryption is a lot faster. To solve this problem, you can generate a random symmetric key, use it to encrypt the message, then use Paul's public key to encrypt that symmetric key and send it to Paul along with the encrypted message. Paul can use his private key to get back the symmetric key and then use it to decrypt the message:

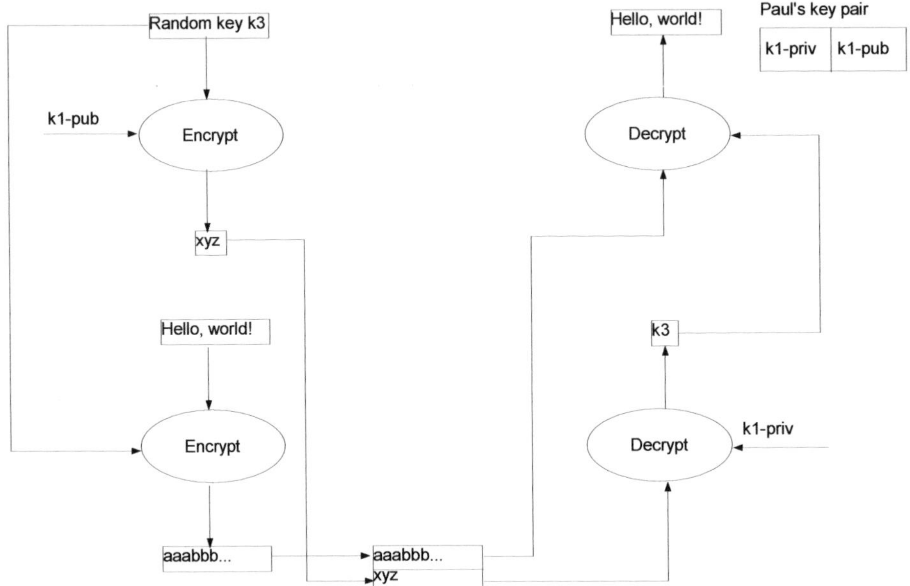

Keeping key pair and certificates in Java

In order to use PKI, typically you should have a private key for yourself (see the diagram below), a certificate for yourself so that you can send to others, a certificate for each person that you need to send something confidential to (e.g., Paul and Mary) and the public keys of the CA's that you trust. For the public key of the CA, you don't directly store its public key. Instead, you store its certificate which contains its public key. But who issued that certificate to it? It was issued by itself (signed by its own private key):

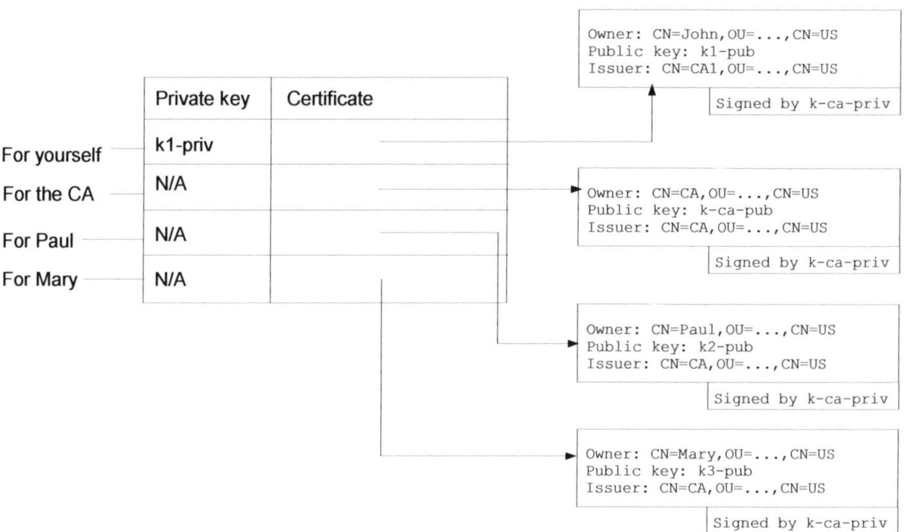

Such a table is called a "keystore" in Java (see the diagram below). A keystore is stored in a file. In addition, each entry in the table has a name called the "alias" of the entry. This way you can, e.g., tell the software to sign a particular message using the private key in the "john" entry (yourself), or encrypt the message using the public key in "paul" entry. Without the alias you will have to use the DN to refer to an entry:

keystore

Alias	Private key	Certificate
john	k1-priv	→
CA	N/A	→
paul	N/A	→
mary	N/A	→

Generating a key pair

In order to generate a key pair, you can use the keytool program in JDK. For example, if your JDK is in c:\Program Files\Java\jdk, then you can find keytool.exe in the bin sub-folder (i.e., c:\Program Files\Java\jdk\bin). For convenience, let's add c:\Program Files\Java\jdk\bin to the PATH:

Note that this PATH setting affects this command prompt only. If later you use a new command prompt, you'll need to set the PATH again. Next, create a folder c:\keys to hold the keys and change into there:

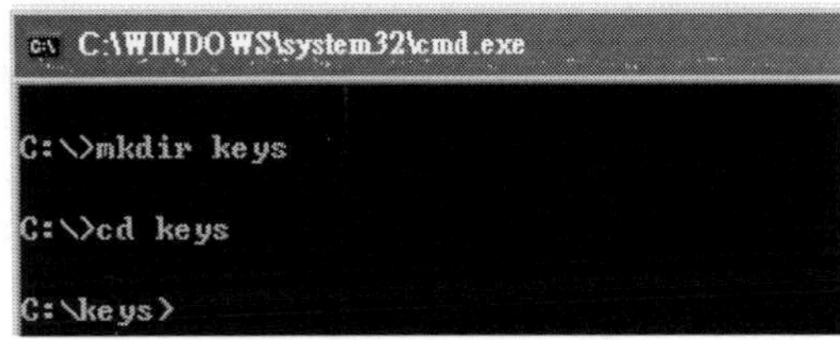

Now, generate a key pair for your web service client:

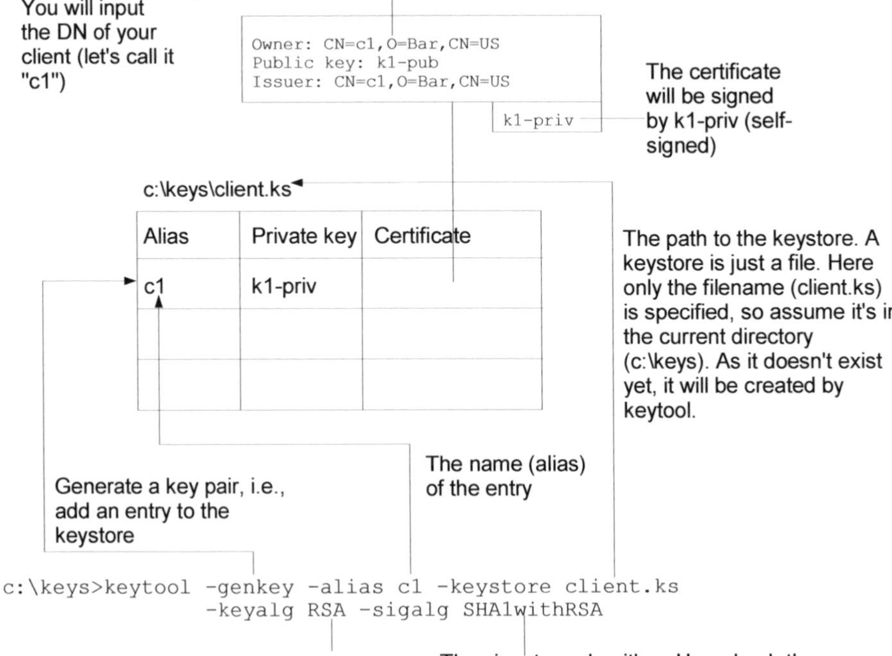


```
c:\keys>keytool -genkey -alias c1 -keystore client.ks
                -keyalg RSA -sigalg SHA1withRSA
```

The key generation algorithm. Commonly it is either DSA or RSA. Java supports both but some of the libraries you use later only support RSA, so use it here.

The signature algorithm. Here, hash the message using SHA1 first and then encrypt it using the RSA private key. If you don't specify it here, keytool will use MD5withRSA. But MD5 is known to be insecure nowadays, so don't use MD5 anymore.

Let's run it:

You need to provide a keystore password to protect the keystore. You can consider that keytool will append this password to the content of the keystore and then generate a hash and store it into the keystore. If someone modifies the keystore without this password, he won't be able to update the hash. The next time you run keytool on this keystore, it will note the mismatch and warn you not to use this keystore anymore.

```
C:\keys>keytool -genkey -alias c1 -keystore client.ks -keyalg RSA -sigalg SHA1wi
thRSA
Enter keystore password:  client-ks-pass
What is your first and last name?
  [Unknown]:  c1
What is the name of your organizational unit?
  [Unknown]:
What is the name of your organization?
  [Unknown]:  Bar
What is the name of your City or Locality?
  [Unknown]:
What is the name of your State or Province?
  [Unknown]:
What is the two-letter country code for this unit?
  [Unknown]:  US
Is CN=c1, OU=Unknown, O=Bar, L=Unknown, ST=Unknown, C=US correct?
  [no]:  yes

Enter key password for <c1>
        (RETURN if same as keystore password):  c1-pass

C:\keys>
```

The DN of John

You need to provide an entry password to protect the entry for c1. You can consider that keytool will use this password to encrypt c1's private key. This way other people won't be able to read c1's private key.

To verify that the entry has been added, you can list the entries:

```
C:\keys>keytool -list -keystore client.ks
Enter keystore password:  client-ks-pass

Keystore type: jks
Keystore provider: SUN

Your keystore contains 1 entry

c1, Dec 12, 2007, keyEntry,
Certificate fingerprint (MD5): AB:58:43:BB:6E:68:7A:AF:2F:FC:B3:67:F5:E7:24:95

C:\keys>
```

Note that it asks for the keystore password so that it can verify the hash. If you'd like to see more details in the entries, use the -v option:

```
C:\keys>keytool -list -v -keystore client.ks
Enter keystore password:  client-ks-pass

Keystore type: jks
Keystore provider: SUN

Your keystore contains 1 entry

Alias name: c1
Creation date: Dec 12, 2007
Entry type: keyEntry
Certificate chain length: 1
Certificate[1]:
Owner: CN=c1, OU=Unknown, O=Bar, L=Unknown, ST=Unknown, C=US
Issuer: CN=c1, OU=Unknown, O=Bar, L=Unknown, ST=Unknown, C=US
Serial number: 475f5119
Valid from: Wed Dec 12 11:10:17 CST 2007 until: Tue Mar 11 11:10:17 CST 2008
Certificate fingerprints:
         MD5:  AB:58:43:BB:6E:68:7A:AF:2F:FC:B3:67:F5:E7:24:95
         SHA1: 33:B8:2E:BB:32:EE:67:8C:73:96:35:10:74:06:91:03:0A:9E:C4:5E


*******************************************
*******************************************
```

You can see that both the "Owner" and the "Issuer" are set to the DN of c1. It shows that it is indeed a self-signed certificate. Having a self-signed certificate is not useful. You need to ask a CA to sign it. To do that, generate a certificate request first:

Generate a certificate request for the entry named "c1":

```
c:\keys>keytool -certreq -alias c1 -keystore client.ks -file c1.csr
```

Put the certificate request into this file

Run it:

```
C:\keys>keytool -certreq -alias c1 -keystore client.ks -file c1.csr
Enter keystore password:  client-ks-pass
Enter key password for <c1>c1-pass

C:\keys>
```

Now it has put the certificate request into c:\keys\c1.csr. You need to send to a CA. In real life, you should send it to VeriSign or some well known CA to get a certificate (of course a payment is required). Here you'll setup your own CA.

Setting up a CA

Go to http://www.openssl.org/related/binaries.html to download the Windows version of OpenSSL. Suppose the file is Win32OpenSSL-v0.9.8a.exe. Login as the Administrator and run it. Follow the instruction to complete the installation. Suppose that it has been installed into c:\OpenSSL. To make it easier to run, add c:\OpenSSL\bin to the PATH:

Next, create a folder say c:\CA to contain the files of the CA. Then create a private key for the CA itself:

Run it and it will prompt you for the DN of the CA and a password to encrypt the private key (e.g., you may use "ca-pass"):

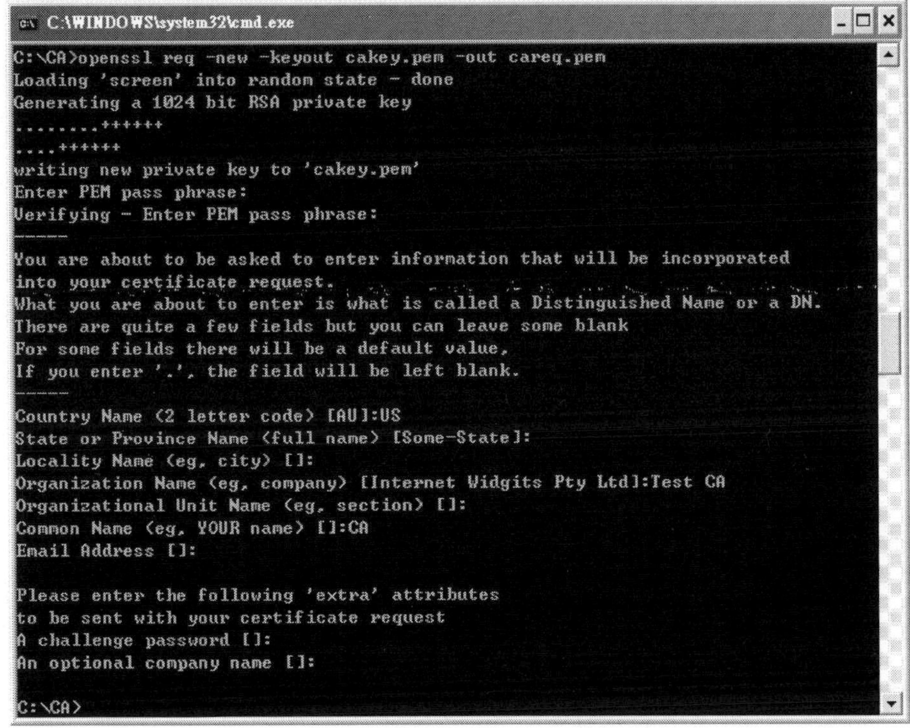

Next, generate a self-signed certificate for it:

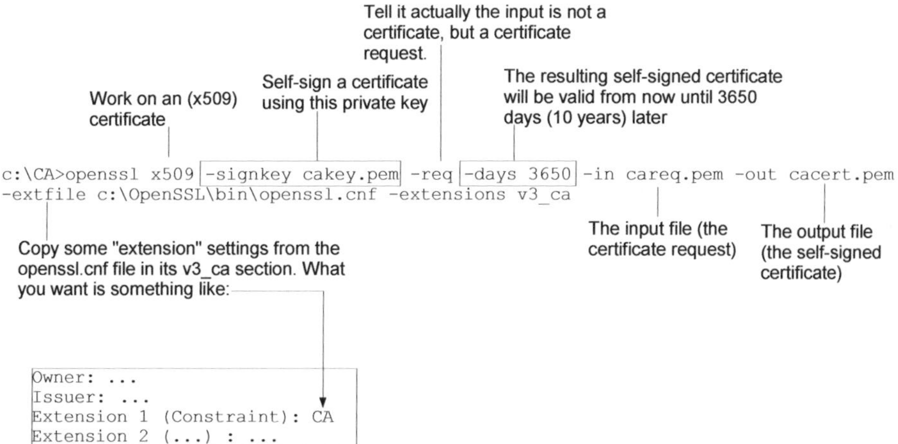

Run it and enter "ca-pass" as the password for the CA key:

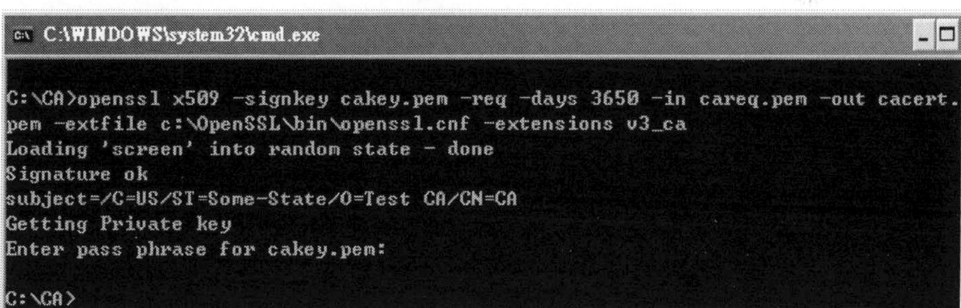

Now you're about to use this CA to sign the certificate request from John (john.csr). However, before that, you need to note that when a CA issues a new certificate, it will put a unique serial number into that certificate. So you need to tell OpenSSL what is the next serial number to use. To do that:

Store the string "02" into a file serial.txt. The file will be created. This way OpenSSL will use 02 as the next serial number. Then it will set it to 03 automatically.

```
c:\CA>echo 02 > serial.txt
```

Note that the "0" is necessary. Using "2" will NOT work because OpenSSL expects a hexadecimal number that contains an even number of digits.

To sign c1's certificate request:

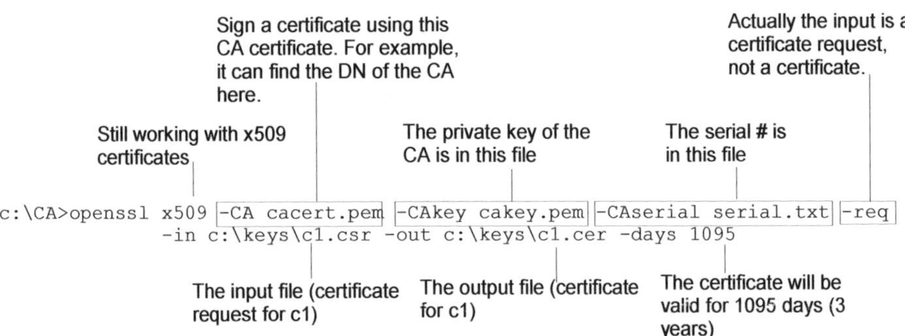
Sign a certificate using this CA certificate. For example, it can find the DN of the CA here.
Actually the input is a certificate request, not a certificate.
Still working with x509 certificates
The private key of the CA is in this file
The serial # is in this file
c:\CA>openssl x509 -CA cacert.pem -CAkey cakey.pem -CAserial serial.txt -req
-in c:\keys\c1.csr -out c:\keys\c1.cer -days 1095
The input file (certificate request for c1)
The output file (certificate for c1)
The certificate will be valid for 1095 days (3 years)

Run it and enter "ca-pass" as the password for the CA key:

```
C:\CA>openssl x509 -CA cacert.pem -CAkey cakey.pem -CAserial serial.txt -req -in
 c:\keys\c1.csr -out c:\keys\c1.cer -days 1095
Loading 'screen' into random state - done
Signature ok
subject=/C=US/ST=Unknown/L=Unknown/O=Bar/OU=Unknown/CN=c1
Getting CA Private Key
Enter pass phrase for cakey.pem:

C:\CA>
```

Importing the certificate into the keystore

Now you have got the certificate in c1.cer, you can import it into the keystore. However, before doing that, you must first import the certificate of the CA itself into your keystore as a trusted CA certficate, otherwise it will refuse to import John's certificate. To do that:

Change back to c:\keys

Import a certificate into the keystore

Create a certificate entry named "testCA". You can use any name that you like and it won't make any difference.

```
c:\CA>cd \keys
c:\keys>keytool -import -alias testCA -file c:\CA\cacert.pem -keystore client.ks
```

The CA's certificate is in this file. In real world, when you receive your certificate from the CA (e.g., VeriSign), it will also give you its own certificate. Or you can probably download it from its web site.

Run it:

```
C:\keys>keytool -import -alias testCA -file c:\CA\cacert.pem -keystore client.ks

Enter keystore password:  client-ks-pass
Owner: CN=CA, O=Test CA, ST=Some-State, C=US
Issuer: CN=CA, O=Test CA, ST=Some-State, C=US
Serial number: d4bf64c2e6aeb694
Valid from: Sat Dec 08 10:26:14 CST 2007 until: Tue Dec 05 10:26:14 CST 2017
Certificate fingerprints:
         MD5:  26:48:1A:1F:8D:57:3F:A7:0F:BD:82:39:F0:AA:5F:6D
         SHA1: 15:35:0F:C6:CD:47:B2:9E:83:61:DB:11:74:9E:40:08:B6:8F:55:79
Trust this certificate? [no]:  yes
Certificate was added to keystore

C:\keys>
```

Note that it asked you to trust this certificate or not. This is a very important decision. If you trust this certificate as a CA certificate, you will trust all certificates issued by it. Next, add John's certificate to the keystore to replace his self-signed certificate. This is also done using the -import option:

When keytool finds an existing entry with the named "c1" in the keystore, it knows you're trying to replace a certificate issued by a CA for the existing self-signed one.

```
c:\keys>keytool -import -alias c1 -file c1.cer -keystore client.ks
```

The certificate is in this file

Run it:

```
C:\keys>keytool -import -alias c1 -file c1.cer -keystore client.ks
Enter keystore password:  client-ks-pass
Enter key password for <c1>c1-pass
Certificate reply was installed in keystore

C:\keys>
```

To verify, you can list the entries in the keystore:

```
C:\keys>keytool -list -v -keystore client.ks
Enter keystore password:  client-ks-pass

Keystore type: jks
Keystore provider: SUN

Your keystore contains 2 entries
```

There are 2 entries in the keystore

Entry 1

```
Alias name: testca
Creation date: Dec 12, 2007
Entry type: trustedCertEntry

Owner: CN=CA, O=Test CA, ST=Some-State, C=US
Issuer: CN=CA, O=Test CA, ST=Some-State, C=US
Serial number: d4bf64c2e6aeb694
Valid from: Sat Dec 08 10:26:14 CST 2007 until: Tue Dec 05 10:26:14 CST 2017
Certificate fingerprints:
         MD5:  26:48:1A:1F:8D:57:3F:A7:0F:BD:82:39:F0:AA:5F:6D
         SHA1: 15:35:0F:C6:CD:47:B2:9E:83:61:DB:11:74:9E:40:08:B6:8F:55:79


*******************************************
*******************************************
```

It is a trusted certificate entry, i.e., a trusted CA certificate.

It is a key entry, i.e., a private key along with a certificate.

It means that there are two certificates in the entry

The first certificate is c1's certificate. From the "Issuer" field you can see it is issued by the test CA, so the next certificate is that of the test CA.

Entry 2

```
Alias name: c1
Creation date: Dec 12, 2007
Entry type: keyEntry
Certificate chain length: 2
Certificate[1]:
Owner: CN=c1, OU=Unknown, O=Bar, L=Unknown, ST=Unknown, C=US
Issuer: CN=CA, O=Test CA, ST=Some-State, C=US
Serial number: 4
Valid from: Wed Dec 12 11:19:58 CST 2007 until: Sat Dec 11 11:19:58 CST 2010
Certificate fingerprints:
         MD5:  83:55:5F:9F:0B:B6:8C:98:29:C9:0B:73:95:80:94:F9
         SHA1: CF:A7:5C:B9:7C:51:6A:FF:44:26:3F:7E:5B:E5:E5:BE:90:41:9D:94
Certificate[2]:
Owner: CN=CA, O=Test CA, ST=Some-State, C=US
Issuer: CN=CA, O=Test CA, ST=Some-State, C=US
Serial number: d4bf64c2e6aeb694
Valid from: Sat Dec 08 10:26:14 CST 2007 until: Tue Dec 05 10:26:14 CST 2017
Certificate fingerprints:
         MD5:  26:48:1A:1F:8D:57:3F:A7:0F:BD:82:39:F0:AA:5F:6D
         SHA1: 15:35:0F:C6:CD:47:B2:9E:83:61:DB:11:74:9E:40:08:B6:8F:55:79


*******************************************
*******************************************
```

The second certificate is the certificate of the test CA

A certificate chain is also called "certificate path". If the certificate of your test CA was issued by yet another CA, then the certificate path would contain the certificate of that other CA as the last certificate.

Installing Rampart

In order to perform signing or encryption, you need an Axis module called "Rampart". So, go to http://ws.apache.org/axis2/modules to download it. Suppose that it is rampart-1.3.zip. Unzip it into say c:\rampart. Rampart needs another library xalan 2.7.0. If you're using JDK 5 or earlier, you probably has only an old version. So, in that case, download xalan-2.7.0.jar from http://www.apache.org/dist/java-repository/xalan/jars and put it into c:\rampart\lib.

To make rampart available to your web services at runtime, copy all the files shown below:

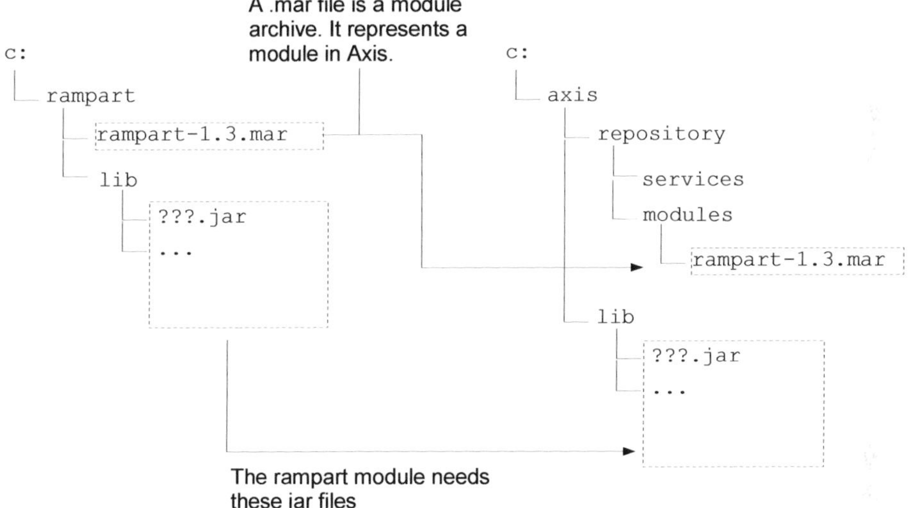

To make it available to your client, copy the WrappedService project and paste it as SecureService. Adjust the linked folder. To make the rampart module available to your client code, add the jar files in c:\rampart\lib to the build path of your project and copy rampart-1.3.mar into your project in such a folder structure:

```
SecureService
 ├─ src
 └─ repository
     └─ modules
         └─ rampart-1.3.mar
```

Just like the Axis server which has a repository, your Axis client can also have a repository.

Rename the WSDL to SecureService.wsdl and replace the word "Secure" for "Wrapped" in it. Update the build.xml file:

```
<project basedir="." default="jar.server">
  ...
```

```
<property name="name" value="SecureService" />
...
<target name="generate-service">
  <wsdl2code
    wsdlfilename="${name}.wsdl"
    serverside="true"
    generateservicexml="true"
    skipbuildxml="true"
    serversideinterface="true"
    namespacetopackages="http://ttdev.com/ss=com.ttdev.secure"
    targetsourcefolderlocation="src"
    targetresourcesfolderlocation="src/META-INF"
    overwrite="true"
    unwrap="true" />
  <replaceregexp
    file="src/META-INF/services.xml"
    match="${name}Skeleton"
    replace="${name}Impl" />
</target>
<target name="generate-client">
  <wsdl2code
    wsdlfilename="${name}.wsdl"
    skipbuildxml="true"
    namespacetopackages="http://ttdev.com/ss=com.ttdev.secure.client"
    targetsourcefolderlocation="src"
    overwrite="true"
    unwrap="true" />
</target>
</project>
```

Signing SOAP messages

In order to sign the SOAP messages, modify the WSDL file:

It belongs to the web service policy namespace

```
<wsdl:definitions xmlns:wsdl="http://schemas.xmlsoap.org/wsdl/"
   xmlns:soap="http://schemas.xmlsoap.org/wsdl/soap/"
   xmlns:tns="http://ttdev.com/ss"
   xmlns:xsd="http://www.w3.org/2001/XMLSchema"
   xmlns:sp="http://schemas.xmlsoap.org/ws/2005/07/securitypolicy"
   xmlns:wsp="http://schemas.xmlsoap.org/ws/2004/09/policy"
   xmlns:wsu="http://docs.oasis-open.org/wss/2004/01/oasis-200401-wss-
wssecurity-utility-1.0.xsd"
   name="SecureService"
   targetNamespace="http://ttdev.com/ss">
   <wsp:Policy wsu:Id="p1">
      <sp:SignedParts>
         <sp:Body />
      </sp:SignedParts>
   </wsp:Policy>
   <wsdl:types>
      ...
   </wsdl:types>
   <wsdl:message name="concatRequest">
      ...
   </wsdl:message>
   <wsdl:message name="concatResponse">
      ...
   </wsdl:message>
   <wsdl:portType name="SecureService">
      <wsdl:operation name="concat">
         <wsdl:input message="tns:concatRequest" />
         <wsdl:output message="tns:concatResponse" />
      </wsdl:operation>
   </wsdl:portType>
   <wsdl:binding name="SecureServiceSOAP" type="tns:SecureService">
      <soap:binding style="document"
         transport="http://schemas.xmlsoap.org/soap/http" />
      <wsdl:operation name="concat">
         <wsp:PolicyReference URI="#p1" wsdl:required="true" />
         <soap:operation .../>
         <wsdl:input>
            <soap:body use="literal" />
         </wsdl:input>
         <wsdl:output>
            <soap:body use="literal" />
         </wsdl:output>
      </wsdl:operation>
   </wsdl:binding>
   <wsdl:service name="SecureService">
      <wsdl:port binding="tns:SecureServiceSOAP"
         name="SecureServiceSOAP">
         <soap:address
            location="http://localhost:
8080/axis2/services/SecureService" />
      </wsdl:port>
   </wsdl:service>
</wsdl:definitions>
```

It belongs to the security policy namespace

This is a "policy". A policy specifies non-functional requirements of the web service (e.g., security, quality of service). The syntax of specifying a policy is governed by the WS-Policy standard.

This is a "policy assertion". It requires certain parts of the SOAP message be signed.

The parts should be signed are listed here. Here, only the <Body> of the SOAP message should be signed.

Apply the policy "p1" to the SOAP binding of the concat operation. It means the <Body> of all the messages for the concat operation must be signed as long as they're using SOAP over HTTP. Without this the policy would be sitting there idle and would have no effect.

As the <PolicyReference> element belongs to a foreign namespace (wsp), there is no guarantee that the program processing the WSDL file (e.g., <wsdl2code>) understands it. This attribute requires that the program understand it, otherwise it should abort the processing.

If you had multiple operations in the port type and they all required signed messages, you would move the <PolicyReference> to there so that it would apply to the SOAP binding of the SecureService port type.

Saying that the <Body> should be signed is not enough. You still need to specify that asymmetric encryption should be used and what signature algorithms are supported and etc.:

Why have an extra <Policy> element? For example, the <x509Token> element can be reused in another place (e.g., <RecipientToken> below), then it will be designed as a policy assertion. One assertion cannot directly include another assertion. It has to include a policy first. This way, different policy assertions could be put inside.

This policy assertion states that asymmetric encryption should be used. This assertion and the <SignedParts> assertion are AND'ed together.

The 1st assertion in the asymmetric assertion: What kind of token (certificate here) should be used by the initiator (i.e., the client)?

It should use an X509 token, which means an certificate. X509 is the official name.

```
<wsdl:definitions ...
  name="SecureService"
  targetNamespace="http://ttdev.com/ss">
  <wsp:Policy wsu:Id="p1">
    <sp:AsymmetricBinding>
      <wsp:Policy>
        <sp:InitiatorToken>
          <wsp:Policy>
            <sp:X509Token sp:IncludeToken="http://schemas.xmlsoap.org/
ws/2005/07/securitypolicy/IncludeToken/AlwaysToRecipient">
              <wsp:Policy>
                <sp:WssX509V3Token10 />
              </wsp:Policy>
            </sp:X509Token>
          </wsp:Policy>
        </sp:InitiatorToken>
        <sp:RecipientToken>
          <wsp:Policy>
            <sp:X509Token sp:IncludeToken="http://schemas.xmlsoap.org/
ws/2005/07/securitypolicy/IncludeToken/Never">
              <wsp:Policy>
                <sp:WssX509V3Token10 />
              </wsp:Policy>
            </sp:X509Token>
          </wsp:Policy>
        </sp:RecipientToken>
        <sp:AlgorithmSuite>
          <wsp:Policy>
            <sp:TripleDesRsa15 />
          </wsp:Policy>
        </sp:AlgorithmSuite>
      </wsp:Policy>
    </sp:AsymmetricBinding>
    <sp:SignedParts>
      <sp:Body />
    </sp:SignedParts>
  </wsp:Policy>
  ...
</wsdl:definitions>
```

X509 certificates have different versions and presentations. Here use v3 and the XML presentation as specified in the web service security (WSS) X509 token profile 1.0.

Always include the token (certificate) in the message to the web service

The 2nd assertion in the asymmetric assertion: What kind of token (certificate here) should be used by the recipient (i.e., the web service)?

Also use X509 v3 certificate for the web service, but do not send its certificate to the client. Instead, send enough information to the client so that the client can retrieve it. How? You'll see later.

The 3rd assertion in the asymmetric assertion. It supports the use of 3DES for encryption and RSA 1.5 algorithm for digital signatures.

In principle you could have multiple elements like this to say that it supports multiple algorithm suites and let the client and the service negotiate to decide which one to use. However, for the moment this negotiation is not supported in Axis. It means what is supported will actually be used. So, do not list multiple alternatives in the policy.

Finally, you still need to say that it supports the Web Service Security (WSS) standard v1.0:

```
<wsdl:definitions ...
  name="SecureService"
  targetNamespace="http://ttdev.com/ss">
  <wsp:Policy wsu:Id="p1">
    <sp:AsymmetricBinding>
      ...
    </sp:AsymmetricBinding>
    <sp:Wss10>
      <wsp:Policy>
        <sp:MustSupportRefEmbeddedToken />
        <sp:MustSupportRefIssuerSerial />
      </wsp:Policy>
    </sp:Wss10>
    <sp:SignedParts>
      <sp:Body />
    </sp:SignedParts>
  </wsp:Policy>
  ...
</wsdl:definitions>
```

Supports WSS 1.0

It can deal with tokens (certificates) directly included in the messages

It can also use the issuer DN and serial number to look up the certificate

Generate the service stub and client stub. Fill out the code in the implementation class:

```
public class SecureServiceImpl implements SecureServiceSkeletonInterface {
    public String concat(String s1, String s2) {
        return s1 + s2;
    }
}
```

Create SecureClient.java in the client package:

Tell the Axis client to load configurations from the "repository" folder in the current folder (project root). Here it will find the module archive for rampart.

```
import org.apache.axis2.context.ConfigurationContext;
import org.apache.axis2.context.ConfigurationContextFactory;

public class SecureClient {
  public static void main(String[] args) throws RemoteException {
    ConfigurationContext context = ConfigurationContextFactory
          .createConfigurationContextFromFileSystem("repository");
    SecureServiceStub stub = new SecureServiceStub(context);
    stub._getServiceClient().engageModule("rampart");
    String result = stub.concat("xyz", "111");
    System.out.println(result);
  }
}
```

Having rampart available is not enough, you must engage it.

For rampart to sign the <Body>, it needs access to the policy. Fortunately <wsdl2code> has extracted the policy information from the WSDL and put it into the Java code generated. What is missing is, what is the alias of the certificate to use, the password, the location of the keystore and etc. All this information can be specified in a Java String or in a text file. Here, let's put it into a text file rampart-config.xml in the project root:

The rampart configuration happens to be also in the form of a policy, although it is supposed to be used by the client itself.

All the other elements here are in the rampart namespace

```
<?xml version="1.0" encoding="UTF-8"?>
<wsp:Policy xmlns:wsp="http://schemas.xmlsoap.org/ws/2004/09/policy"
  xmlns="http://ws.apache.org/rampart/policy">
  <RampartConfig>
    <user>c1</user>
    <passwordCallbackClass>
      com.ttdev.secure.client.PasswordCallbackHandler
    </passwordCallbackClass>
    <signatureCrypto>
      <crypto
        provider="org.apache.ws.security.components.crypto.Merlin">
        <property
          name="org.apache.ws.security.crypto.merlin.keystore.type">
          JKS
        </property>
        <property
          name="org.apache.ws.security.crypto.merlin.file">
          c:/keys/client.ks
        </property>
        <property
          name="org.apache.ws.security.crypto.merlin.keystore.password">
          client-ks-pass
        </property>
      </crypto>
    </signatureCrypto>
  </RampartConfig>
</wsp:Policy>
```

The alias of the entry in the keystore. Use its private key to sign the message.

It will create an instance of this class and ask it for the password

Configurations for signing

A Java keystore supports different formats. JKS is the default.

The path to the keystore

The keystore password

Rampart uses a cryptographic provider to perform signing, encryption and etc. You specify the class of the provider to use this. Here you're telling it to use the Merlin provider which comes with rampart and uses the JDK to perform these tasks.

Three properties for Merlin only. It has the concept of keystore (a Java concept) and etc.

To load the configuration file into rampart, modify the SecureClient.java:

```
import org.apache.axiom.om.impl.builder.StAXOMBuilder;
import org.apache.axis2.description.PolicyInclude;
import org.apache.neethi.Policy;
import org.apache.neethi.PolicyEngine;

public class SecureClient {
  public static void main(String[] args) throws RemoteException,
        FileNotFoundException, XMLStreamException {
    ConfigurationContext context = ConfigurationContextFactory
        .createConfigurationContextFromFileSystem("repository");
    SecureServiceStub stub = new SecureServiceStub(context);
    stub._getServiceClient().engageModule("rampart");
    StAXOMBuilder builder = new StAXOMBuilder("rampart-config.xml");
    OMElement configElement = builder.getDocumentElement();
    Policy rampartConfig = PolicyEngine.getPolicy(configElement);
    stub._getServiceClient().getAxisService().getPolicyInclude()
        .addPolicyElement(PolicyInclude.SERVICE_POLICY, rampartConfig);
    String result = stub.concat("xyz", "111");
    System.out.println(result);
  }
}
```

Load the rampart-config.xml file and get the <Policy> element

Convert the <Policy> XML element into a Policy Java object

This AxisService object represents your web service as it is described by the WSDL (including the policy in there)

Add that Policy object to the existing policy. Apply this extra Policy to the whole web service.

Of course you need to create a PasswordCallbackHandler class in the client package:

```
public class PasswordCallbackHandler implements CallbackHandler {
    public void handle(Callback[] callbacks)
```

```
            throws IOException, UnsupportedCallbackException {
            for (int i = 0; i < callbacks.length; i++) {
                WSPasswordCallback pwcb = (WSPasswordCallback) callbacks[i];
                String id = pwcb.getIdentifer();
                if (id.equals("c1")) {
                    pwcb.setPassword("c1-pass");
                }
            }
        }
    }
```

You may wonder why it is so complicated just to tell it the password and why not just specify the password in the rampart-config.xml file. It is so that you can look it up in a database and etc.

Now launch the TCP Monitor and let it listen on port 1234. For it to work, specify the port 1234 in the client:

```
public class SecureClient {
  public static void main(String[] args) throws RemoteException,
        FileNotFoundException, XMLStreamException {
    ConfigurationContext context = ConfigurationContextFactory
          .createConfigurationContextFromFileSystem("repository");
    SecureServiceStub stub = new SecureServiceStub(context,
          "http://localhost:1234/axis2/services/SecureService");
    stub._getServiceClient().engageModule("rampart");
    StAXOMBuilder builder = new StAXOMBuilder("rampart-config.xml");
    OMElement configElement = builder.getDocumentElement();
    Policy rampartConfig = PolicyEngine.getPolicy(configElement);
    stub._getServiceClient().getAxisService().getPolicyInclude()
          .addPolicyElement(PolicyInclude.SERVICE_POLICY, rampartConfig);
    String result = stub.concat("xyz", "111");
    System.out.println(result);
  }
}
```

Run it and you will see an error in the console saying the a header was not understood:

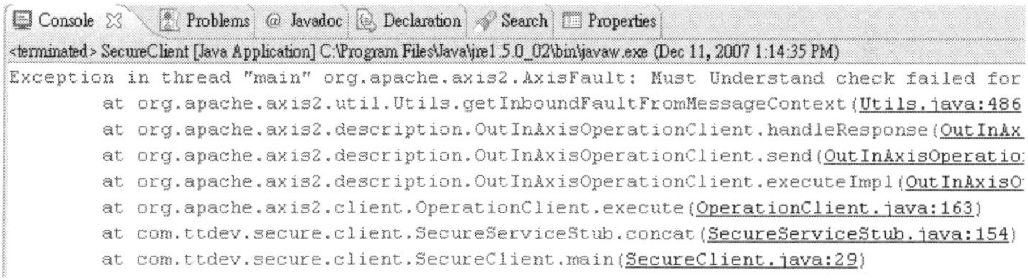

```
Console ⌧  Problems  @ Javadoc  Declaration  Search  Properties
<terminated> SecureClient [Java Application] C:\Program Files\Java\jre1.5.0_02\bin\javaw.exe (Dec 11, 2007 1:14:35 PM)
Exception in thread "main" org.apache.axis2.AxisFault: Must Understand check failed for
        at org.apache.axis2.util.Utils.getInboundFaultFromMessageContext(Utils.java:486
        at org.apache.axis2.description.OutInAxisOperationClient.handleResponse(OutInAx
        at org.apache.axis2.description.OutInAxisOperationClient.send(OutInAxisOperatio
        at org.apache.axis2.description.OutInAxisOperationClient.executeImpl(OutInAxisO
        at org.apache.axis2.client.OperationClient.execute(OperationClient.java:163)
        at com.ttdev.secure.client.SecureServiceStub.concat(SecureServiceStub.java:154)
        at com.ttdev.secure.client.SecureClient.main(SecureClient.java:29)
```

This is fine as the web service is not yet prepared to handle the digital signature. What is interesting is in the request message as shown in the TCP Monitor:

A <Security> element is added. It is a header entry.

The "mustUnderstand" attribute is set to 1, meaning that the receiver (the service) must handle this header, otherwise it must return a SOAP fault (which is the case here).

```
<soapenv:Envelope
  xmlns:soapenv="http://schemas.xmlsoap.org/soap/envelope/">
  <soapenv:Header>
    <wsse:Security
      xmlns:wsse="..."
      soapenv:mustUnderstand="1">
      <wsse:BinarySecurityToken
        xmlns:wsu="..."
        EncodingType="...Base64Binary"
        ValueType="...X509v3"
        wsu:Id="CertId-1534652">
        MIICEzCC...
      </wsse:BinarySecurityToken>
      <ds:Signature xmlns:ds="http://www.w3.org/2000/09/xmldsig#"
        Id="Signature-18687346">
        <ds:SignedInfo>
          <ds:CanonicalizationMethod
            Algorithm="http://www.w3.org/2001/10/xml-exc-c14n#" />
          <ds:SignatureMethod
            Algorithm="http://www.w3.org/2000/09/xmldsig#rsa-sha1" />
          <ds:Reference URI="#Id-4779445">
            <ds:Transforms>
              <ds:Transform
                Algorithm="http://www.w3.org/2001/10/xml-exc-c14n#" />
            </ds:Transforms>
            <ds:DigestMethod
              Algorithm="http://www.w3.org/2000/09/xmldsig#sha1" />
            <ds:DigestValue>
              uPNVEvSdKiBJp+xXNwqjaFgUZHc=
            </ds:DigestValue>
          </ds:Reference>
        </ds:SignedInfo>
        <ds:SignatureValue>
          DHA84dS...
        </ds:SignatureValue>
        <ds:KeyInfo Id="KeyId-22831804">
          <wsse:SecurityTokenReference
            xmlns:wsu="..."
            wsu:Id="STRId-15696851">
            <wsse:Reference URI="#CertId-1534652" ValueType="...X509v3" />
          </wsse:SecurityTokenReference>
        </ds:KeyInfo>
      </ds:Signature>
    </wsse:Security>
  </soapenv:Header>
  <soapenv:Body
    xmlns:wsu="..."
    wsu:Id="Id-4779445">
    <ns1:concat xmlns:ns1="http://ttdev.com/ss">
      <s1>xyz</s1>
      <s2>111</s2>
    </ns1:concat>
  </soapenv:Body>
</soapenv:Envelope>
```

The token (certificate) is directly included here

A <Signature> element represents a digital signature. You don't need to fully understand its details. If later you encrypt the message, there will be an <EncryptedData> element as its sibling.

The signature is signing over this element, i.e., the <Body> element.

The signature was created using this token (certificate)

The <Body> element is basically unchanged. The only exception is that an id has been added so that the signature can refer to it.

Supporting digital signatures in the web service

Ideally, when generating the service stub, <wsdl2code> should consult the policy in the WSDL and setup rampart properly. However, the current version of Axis is not doing that. That's why the web service is not understanding the <Security> header element. To fix the problem, add the policy to services.xml:

```
<?xml version="1.0" encoding="UTF-8"?>
<serviceGroup>
  <service name="SecureService">
    <messageReceivers>
      <messageReceiver mep="http://www.w3.org/ns/wsdl/in-out"
        class="com.ttdev.secure.SecureServiceMessageReceiverInOut" />
    </messageReceivers>
    <parameter name="ServiceClass">
      com.ttdev.secure.SecureServiceImpl
```

```
    </parameter>
    <parameter name="useOriginalwsdl">true</parameter>
    <parameter name="modifyUserWSDLPortAddress">true</parameter>
    <operation name="concat"
      mep="http://www.w3.org/ns/wsdl/in-out">
      <actionMapping>
        http://ttdev.com/ss/NewOperation
      </actionMapping>
      <outputActionMapping>
        http://ttdev.com/ss/SecureService/concatResponse
      </outputActionMapping>
    </operation>
    <wsp:Policy
      xmlns:sp="http://schemas.xmlsoap.org/ws/2005/07/securitypolicy"
      xmlns:wsp="http://schemas.xmlsoap.org/ws/2004/09/policy"
      xmlns:wsu="http://docs.oasis-open.org/wss/2004/01/
oasis-200401-wss-wssecurity-utility-1.0.xsd"
      wsu:Id="p1">
      <sp:AsymmetricBinding>
        <wsp:Policy>
          <sp:InitiatorToken>
            <wsp:Policy>
              <sp:X509Token
                sp:IncludeToken="http://schemas.xmlsoap.org/ws/2005/07/
securitypolicy/IncludeToken/AlwaysToRecipient">
                <wsp:Policy>
                        <sp:WssX509V3Token10 />
                </wsp:Policy>
              </sp:X509Token>
            </wsp:Policy>
          </sp:InitiatorToken>
          <sp:RecipientToken>
            <wsp:Policy>
              <sp:X509Token
                sp:IncludeToken="http://schemas.xmlsoap.org/ws/2005/07/
securitypolicy/IncludeToken/Never">
                <wsp:Policy>
                        <sp:WssX509V3Token10 />
                </wsp:Policy>
              </sp:X509Token>
            </wsp:Policy>
          </sp:RecipientToken>
          <sp:AlgorithmSuite>
            <wsp:Policy>
              <sp:TripleDesRsa15 />
            </wsp:Policy>
          </sp:AlgorithmSuite>
        </wsp:Policy>
      </sp:AsymmetricBinding>
      <sp:Wss10>
        <wsp:Policy>
          <sp:MustSupportRefEmbeddedToken />
          <sp:MustSupportRefIssuerSerial />
        </wsp:Policy>
      </sp:Wss10>
      <sp:SignedParts>
        <sp:Body />
      </sp:SignedParts>
  </service>
</serviceGroup>
```

Then engage the rampart module and add the rampart configuration as a policy assertion:

```
<?xml version="1.0" encoding="UTF-8"?>
<serviceGroup>
  <service name="SecureService">
    <messageReceivers>
      ...
    </messageReceivers>
    <parameter ...>
    <parameter ...>
    <operation name="concat" ...>
      ...
    </operation>
    <module ref="rampart" />
    <wsp:Policy ...>
      <sp:AsymmetricBinding>
        ...
      </sp:AsymmetricBinding>
      <sp:Wss10>
        ...
      </sp:Wss10>
      <sp:SignedParts>
        <sp:Body />
      </sp:SignedParts>
      <RampartConfig
        xmlns="http://ws.apache.org/rampart/policy">
        <user>s1</user>
        <passwordCallbackClass>
          com.ttdev.secure.PasswordCallbackHandler
        </passwordCallbackClass>
        <signatureCrypto>
          <crypto
            provider="org.apache.ws.security.components.crypto.Merlin">
            <property
              name="org.apache.ws.security.crypto.merlin.keystore.type">
              JKS
            </property>
            <property
              name="org.apache.ws.security.crypto.merlin.file">
              c:/keys/service.ks
            </property>
            <property
              name="org.apache.ws.security.crypto.merlin.keystore.password">
              service-ks-pass
            </property>
          </crypto>
        </signatureCrypto>
      </RampartConfig>
    </wsp:Policy>
  </service>
</serviceGroup>
```

Engage the rampart module. The ordering of the <module> element doesn't really matter as long as it is directly in the <service> element.

c:\keys\service.ks

Alias	Private key	Certificate
s1	...	...

It is used as a policy assertion

You'll create this keystore entry later for the web service

You'll create this class later

You'll create this keystore later

The keystore password

Next, create PasswordCallbackHandler.java in the com.ttdev.secure package to provide the password to decrypt the private key in the "s1" alias:

```
public class PasswordCallbackHandler implements CallbackHandler {
  public void handle(Callback[] callbacks)
    throws IOException, UnsupportedCallbackException {
    for (int i = 0; i < callbacks.length; i++) {
      WSPasswordCallback pwcb = (WSPasswordCallback) callbacks[i];
      String id = pwcb.getIdentifer();
      if (id.equals("s1")) {
        pwcb.setPassword("s1-pass");
      }
    }
  }
}
```

To get a certificate for the service, open a command prompt and then:

```
c:\>cd \keys

c:\keys>keytool -genkey -alias s1 -keystore service.ks -keyalg RSA -sigalg
SHA1withRSA
Enter keystore password:  service-ks-pass
What is your first and last name?
  [Unknown]:  s1
What is the name of your organizational unit?
  [Unknown]:
What is the name of your organization?
  [Unknown]:  Foo
What is the name of your City or Locality?
  [Unknown]:
What is the name of your State or Province?
  [Unknown]:
What is the two-letter country code for this unit?
  [Unknown]:  US
Is CN=s1, OU=Unknown, O=Foo, L=Unknown, ST=Unknown, C=US correct?
  [no]:  yes
Enter key password for <s1>
        (RETURN if same as keystore password):  s1-pass
```

Generate a certificate request for it:

```
c:\keys>keytool -certreq -alias s1 -keystore service.ks -file s1.csr
Enter keystore password:  service-ks-pass
Enter key password for <s1>s1-pass
```

Use your test CA to create a certificate for it (remember that "ca-pass" is the password for the CA key):

```
c:\keys>cd \CA

c:\CA>openssl x509 -CA cacert.pem -CAkey cakey.pem -CAserial serial.txt -req -in
c:\keys\s1.csr -out c:\keys\s1.cer -days 1095
```

Import the certificate of the CA and that for the service into the keystore for the service:

```
c:\CA>cd \keys

c:\keys>keytool -import -alias testCA -keystore service.ks -file c:\CA\cacert.pem
Enter keystore password:  service-ks-pass
Owner: CN=CA, O=Test CA, ST=Some-State, C=US
Issuer: CN=CA, O=Test CA, ST=Some-State, C=US
Serial number: d4bf64c2e6aeb694
Valid from: Sat Dec 08 10:26:14 CST 2007 until: Tue Dec 05 10:26:14 CST 2017
Certificate fingerprints:
         MD5:  26:48:1A:1F:8D:57:3F:A7:0F:BD:82:39:F0:AA:5F:6D
         SHA1: 15:35:0F:C6:CD:47:B2:9E:83:61:DB:11:74:9E:40:08:B6:8F:55:79
Trust this certificate? [no]:  yes
Certificate was added to keystore

c:\keys>keytool -import -alias s1 -keystore service.ks -file s1.cer
Enter keystore password:  service-ks-pass
Enter key password for <s1>s1-pass
Certificate reply was installed in keystore
```

Do you need to import c1's certificate? No. As the client will include it in the message, you don't need it in the keystore. On the other hand, do you need to import s1's certificate into the keystore for the client? Yes. This is because the web service will not send its certificate to the client, but just the issuer's DN and serial number of the certificate. So the client needs this certificate in its keystore. So, import it:

```
c:\keys>keytool -import -alias s1 -keystore client.ks -file s1.cer
Enter keystore password:  client-ks-pass
Certificate was added to keystore
```

Now, run the client again. This time it will work. If you check the SOAP response message in TCP Monitor, you'll see:

```
<soapenv:Envelope
  xmlns:soapenv="http://schemas.xmlsoap.org/soap/envelope/">
  <soapenv:Header>
    <wsse:Security
      xmlns:wsse="..."
      soapenv:mustUnderstand="1">
      <ds:Signature xmlns:ds="http://www.w3.org/2000/09/xmldsig#"
        Id="Signature-25591289">
        <ds:SignedInfo>
          <ds:CanonicalizationMethod
            Algorithm="http://www.w3.org/2001/10/xml-exc-c14n#" />
          <ds:SignatureMethod
            Algorithm="http://www.w3.org/2000/09/xmldsig#rsa-sha1" />
          <ds:Reference URI="#Id-6923467">
            <ds:Transforms>
              <ds:Transform
                Algorithm="http://www.w3.org/2001/10/xml-exc-c14n#" />
            </ds:Transforms>
            <ds:DigestMethod
              Algorithm="http://www.w3.org/2000/09/xmldsig#sha1" />
            <ds:DigestValue>
              UPGGHvigdM6mQrGJ3lFGFWdWBk4=
            </ds:DigestValue>
          </ds:Reference>
        </ds:SignedInfo>
        <ds:SignatureValue>
          M680t...
        </ds:SignatureValue>
        <ds:KeyInfo Id="KeyId-17240206">
          <wsse:SecurityTokenReference
            xmlns:wsu="..."
            wsu:Id="STRId-13623369">
            <ds:X509Data>
              <ds:X509IssuerSerial>
                <ds:X509IssuerName>
                  CN=CA,O=Test CA,ST=Some-State,C=US
                </ds:X509IssuerName>
                <ds:X509SerialNumber>5</ds:X509SerialNumber>
              </ds:X509IssuerSerial>
            </ds:X509Data>
          </wsse:SecurityTokenReference>
        </ds:KeyInfo>
      </ds:Signature>
    </wsse:Security>
  </soapenv:Header>
  <soapenv:Body
    xmlns:wsu="..."
    wsu:Id="Id-6923467">
    <ns1:concatResponse xmlns:ns1="http://ttdev.com/ss">
      <r>xyz111</r>
    </ns1:concatResponse>
  </soapenv:Body>
</soapenv:Envelope>
```

There is no <BinarySecurityToken> here. It means the s1 certificate is not sent.

Use the issuer DN and certificate serial number (5 here) to identify the certificate. It is up to the client to look it up.

That is, it is telling the service that the certificate used to sign the message is issued by CN=CA,O=Test CA,ST=Some-State,C=US and the serial number of the certificate is 5. It is hoping that the client can use this information to locate the certificate and then use the public key in it to verify the signature. For this to work, the client may scan all the certificates in the keystore to try to find it. It means you must import s1's certificate into the keystore on the client.

To check that the service is really verifying the signature, note messages like below in the console:

```
[INFO] Deploying module: soapmonitor-1.3
[INFO] script module activated
[INFO] Deploying Web service: BizService
[INFO] Deploying Web service: ImageService
[INFO] Deploying Web service: ManualService
[INFO] Deploying Web service: SecureService
[INFO] Deploying Web service: SimpleService
[INFO] Deploying Web service: version.aar
[INFO] Deploying Web service: WrappedService
[INFO] [SimpleAxisServer] Started
[SimpleAxisServer] Started
[INFO] Listening on port 8080
[INFO] Undeploying Web service: SecureService
[INFO] Deploying Web service: SecureService
[INFO] Undeploying Web service: SecureService
[INFO] Deploying Web service: SecureService
[INFO] Verification successful for URI "#Id-4779445"
[INFO] Verification successful for URI "#Id-4779445"
```

Encrypting SOAP messages

At the moment the messages are signed, but they aren't encrypted and thus people on the Internet can see them. If the information is confidential, you should encrypt it. To do that, modify the policy in the WSDL file:

```
<?xml version="1.0" encoding="UTF-8"?>
<wsdl:definitions ...>
  <wsp:Policy wsu:Id="p1">
    <sp:AsymmetricBinding>
      ...
    </sp:AsymmetricBinding>
    <sp:Wss10>
      ...
    </sp:Wss10>
    <sp:SignedParts>
      <sp:Body />
    </sp:SignedParts>
    <sp:EncryptedParts>
      <sp:Body />
    </sp:EncryptedParts>
  </wsp:Policy>
  ...
</wsdl:definitions>
```

The <Body> element of the SOAP message should be encrypted

Generate the service stub and client stub again. Modify rampart-config.xml for the client:

```
<wsp:Policy ...>
  <RampartConfig>
    <user>c1</user>
    <encryptionUser>s1</encryptionUser>
    <passwordCallbackClass>
      com.ttdev.secure.client.PasswordCallbackHandler
    </passwordCallbackClass>
    <signatureCrypto>
      <crypto
        provider="org.apache.ws.security.components.crypto.Merlin">
        <property
          name="org.apache.ws.security.crypto.merlin.keystore.type">
          JKS
        </property>
        <property
          name="org.apache.ws.security.crypto.merlin.file">
          c:/keys/client.ks
        </property>
        <property
          name="org.apache.ws.security.crypto.merlin.keystore.password">
          client-ks-pass
        </property>
      </crypto>
    </signatureCrypto>
    <encryptionCrypto>
      <crypto
        provider="org.apache.ws.security.components.crypto.Merlin">
        <property
          name="org.apache.ws.security.crypto.merlin.keystore.type">
          JKS
        </property>
        <property
          name="org.apache.ws.security.crypto.merlin.file">
          c:/keys/client.ks
        </property>
        <property
          name="org.apache.ws.security.crypto.merlin.keystore.password">
          client-ks-pass
        </property>
      </crypto>
    </encryptionCrypto>
  </RampartConfig>
</wsp:Policy>
```

This is a keystore alias. Get the certificate for the alias "s1" from the keystore and use the public key there to encrypt the message. Note that you don't need the password to get the public key.

Specify the cryptographic provider to perform encryption. Here, you still use the Merlin provider (JDK). You also specify its configurations (the path to the keystore and the keystore password). Here, everything is the same as the cryptographic provider for signing.

For the web service, modify services.xml:

```
<serviceGroup>
  <service name="SecureService">
    ...
    <wsp:Policy ... wsu:Id="p1">
      <sp:AsymmetricBinding>
        ...
      </sp:AsymmetricBinding>
      <sp:Wss10>
        ...
      </sp:Wss10>
      <sp:SignedParts>
        <sp:Body />
      </sp:SignedParts>
      <sp:EncryptedParts>
        <sp:Body />
      </sp:EncryptedParts>
      <RampartConfig
        xmlns="http://ws.apache.org/rampart/policy">
        <user>s1</user>
        <encryptionUser>c1</encryptionUser>
        <passwordCallbackClass>
          com.ttdev.secure.PasswordCallbackHandler
        </passwordCallbackClass>
        <signatureCrypto>
          <crypto
            provider="org.apache.ws.security.components.crypto.Merlin">
            <property
              name="org.apache.ws.security.crypto.merlin.keystore.type">
              JKS
            </property>
            <property
              name="org.apache.ws.security.crypto.merlin.file">
              c:/keys/service.ks
            </property>
            <property
              name="org.apache.ws.security.crypto.merlin.keystore.password">
              service-ks-pass
            </property>
          </crypto>
        </signatureCrypto>
        <encryptionCrypto>
          <crypto
            provider="org.apache.ws.security.components.crypto.Merlin">
            <property
              name="org.apache.ws.security.crypto.merlin.keystore.type">
              JKS
            </property>
            <property
              name="org.apache.ws.security.crypto.merlin.file">
              c:/keys/service.ks
            </property>
            <property
              name="org.apache.ws.security.crypto.merlin.keystore.password">
              service-ks-pass
            </property>
          </crypto>
        </encryptionCrypto>
      </RampartConfig>
    </wsp:Policy>
  </service>
</serviceGroup>
```

The <Body> element of the SOAP message should be encrypted

Encrypt the response using c1's public key

Specify the cryptographic provider to perform encryption. It is the same as the one used for signing. It is also identical to the one used by the client except that it uses a different keystore file.

However, there is a problem here. As you're encrypting the response message using c1's public key, how can it find out c1's public key? You'll need to put c1's certificate in the keystore for the web service. In addition, this web service can only talk to a single client c1 (see the diagram below). If there is another client c2, it can encrypt the request using s1's public key, but s1 will encrypt the response using the public key of c1 (NOT c2), making c2 fail to decrypt it:

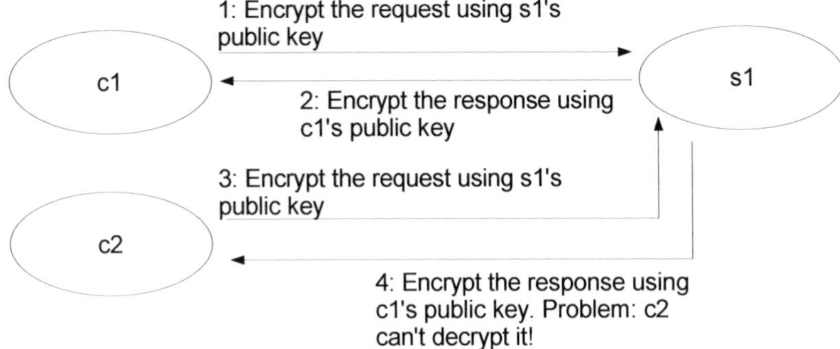

To solve this problem, rampart supports a special way of operation. If c1 both signs and encrypts the request, it will sign it using its own private key. If it also includes its certificate in the request, then rampart can be instructed to look up this certificate in the request and use it to encrypt the response. Therefore, it will use c1's certificate to encrypt the response. If c2 sends it a request, it will encrypt the response using c2's certificate:

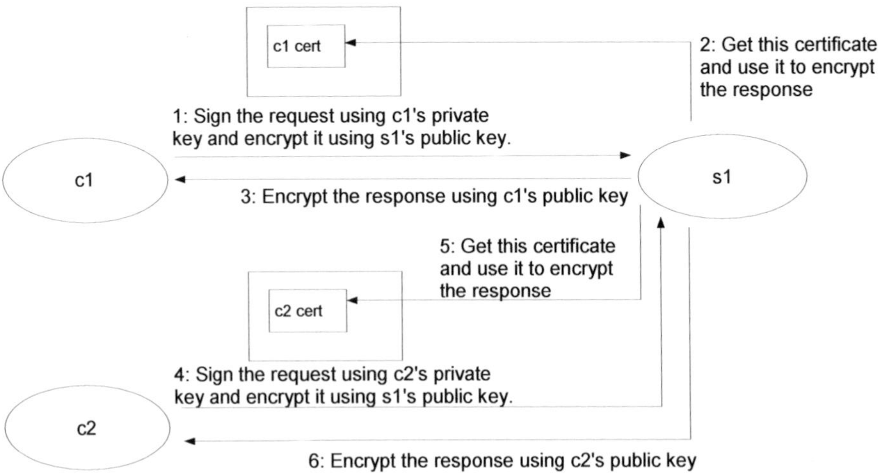

To enable this operation, put a special value "useRegSigCert" into the <encryptionUser> element:

It stands for "use request signing certificate". That is, use the certificate that signed the request message.

```
<serviceGroup>
  <service name="SecureService">
    ...
    <wsp:Policy ... wsu:Id="p1">
      ...
      <RampartConfig
        xmlns="http://ws.apache.org/rampart/policy">
        <user>s1</user>
        <encryptionUser>useReqSigCert</encryptionUser>
        ...
      </RampartConfig>
    </wsp:Policy>
  </service>
</serviceGroup>
```

Now run the client and it should work. To verify that the messages are indeed encrypted, check them out in the TCP Monitor:

```
<soapenv:Envelope ...>
  <soapenv:Header>
    <wsse:Security xmlns:wsse="..." soapenv:mustUnderstand="1">
      <xenc:EncryptedKey Id="EncKeyId-10630672">
        <xenc:EncryptionMethod
          Algorithm="http://www.w3.org/2001/04/xmlenc#rsa-1_5" />
        <ds:KeyInfo
          xmlns:ds="http://www.w3.org/2000/09/xmldsig#">
          <wsse:SecurityTokenReference>
            <ds:X509Data>
              <ds:X509IssuerSerial>
                <ds:X509IssuerName>
                  CN=CA,O=Test CA,ST=Some-State,C=US
                </ds:X509IssuerName>
                <ds:X509SerialNumber>
                  5
                </ds:X509SerialNumber>
              </ds:X509IssuerSerial>
            </ds:X509Data>
          </wsse:SecurityTokenReference>
        </ds:KeyInfo>
        <xenc:CipherData>
          <xenc:CipherValue>
            AB19mZuB1...
          </xenc:CipherValue>
        </xenc:CipherData>
        <xenc:ReferenceList>
          <xenc:DataReference URI="#EncDataId-26622782" />
        </xenc:ReferenceList>
      </xenc:EncryptedKey>
      <wsse:BinarySecurityToken ... wsu:Id="CertId-571295">
        MIICD...
      </wsse:BinarySecurityToken>
      <ds:Signature ... Id="Signature-22831804">
        ...
      </ds:Signature>
    </wsse:Security>
  </soapenv:Header>
  <soapenv:Body ... wsu:Id="Id-26622782">
    <xenc:EncryptedData Id="EncDataId-26622782"
      Type="http://www.w3.org/2001/04/xmlenc#Content">
      <xenc:EncryptionMethod
        Algorithm="http://www.w3.org/2001/04/xmlenc#tripledes-cbc" />
      <ds:KeyInfo xmlns:ds="http://www.w3.org/2000/09/xmldsig#">
        <wsse:SecurityTokenReference ...>
          <wsse:Reference URI="#EncKeyId-10630672" />
        </wsse:SecurityTokenReference>
      </ds:KeyInfo>
      <xenc:CipherData>
        <xenc:Ciph1f5erValue>
          C2wnpTtd...
        </xenc:CipherValue>
      </xenc:CipherData>
    </xenc:EncryptedData>
  </soapenv:Body>
</soapenv:Envelope>
```

All encryption and signing information is included in the <Security> header
This represents the encrypted symmetric key
How the symmetric key was encrypted
Information about the private key that was used to encrypt this symmetric key. Here it refers to s1's certificate using the issuer DN and serial number.
The encrypted symmetric key
The certificate used for signing (c1's certificate)
The symmetric key used to encrypt the data
How was the content of the <Body> encrypted? It used 3DES
The encrypted content of the <Body>
The content of the <Body> has been encrypted

Security issues when performing both signing and encrypting

When you're performing both signing and encryption, there are security issues. For example, if you sign the <Body> and then encrypt it, then the resulting message will be like:

```
<Header>
  <Security>
    <EncryptedKey>...</EncryptedKey>
    <Signature>
      <ds:SignedInfo>
        <ds:CanonicalizationMethod .../>
        <ds:SignatureMethod .../>
        <ds:Reference URI="#Id-26622782">
          ...
          <ds:DigestMethod .../>
          <ds:DigestValue>JOO/ATRze2p/BUBwlq1ZJ8xX9v4=</ds:DigestValue>
        </ds:Reference>
      </ds:SignedInfo>
      ...
    </Signature>
  </Security>
</Header>
<Body>
  encrypted data...
</Body>
```

The digest of the content of the <Body> element

The problem is that, if you run the client multiple times, the digest will be the same. This is the way it should be. Given some particular plain text, anyone can calculate the digest and it should be the same. This means that a hacker could calculate the digest of some common plain text to build a lookup table like:

Plain text

```
<ns1:concat xmlns:ns1="http://ttdev.com/ss">
  <s1>xyz</s1>
  <s2>111</s2>
</ns1:concat>
```

→ khg8fryfs37ufaeG

```
<ns1:concat xmlns:ns1="http://ttdev.com/ss">
  <s1>xyz</s1>
  <s2>abc</s2>
</ns1:concat>
```

→ HTsfjdiDFfhk

```
...
```

→ ...

Then he can capture your message, get the digest and use the lookup table above to recover the plain text, even though you've encrypted the content of the <Body> element. It means the digest is actually leaking the plain text.

You may wonder if the hacker can do the same thing using the encrypted content of the <Body> element?

```
<soapenv:Body ...>
  <xenc:EncryptedData Id="EncDataId-26622782" ...>
    <xenc:EncryptionMethod .../>
    <ds:KeyInfo ...>
      ...
    </ds:KeyInfo>
    <xenc:CipherData>
      <xenc:Ciph1f5erValue>
        dKeF1WLDqSV...
      </xenc:CipherValue>
    </xenc:CipherData>
  </xenc:EncryptedData>
</soapenv:Body>
```

The encrypted content of the <Body> element

If you run the client multiple times, you'll see that the encrypted content of the <Body> element will change every time. This is a basic requirement of encryption algorithms to prevent such a lookup attack (called "dictionary attack").

Now the question is how to prevent the digest from leaking information? There are three alternative solutions.

The first solution is to perform encryption first and then sign on the encrypted <Body> content. As the encrypted content changes every time, the digest will change every time. However, this is not a very good solution as digital signatures should be performed on what is seen by the users (i.e., plain text, not encrypted text). For the case on hand, as it is the client (not user) signing it, it may be good enough.

The second solution is to sign and then encrypt and finally also encrypt the signature. This works for the case on hand. However, if the web service was supposed to verify the signature but needed to pass the encrypted data to a 3rd party, then the web service wouldn't have the key to decrypt the signature and couldn't verify it.

The third solution is to include a random element (usually called "nonce" or "salt") into the plain text so that the digest changes every time. For example, you could add a third element to the request:

```
<ns1:concat xmlns:ns1="http://ttdev.com/ss">
  <s1>xyz</s1>
  <s2>111</s2>
  <salt>kguy8FDsfDFAfa389r</salt>
</ns1:concat>
```

This is the most flexible solution but it means a lot of extra work on you. Anyway, in order to implement the first solution (encrypt and then sign), modify the policy:

```
<wsp:Policy wsu:Id="p1">
  <sp:AsymmetricBinding>
    <wsp:Policy>
      <sp:InitiatorToken>
        ...
      </sp:InitiatorToken>
      <sp:RecipientToken>
        ...
```

```
      </sp:RecipientToken>
      <sp:AlgorithmSuite>
        ...
      </sp:AlgorithmSuite>
      <sp:EncryptBeforeSigning/>
    </wsp:Policy>
  </sp:AsymmetricBinding>
  ...
</wsp:Policy>
```

To implement the second solution, modify the policy:

```
<wsp:Policy wsu:Id="p1">
  <sp:AsymmetricBinding>
    ...
    <sp:EncryptBeforeSigning/>
    ...
  </sp:AsymmetricBinding>
  <sp:Wss10>
    ...
  </sp:Wss10>
  <sp:SignedParts>
    <sp:Body />
  </sp:SignedParts>
  <sp:EncryptedParts>
    <sp:Body />
  </sp:EncryptedParts>
  <sp:EncryptedElements>
    <sp:XPath>
      //*[local-name()='Signature']
    </sp:XPath>
  </sp:EncryptedElements>
</wsp:Policy>
```

Don't need this any more

It is like <EncryptedParts> but it is not using SOAP structures such as <Body> to refer the message. Instead, it uses something called XPath to refer to elements in the XML document.

Then select those whose element name (ignoring the namespace) is "Signature".

Look for any descendant of XML root element (<Envelope> here)

```
<soapenv:Envelope ...>
  <soapenv:Header>
    <wsse:Security ...>
      <xenc:EncryptedKey ...>...</xenc:EncryptedKey>
      <ds:Signature ...>
        ...
      </ds:Signature>
    </wsse:Security>
  </soapenv:Header>
</soapenv:Envelope>
```

BUG ALERT: Due to a bug in the current version of Rampart, the <EncryptedElements> feature is not working.

Protecting WS-Addressing header elements

If you're using WS-Addressing, most likely you'd like to ensure that the WS-Addressing header elements are not tampered with. To do that, you can modify the policy to require signing on header elements:

```
<wsp:Policy wsu:Id="p1">
  <sp:AsymmetricBinding>
    ...
  </sp:AsymmetricBinding>
  <sp:Wss10>
    ...
  </sp:Wss10>
  <sp:SignedParts>
    <sp:Body />
    <sp:Header Name="To" Namespace="http://www.w3.org/2005/08/addressing"/>
  </sp:SignedParts>
  <sp:EncryptedParts>
    <sp:Body />
  </sp:EncryptedParts>
</wsp:Policy>
```

Encrypt the <To> element in the http://www.w3.org/2005/08/addressing namespace

```
<soapenv:Envelope
  xmlns:wsa="http://www.w3.org/2005/08/addressing" ...>
  <soapenv:Header>
    <wsse:Security>
      ...
    </wsse:Security>
    <wsa:To>http://localhost:1234/axis2/services/SecureService</wsa:To>
    <wsa:MessageID>urn:uuid:59F3153E977EDEDE471197688498788</wsa:MessageID>
    <wsa:Action>http://ttdev.com/ss/New4b4Operation</wsa:Action>
  </soapenv:Header>
</soapenv:Envelope>
```

To protect all such elements, you may list them one by one:

```
<sp:SignedParts>
  <sp:Body />
  <sp:Header Name="To" Namespace="http://www.w3.org/2005/08/addressing"/>
  <sp:Header Name="MessageID" Namespace="http://www.w3.org/2005/08/addressing"/>
  <sp:Header Name="Action" Namespace="http://www.w3.org/2005/08/addressing"/>
  <sp:Header Name="RelatesTo" Namespace="http://www.w3.org/2005/08/addressing"/>
</sp:SignedParts>
```

However, this is too much trouble. A better way is not to specify the Name attribute and specify only the Namespace attribute. This way all header elements in the WS-Addressing namespace will be signed:

```
<sp:SignedParts>
  <sp:Body />
  <sp:Header Name="To" Namespace="http://www.w3.org/2005/08/addressing"/>
</sp:SignedParts>
```

BUG ALERT: Due to a bug in the current version of Rampart, this feature is not working. Therefore, for the moment, you'll have to list them one by one.

Sending login information

Suppose that the web service will perform the requested operation only for selected users only. To do that, you can configure your client to send the user name and password to the web service. Such information is called a Username Token. To require a Username token in the request message, modify the policy:

```
<wsp:Policy wsu:Id="p1">
   <sp:AsymmetricBinding>
      ...
   </sp:AsymmetricBinding>
   <sp:Wss10>
      ...
   </sp:Wss10>
   <sp:SignedParts>
      ...
   </sp:SignedParts>
   <sp:EncryptedParts>
      ...
   </sp:EncryptedParts>
   <sp:SignedSupportingTokens>
         <wsp:Policy>
            <sp:UsernameToken sp:IncludeToken="http://docs.oasis-open.org/ws-sx/
ws-securitypolicy/200702/IncludeToken/AlwaysToRecipient"/>
         </wsp:Policy>
   </sp:SignedSupportingTokens>
</wsp:Policy>
```

A Username Token is not like the certificate token which is required for signing or encryption. Therefore it is just a supporting token. Here, you also require that it be signed to make sure that it has not been tampered with.

Always include it in the request message

There can be other types of supporting tokens. Username token is just one possible type.

How to specify the user name? For the moment rampart will always use the <user> configuration (in your rampart-config.xml file):

It is used both as the user name in the Username token and as the alias for the client certificate

```
<wsp:Policy xmlns:wsp="http://schemas.xmlsoap.org/ws/2004/09/policy"
   xmlns="http://ws.apache.org/rampart/policy">
   <RampartConfig>
      <user>c1</user>
      <encryptionUser>s1</encryptionUser>
      <passwordCallbackClass>
         com.ttdev.secure.client.PasswordCallbackHandler
      </passwordCallbackClass>
      <signatureCrypto>
         ...
      </signatureCrypto>
      <encryptionCrypto>
         ...
      </encryptionCrypto>
   </RampartConfig>
</wsp:Policy>
```

This is a problem as you probably want the client to allow different users to use it to talk to the web service. In the latest snapshot of rampart these concepts can be separated:

It is used only as the user name in the Username token

It is used only as the alias for the client certificate

```
<wsp:Policy xmlns:wsp="http://schemas.xmlsoap.org/ws/2004/09/policy"
  xmlns="http://ws.apache.org/rampart/policy">
  <RampartConfig>
    <user>u1</user>
    <userCertAlias>c1</userCertAlias>
    <encryptionUser>s1</encryptionUser>
    <passwordCallbackClass>
      com.ttdev.secure.client.PasswordCallbackHandler
    </passwordCallbackClass>
    <signatureCrypto>
      ...
    </signatureCrypto>
    <encryptionCrypto>
      ...
    </encryptionCrypto>
  </RampartConfig>
</wsp:Policy>
```

As that version has not been released yet, here you can only use c1 for both purposes. So rampart has the user name, how does it know the password? It can use the password callback. So modify PasswordCallbackHandler.java in the client package:

```
public class PasswordCallbackHandler implements CallbackHandler {
    public void handle(Callback[] callbacks)
        throws IOException, UnsupportedCallbackException {
        for (int i = 0; i < callbacks.length; i++) {
            WSPasswordCallback pwcb = (WSPasswordCallback) callbacks[i];
            String id = pwcb.getIdentifer();
            switch (pwcb.getUsage()) {
            case WSPasswordCallback.SIGNATURE:
            case WSPasswordCallback.DECRYPT:{
                if (id.equals("c1")) {
                    pwcb.setPassword("c1-pass");
                }
                break;
            }
            case WSPasswordCallback.USERNAME_TOKEN: {
                if (id.equals("c1")) {
                    pwcb.setPassword("c1-as-user-pass");
                }
                break;
            }
            }
        }
    }
}
```

When rampart needs to sign or decrypt, c1 is acting as the alias.

When rampart needs to send a Username token, c1 is acting as the user name.

Here use a different password to verify that they are different

How can the web service verify the password? Again, rampart replies on the password callback to get the correct password for comparison. So, modify PasswordCallbackHandler.java in the com.ttdev.secure package:

```
public class PasswordCallbackHandler implements CallbackHandler {
    public void handle(Callback[] callbacks)
        throws IOException, UnsupportedCallbackException {
        for (int i = 0; i < callbacks.length; i++) {
            WSPasswordCallback pwcb = (WSPasswordCallback) callbacks[i];
            String id = pwcb.getIdentifer();
            switch (pwcb.getUsage()) {
            case WSPasswordCallback.DECRYPT:
            case WSPasswordCallback.SIGNATURE: {
                if (id.equals("s1")) {
                    pwcb.setPassword("s1-pass");
                }
                break;
            }
            case WSPasswordCallback.USERNAME_TOKEN: {
                if (id.equals("c1")) {
                    pwcb.setPassword("c1-as-user-pass");
                }
                break;
            }
            }
        }
    }
}
```

When rampart needs to sign or decrypt, it needs its own (s1) password.

When rampart needs to verify a Username token, it needs to return the password for the known users (c1).

Now generate the service stub and client stub again. Run it. You should see the Username token in the TCP Monitor:

```
<soapenv:Envelope ...>
  <soapenv:Header>
    <wsse:Security ...>
      <xenc:EncryptedKey Id="EncKeyId-29857804">
        ...
      </xenc:EncryptedKey>
      <wsse:UsernameToken
        xmlns:wsu="..."
        wsu:Id="UsernameToken-6659511">
        <wsse:Username>c1</wsse:Username>
        <wsse:Password
          Type="http://docs.oasis-open.org/wss/
2004/01/oasis-200401-wss-username-token-profile-1.0#PasswordDigest">
          6GW32nj7XJ0sTyIjDZrcQWn3X0E=
        </wsse:Password>
        <wsse:Nonce>/D2oMduF226uzRd4Rs3Bkw==</wsse:Nonce>
        <wsu:Created>2007-12-15T06:16:55.765Z</wsu:Created>
      </wsse:UsernameToken>
      ...
      <ds:Signature xmlns:ds="http://www.w3.org/2000/09/xmldsig#"
        Id="Signature-25421790">
        <ds:SignedInfo>
          ...
          <ds:Reference URI="#UsernameToken-6659511">
              Algorithm="http://www.w3.org/2000/09/xmldsig#sha1" />
            <ds:DigestValue>
              Ht4ubB6JdHcLyaJUxYiwdnSQVj0=
            </ds:DigestValue>
          </ds:Reference>
        </ds:SignedInfo>
        ...
      </ds:Signature>
    </wsse:Security>
  ...
</soapenv:Envelope>
```

The Username token

c1 is the user name

For security, the password is not sent as clear text but as a digest.

The token is signed

To fight against dictionary attack, a nonce and a time stamp are included when calculating the digest:

password + nonce + time stamp

digest

In addition, the web service can remember the nonces seen in a short recent period. If the same nonce is used again, it is a replay attack.

If you don't want others to even see the user name of "c1", you can encrypt the Username token. All that is required is to change <SignedSupportingTokens> to <SignedEncryptedSupportingTokens> in the policy.

What if different users have different permissions? You can retrieve the user name in your own code and decide what permissions he has. To do that, you need to understand the data structure created by rampart after processing the request message. There could be multiple rampart module instances running. Each will store its result into an element of a Vector (see the diagram below). Each rampart module instance may perform multiple actions, e.g., verify its signature, verify a Username token or decrypt a message. Therefore, for each action it will create a WSSecurityEngineResult to represent the result of that action. So, for each instance it creates a vector-like structure to store all such results. This is the WSHandlerResult. For example, in the diagram, the first action is SIGN, which means verifying a signature, the result contains the certificate used and etc. The second action is UT, which means verifying a Username token, the result contains the user name:

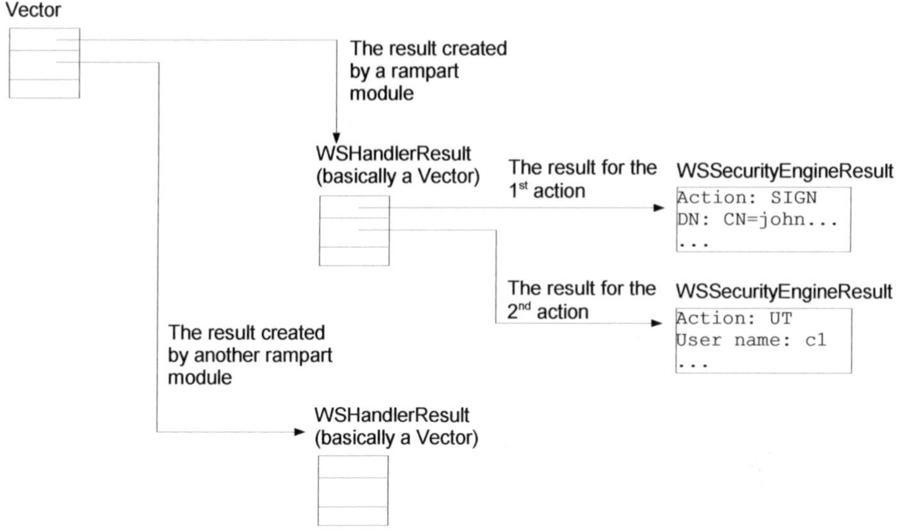

Now, to retrieve the DN of the user in the back end object, modify SecureServiceImpl.java:

```
public class SecureServiceImpl implements SecureServiceSkeletonInterface {
  public String concat(String s1, String s2) {
    checkUser();
    return s1 + s2;
  }
  private void checkUser() {
    MessageContext context = MessageContext.getCurrentMessageContext();
    Vector handlersResults = (Vector) context
          .getProperty(WSHandlerConstants.RECV_RESULTS);
    for (Iterator iter = handlersResults.iterator(); iter.hasNext();) {
      WSHandlerResult handlerResult = (WSHandlerResult) iter.next();
      Vector actionsResults = handlerResult.getResults();
      for (Iterator iterator = actionsResults.iterator(); iterator
            .hasNext();) {
        WSSecurityEngineResult actionResult = (WSSecurityEngineResult) iterator
              .next();
        int action = ((Integer) actionResult
              .get(WSSecurityEngineResult.TAG_ACTION)).intValue();
        if (action == WSConstants.UT) {
          Principal p = (Principal) actionResult
                .get(WSSecurityEngineResult.TAG_PRINCIPAL);
          if (p != null) {
            System.out.println("Checking " + p.getName());
            return; //return if the user has the required permission
          }
        }
      }
    }
    // throw an exception if the user is not allowed
  }
}
```

Get the result Vector from the property for all rampart instances

Get the action results for a rampart instance

Get the result for a single action

Get the action and check if it is UT (verify a Username token)

For testing, just print out the name.

Get the user principal. A Principal object represents a user id. It only has a "name" field.

Now run the client and you should see the output in the Tomcat console:

```
[INFO] Verification successful for URI "#Id-24880015"
[INFO] Verification successful for URI "#id-23447542"
[INFO] Verification successful for URI "#id-19589694"
[INFO] Verification successful for URI "#id-7912507"
[INFO] Verification successful for URI "#UsernameToken-6659511"
Checking c1
```

Modifying services.xml programatically

Currently you're adding the <Policy> and the <module ref="rampart" /> elements to the services.xml file manually. This is no good as it will be overwritten if you run <wsdl2code> again (it is not deleted due to a BUG). A better way is to let Ant modify the services.xml file every time it is generated by <wsdl2code>. To do that, create a file add-policy.xsl in the project root:

```
<?xml version="1.0" encoding="ISO-8859-1"?>
<xsl:stylesheet version="1.0"
  xmlns:xsl="http://www.w3.org/1999/XSL/Transform">
  <xsl:template match="@*|node()">
    <xsl:copy>
      <xsl:apply-templates select="@*|node()" />
    </xsl:copy>
  </xsl:template>
</xsl:stylesheet>
```

1: This pattern will match any element or attribute. So this template will be applied to the <serviceGroup>. So, the body of the template will be output.

4: Only this template is applicable. So, it will be copied and so will its children.

2: The <xsl:copy> element has special meaning. It will output the start tag of the current node (<serviceGroup>), then output its own body and then output the end tag (</serviceGroup>).

```
<serviceGroup>
  <service name="SecureService">
    ...
  </service>
</serviceGroup>
```

```
<serviceGroup>
  ...
</serviceGroup>
```

3: Here <xsl:apply-templates> is the body of the <xsl:copy> element. It also has special meaning. It will apply a template to each child element of the current node (here, there is only one: the <service> element). The output will be put after <serviceGroup> tag and before the </serviceGroup> tag in the output.

Such a file is called an "XSL Transformations (XSLT)". XSL stands for "Extensible Stylesheet Language". What this file does is to copy the services.xml file to the output. In order to add the <Policy> and the <module ref="rampart" /> elements to it, further modify the add-policy.xsl file:

```
<?xml version="1.0" encoding="ISO-8859-1"?>
<xsl:stylesheet version="1.0"
  xmlns:xsl="http://www.w3.org/1999/XSL/Transform">
  <xsl:template match="@*|node()">
    <xsl:copy>
      <xsl:apply-templates select="@*|node()" />
    </xsl:copy>
  </xsl:template>
  <xsl:template match="operation">
    <xsl:copy>
      <xsl:apply-templates select="@*|node()" />
    </xsl:copy>
    <module ref="rampart" />
    <wsp:Policy
      xmlns:wsp="http://schemas.xmlsoap.org/ws/2004/09/policy"
      xmlns:sp="http://schemas.xmlsoap.org/ws/2005/07/securitypolicy"
      xmlns:wsu="..."
      wsu:Id="p1">
      ...
    </wsp:Policy>
  </xsl:template>
</xsl:stylesheet>
```

1: This template and the previous one will match this <operation> element, but this template is more specific so it will be applied. Therefore its content will be output.

```
<serviceGroup>
  <service name="SecureService">
    ...
    <operation name="concat" ...>
      ...
    </operation>
  </service>
</serviceGroup>
```

2: <xsl:copy> will copy it and its children as usual

```
<operation name="concat" ...>
  ...
</operation>
<module ref="rampart" />
<wsp:Policy ...>
  ...
</wsp:Policy>
```

3: This part will be output verbatim as it is no special meaning to XSLT. It will be put after the <operation> element that was output.

To apply this add-policy.xml file, modify build.xml:

As you'll be using the path to the services.xml file for many times, define a property for it.

```
<project basedir="." default="jar.server">
  <property name="name" value="SecureService" />
  <property name="servicesFile" value="src/META-INF/services.xml" />
  ...
  <target name="generate-service">
    <delete file="${servicesFile}"/>
    <wsdl2code
      .../>
    <replaceregexp
      file="${servicesFile}"
      match="${name}Skeleton"
      replace="${name}Impl" />
    <xslt
      in="${servicesFile}"
      out="${servicesFile}.tmp"
      style="add-policy.xsl"/>
    <move
      file="${servicesFile}.tmp"
      tofile="${servicesFile}"/>
  </target>
</project>
```

Due to the bug, <wsdl2code> won't overwrite the file, so delete it to simulate the correct behavior.

Apply an XSLT file

The input file is the services.xml file

The output file is services.xml.tmp

The XSLT file

Move the services.xml.tmp file into services.xml. It is essentially a rename.

Now run the build.xml file and the services.xml will be setup properly. Run the client and it should continue to work.

Summary

WS-Policy allows you to specify non-functional requirements such as security on web services. You include a policy in the WSDL file and the generated client stub will use it. For the web service, you still need to include it into the services.xml file.

To sign or encrypt a message, specify in the policy the configuration settings such as algorithms to use, whether to include the certificate (token) and how (direct include or issuer DN plus serial number and etc.). You also specify which parts should be signed and which parts should be encrypted.

The Rampart module implements the WS-Security standard and can be used to satisfy security requirements expressed in policies. It gets information from the policy. In addition, you also need to provide further configurations to it using an XML file or a string. Such configurations include the user name alias, password callback class, what cryptographic provider to use (e.g., JDK), the location of the keystore and the keystore password.

When performing both signing and encrypting, to fight against dictionary attacks, you should encrypt the signature, encrypt before signing or include a nonce into the digest.

To send authentication information, you can use a Username token. This is also specified in a policy. Your password callback class should provide the password. The Username token should be signed and probably also be encrypted. You can retrieve the user name in your web service to perform authorization.

To modify XML file using Ant, you can use XSLT. This allows you to modify the services.xml file programmatically.

Chapter 10

Integrating Your Web Services with Tomcat and Spring

What's in this chapter?

In this chapter you'll learn how to run the Axis server inside Tomcat and let your web service invoke business logic in Spring beans.

Axis server as a mini-web server

Up until now you've been running the Axis server as a separate process listening for SOAP messages in HTTP requests on port 8080. Essentially it is acting as a mini-web server. If you're already running a web server such as Tomcat, you probably want to run the Axis server as a web application in Tomcat.

Installing Tomcat

If you already have Tomcat installed, skip to the next section. Otherwise, go to http://tomcat.apache.org to download a binary package of Tomcat. Download the zip version instead of the Windows exe version. Suppose that it is apache-tomcat-6.0.13.zip. Unzip it into a folder say c:\tomcat. Note that Tomcat 6.x works with JDK 5 or above.

Before you can run it, make sure the environment variable JAVA_HOME is defined to point to your JDK folder (e.g., C:\Program Files\Java\jdk1.5.0_02):

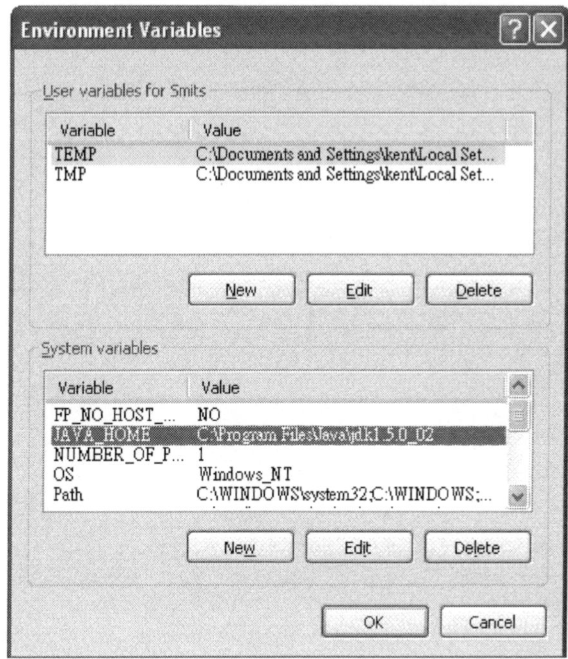

If you don't have it, define it now. Now, open a command prompt, change to c:\tomcat\bin and then run startup.bat. If it is working, you should see:

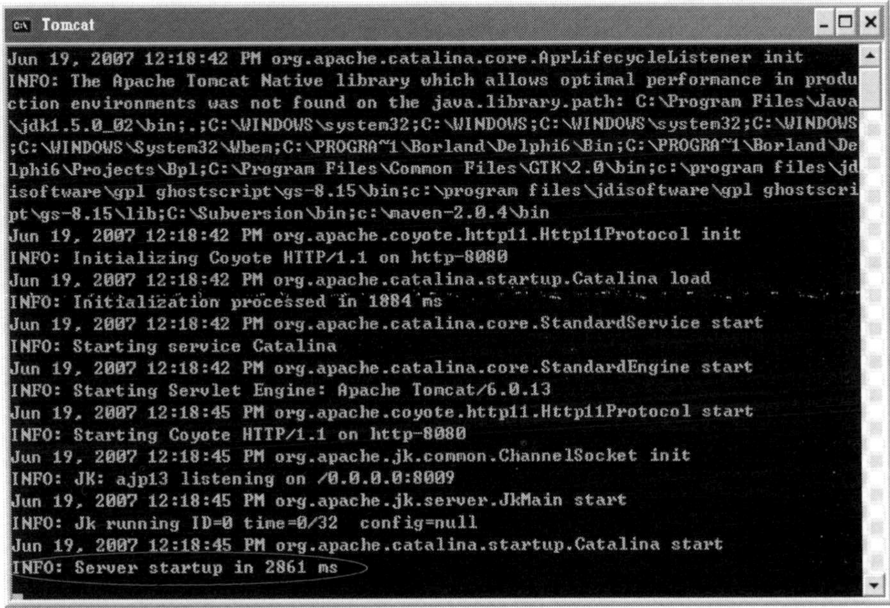

Open a browser and go to http://localhost:8080 and you should see:

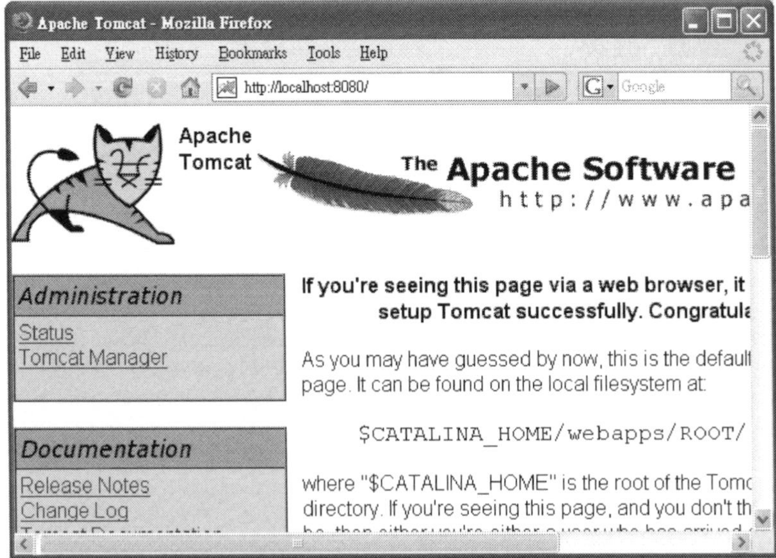

Let's shut it down by changing to c:\tomcat\bin and running shutdown.bat.

Running the Axis server inside Tomcat

Next, go to http://ws.apache.org/axis2 to download the "WAR (Web Archive) Distribution" (e.g. axis2-1.3-war.zip). There are just a handful of files in the zip file. Unzip it and put the files into c:\axis. The only important file there is the axis2-1.3.war file. To install it into Tomcat, copy it into c:\tomcat\webapps. Then start Tomcat by running startup.bat. You should see:

```
INFO: Deploying web application archive axis2.war
[INFO] Deploying module: addressing-1.3
[INFO] Deploying module: script-1.3
[INFO] Deploying module: metadataExchange-1.3
[INFO] Deploying module: ping-1.3
[INFO] Deploying module: soapmonitor-1.3
[INFO] script module activated
[INFO] Deploying Web service: version-1.3.aar
Dec 16, 2007 11:50:16 AM org.apache.coyote.http11.Http11Protocol start
INFO: Starting Coyote HTTP/1.1 on http-8080
Dec 16, 2007 11:50:16 AM org.apache.jk.common.ChannelSocket init
INFO: JK: ajp13 listening on /0.0.0.0:8009
Dec 16, 2007 11:50:16 AM org.apache.jk.server.JkMain start
INFO: Jk running ID=0 time=0/32  config=null
Dec 16, 2007 11:50:16 AM org.apache.catalina.startup.Catalina start
INFO: Server startup in 35270 ms
```

To further check that the Axis server is running, go to http://localhost:8080/axis2 in a browser. You should see:

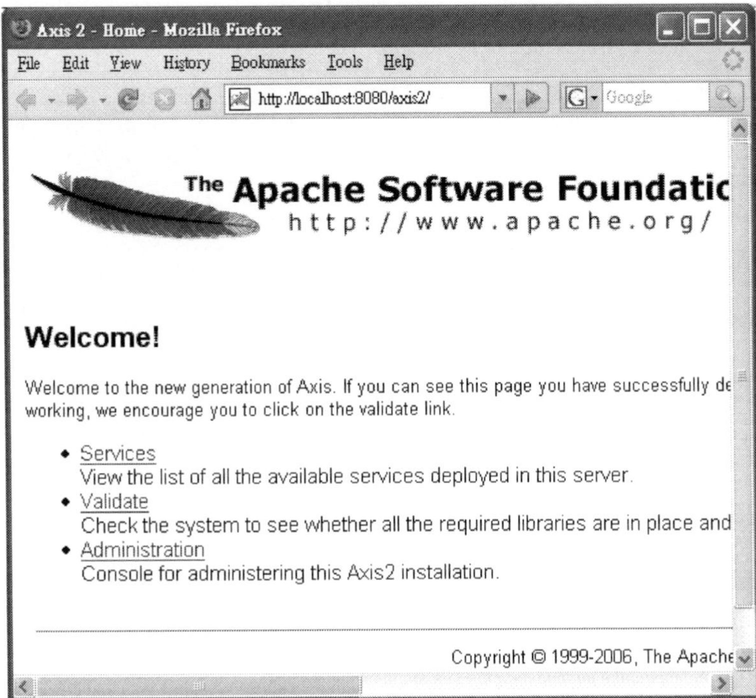

Check c:\tomcat\webapps, you should see that there is an axis2 folder created with the following structure:

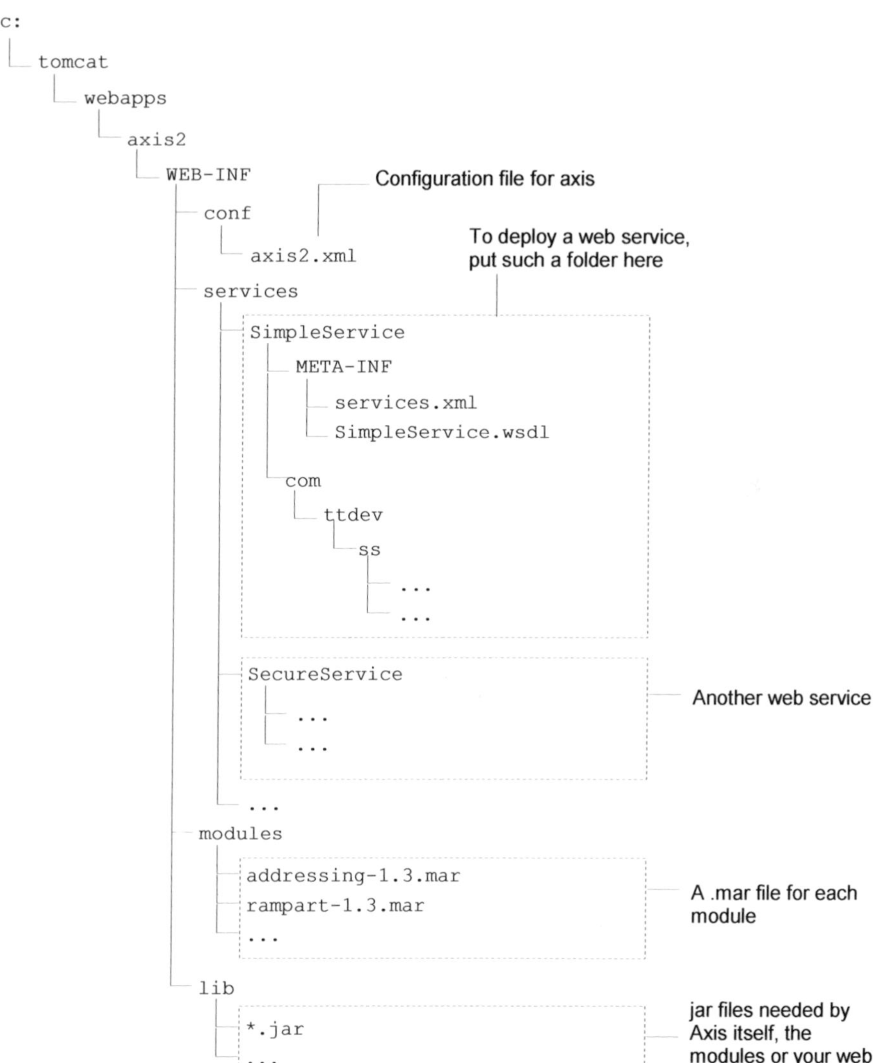

To deploy the web services you developed in the previous chapters, just copy their folders over:

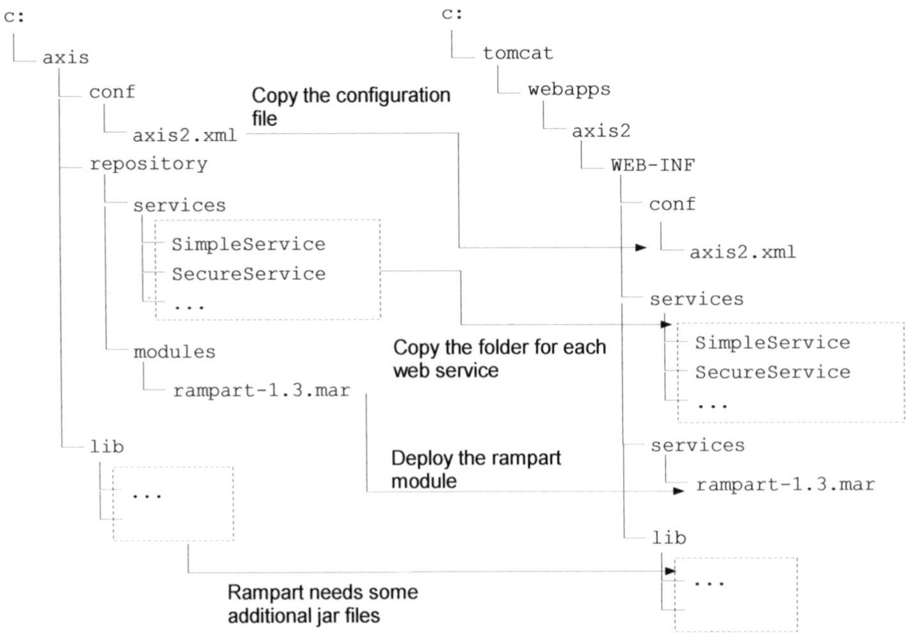

Restart Tomcat for the changes to take effect. Run a client such as the SecureClient and it should continue to work.

Invoking Spring beans from your web service

Up until now all your web services perform very simple operations such as concatenating two strings. In practice, they should really invoke business logic such as placing an order for some goods. Typically such business logic may have been implemented as Spring beans. Next, let's work on one such example.

In Eclipse copy the WrappedService project and paste it as SpringService. Link the "out" folder to C:\tomcat\webapps\axis2\WEB-INF\services\SpringService. Rename WrappedService.wsdl to SpringService.wsdl and changes the word "Wrapped" to "Spring" in the file. Then modify build.xml:

```
<?xml version="1.0" encoding="UTF-8"?>
<project basedir="." default="jar.server">
  ...
  <property name="name" value="SpringService" />
  ...
  <target name="generate-service">
    <wsdl2code
      wsdlfilename="${name}.wsdl"
      serverside="true"
      generateservicexml="true"
      skipbuildxml="true"
      serversideinterface="true"
      namespacetopackages="http://ttdev.com/ss=com.ttdev.spring"
      targetsourcefolderlocation="src"
```

```
        targetresourcesfolderlocation="src/META-INF"
        overwrite="true"
        unwrap="true" />
      <replaceregexp
        file="src/META-INF/services.xml"
        match="${name}Skeleton"
        replace="${name}Impl" />
    </target>
    <target name="generate-client">
      <wsdl2code
        wsdlfilename="${name}.wsdl"
        skipbuildxml="true"
        namespacetopackages="http://ttdev.com/ss=com.ttdev.spring.client"
        targetsourcefolderlocation="src"
        overwrite="true"
        unwrap="true" />
    </target>
  </project>
```

Run it to generate the stubs.

To setup Spring, go to http://www.springframework.org to download it. Suppose that the file is spring-framework-2.0.6-with-dependencies.zip. Unzip it into say c:\spring-framework. To make the Spring classes available to your application, copy the following jar files into c:\tomcat\webapps\axis2\WEB-INF\lib:

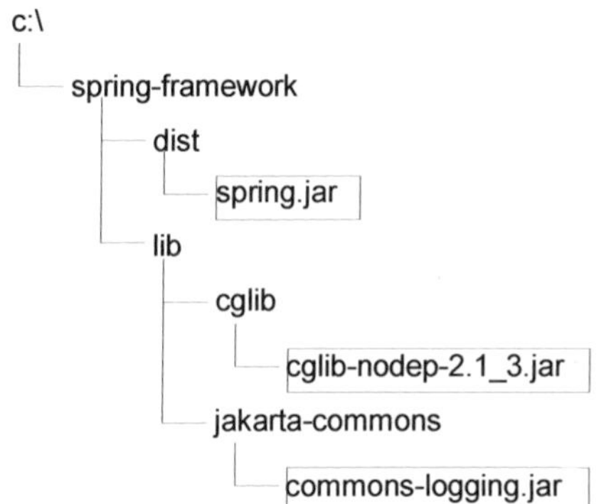

You'll also need to access the Spring classes in Eclipse, so add spring.jar to the build path of your project in Eclipse. Then modify c:\tomcat\webapps\axis2\WEB-INF\web.xml as shown below. You add a <listener> element. When Tomcat notes that there is a <listener> element, when it is starting the Axis server (as a web application), it will create a listener object of the specified class (here, the ContextLoaderListener class provided by Spring) and call it. The ContextLoaderListener will initialize the Spring framework, or rather, it will create a Spring application context which is basically a collection of Spring beans. As the listener is loading the context, that's why it is called ContextLoaderListener:

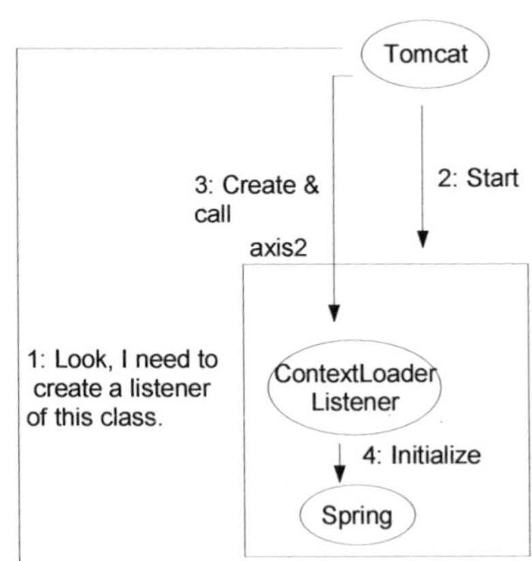


```
<?xml version="1.0" encoding="ISO-8859-1"?>
<!DOCTYPE web-app PUBLIC "-//Sun Microsystems, Inc.//DTD Web Application
2.3//EN" "http://java.sun.com/dtd/web-app_2_3.dtd">
<web-app>
   <display-name>Apache-Axis2</display-name>
   <listener>
      <listener-class>
         org.springframework.web.context.ContextLoaderListener
      </listener-class>
   </listener>
   <servlet>
      ...
   </servlet>
   ...
</web-app>
```

When Spring is creating the application context, it will try to read a configuration file WEB-INF/applicationContext.xml to find out what beans are available. So, create that file now:

Define a bean named "concatBean"

1: Give me the bean named "concatBean".

Spring

```
<?xml version="1.0" encoding="UTF-8"?>
<beans xmlns="http://www.springframework.org/schema/beans"
      xmlns:xsi="http://www.w3.org/2001/XMLSchema-instance"
      xsi:schemaLocation="http://www.springframework.org/schema/beans
http://www.springframework.org/schema/beans/spring-beans-2.0.xsd">
   <bean
      id="concatBean"
      class="com.ttdev.spring.middletier.ConcatService"/>
   <bean
      id="appContextHolder"
      class="org.apache.axis2.extensions.spring.
            receivers.ApplicationContextHolder"/>
</beans>
```

2: Create an instance of this class

ConcatService

Assume that this middletier package contains all the business logic classes in your system

Define another bean. It will get access to the application context and allow others to access it.

Next, create ConcatService.java in the com.ttdev.spring.middletier package:

```
package com.ttdev.spring.middletier;

public class ConcatService {
  public String concat(String s1, String s2) {
    return s1+s2;
  }
}
```

To make the classes in this middletier package available to Spring, they should be packed into a jar file and then copied into WEB-INF/lib. To do that, right click the middletier package and choose Export, then choose Java | JAR file:

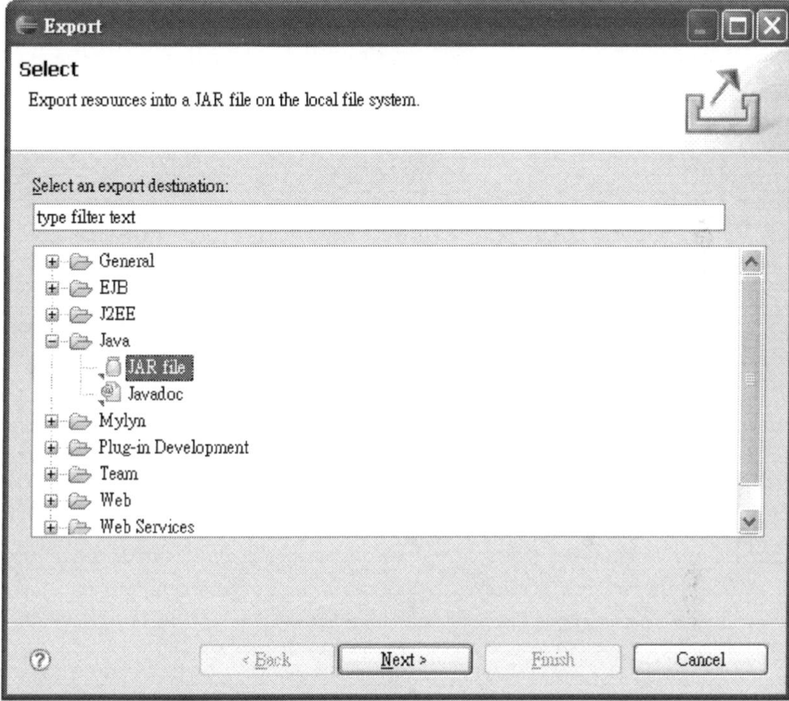

Enter the destination path as shown below:

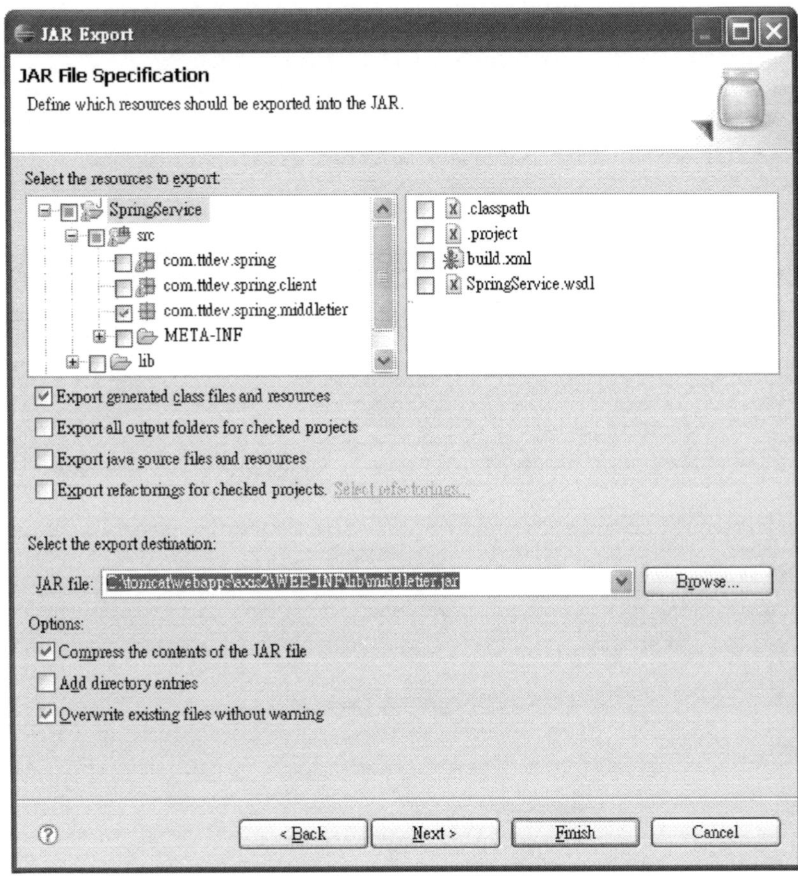

Click Finish to create the jar file.

To invoke the concatBean in your web service code, create SpringServiceImpl.java:

Get the application context

```
public class SpringServiceImpl implements SpringServiceSkeletonInterface {
  public String concat(String s1, String s2) {
    ApplicationContext context = ApplicationContextHolder.getContext();
    ConcatService bean = (ConcatService) context.getBean("concatBean");
    return bean.concat(s1, s2);
  }
}
```

Get the "concatBean"

Call the business logic

Now, restart Tomcat for the changes to take effect. To test it, create a SpringClient in the client package:

```
public class SpringClient {
  public static void main(String[] args) throws RemoteException {
```

```
      SpringServiceStub stub = new SpringServiceStub();
      String result = stub.concat("xyz", "abc");
      System.out.println(result);
    }
  }
```

Run it and it should work.

Summary

The Axis server can be run inside Tomcat as a web application. This is most useful when you are already running Tomcat. In particular, when you're using Spring beans to implement your business logic, in order for your web service code to access the Spring beans, you have to run the Axis server inside Tomcat.

To access a Spring bean from your web service, the key is to gain access to the Spring application context. This can be done through a special application context holder bean.

References

- Axis2 developers. Axis2 Documentation. http://ws.apache.org/axis2.
- Rampart developers. Rampart Documentation. http://ws.apache.org/axis2/modules/rampart/1_3/security-module.html.
- IBM. Develop asynchronous Web services with Axis2. http://www.ibm.com/developerworks/webservices/library/ws-axis2.
- Interface21. The Spring Framework 2.5 Reference Manual. http://static.springframework.org/spring/docs/2.5.x/reference/index.html.
- Nadana Mihindukulasooriya. WS - Security Policy. http://nandanasm.wordpress.com/2007/10/31/ws-security-policy/
- OASIS. Web Services Security: 3 SOAP Message Security 1.0 (WS-Security 2004). http://docs.oasis-open.org/wss/2004/01/oasis-200401-wss-soap-message-security-1.0.
- OASIS. WS-SecurityPolicy 1.2. http://docs.oasis-open.org/ws-sx/ws-securitypolicy/v1.2/ws-securitypolicy.html
- OASIS. Web Services Security UsernameToken Profile 1.0. http://docs.oasis-open.org/wss/2004/01/oasis-200401-wss-username-token-profile-1.0.
- OASIS. Web Services Security X.509 Certificate Token Profile. http://docs.oasis-open.org/wss/2004/01/oasis-200401-wss-x509-token-profile-1.0.
- Russell Butek. Which style of WSDL should I use? http://www-128.ibm.com/developerworks/webservices/library/ws-whichwsdl/?ca=dgr-devx-WebServicesMVP03.
- Tomcat developers. Tomcat Documentation. http://jakarta.apache.org/tomcat.
- W3C. Decryption Transform for XML Signature. http://www.w3.org/TR/2002/CR-xmlenc-decrypt-20020304.
- W3C. Namespaces in XML. http://www.w3.org/TR/1999/REC-xml-names-19990114.
- W3C. Simple Object Access Protocol (SOAP) 1.1. http://www.w3.org/TR/2000/NOTE-SOAP-20000508.
- W3C. SOAP Message Transmission Optimization Mechanism. http://www.w3.org/TR/soap12-mtom.
- W3C. URIs, URLs, and URNs: Clarifications and Recommendations 1.0. http://www.w3.org/TR/2001/NOTE-uri-clarification-20010921.

- W3C. Web Services Addressing 1.0 – Core. http://www.w3.org/TR/ws-addr-core.
- W3C. Web Services Addressing 1.0 - SOAP Binding. http://www.w3.org/TR/ws-addr-soap.
- W3C. Web Services Addressing 1.0 – Core. http://www.w3.org/TR/ws-addr-core.
- W3C. Web Services Addressing 1.0 - WSDL Binding. http://www.w3.org/TR/ws-addr-wsdl.
- W3C. Web Services Description Language (WSDL) 1.1. http://www.w3.org/TR/2001/NOTE-wsdl-20010315.
- W3C. Web Services Policy 1.2 - Framework. http://www.w3.org/Submission/WS-Policy.
- W3C. XML-binary Optimized Packaging. http://www.w3.org/TR/xop10.
- W3C. XML Encryption Syntax and Processing. http://www.w3.org/TR/2002/REC-xmlenc-core-20021210.
- W3C. XML Schema Part 0: Primer Second Edition. http://www.w3.org/TR/2004/REC-xmlschema-0-20041028.
- W3C. XML Schema Part 1: Structures Second Edition. http://www.w3.org/TR/2004/REC-xmlschema-1-20041028.
- W3C. XML Schema Part 2: Datatypes Second Edition. http://www.w3.org/TR/2004/REC-xmlschema-2-20041028.
- W3C. XML-Signature Syntax and Processing. http://www.w3.org/TR/2002/REC-xmldsig-core-20020212.
- W3C. XSL Transformations (XSLT). http://www.w3.org/TR/xslt.
- Will Provost. WSDL First. http://webservices.xml.com/pub/a/ws/2003/07/22/wsdlfirst.html.
- WS-I. WS-I Basic Profile Version 1.0. http://www.ws-i.org/Profiles/BasicProfile-1.0-2004-04-16.html.
- WSS4J developers. WSS4J Axis Deployment Tutorial. http://ws.apache.org/wss4j/axis.html.

Alphabetical Index

5124467R0

Made in the USA
Lexington, KY
06 April 2010